THE NATURALIST
IN NICARAGUA

Yours very truly
Thomas Belt

THE NATURALIST
IN NICARAGUA

THOMAS BELT

With a Foreword by
DANIEL H. JANZEN

The University of Chicago Press
Chicago and London

The University of Chicago Press, Chicago 60637
The University of Chicago Press, Ltd., London

Originally published 1874
University of Chicago Press edition 1985
Foreword © 1985 by the University of Chicago
All rights reserved
Printed in the United States of America

94 93 92 91 90 89 88 87 86 85   5 4 3 2 1

Library of Congress Cataloging-in-Publication Data

Belt, Thomas, 1832 – 1878.
The naturalist in Nicaragua.

Reprint. Originally published: London : J. Murray,
1874.
Includes index.
1. Natural history—Nicaragua.   2. Nicaragua—
Description and travel.   I. Title.
QH108.N5B45   1985   508.7285   85 – 8502
ISBN 0 – 226 – 04219 – 7 (cloth)
ISBN 0 – 226 – 04220 – 0 (paper)

FOREWORD.

The Naturalist in Nicaragua is rich fare, a generous feast of natural history for the tropical tourist, the student on his or her first tropical foray, and the experienced tropical biologist. It would also make a fantastic script for a tropical film, one that resists the temptation to include mainly cameo shots of exquisite beetles pinned in trays.

Thomas Belt lived his forty-five years matter-of-factly close to nature. It is difficult for us to appreciate how close, for today we travel in an afternoon the distance it took Belt nineteen days to cover on mule-back. When you ride a mule for nineteen days, you have time for the contemplation of your surroundings, and your surroundings have the time to contemplate you. This is not to suggest that perching on a slogging mule in the blazing sun or driving rain, with no food in your stomach, will lead automatically or even at all to a careful, enthusiastic, interpretive examination of nature.

But Belt was an engineer, and he went at nature with the attention to detail one would expect of a man who did not want his bridges or mine shafts to collapse. A man whose life depends on getting a timber baulk at just the right point and angle in a tunnel is someone preconditioned to notice quite carefully how a bee enters a flower. Belt's intensely personal description of tropical nature is a living example of how simple curiosity accompanied by an unabashed devotion to learning how things work can lead to superb descriptions of the natural world and to the guts of generalizations of the kind that are still the starting point for serious scientific work in ecology and evolutionary biology.

On nearly every page of *The Naturalist in Nicaragua*, Belt gives us a superbly drawn description of an animal or plant, and what it is doing, and then he tells us what all this suggests to him and why. Those of us who did not grow up in the tropics may encounter, in Belt's book, just as we do in the tropical forest, a bewildering and intriguing array of unfamiliar animals and plants, facts and ideas. Read on, travel on. If you meet a toucan first in the book, and then in the forest, the meetings reinforce each other as two meetings in either the book or the forest cannot. Few of us can see the natural world with Belt's disciplined and eager inquisitiveness or think about it as clearly and attentively as he.

I am writing this Foreword in Parque Nacional Santa Rosa in Costa Rica, in a tropical forest 100 miles southwest of Belt's house. There is a peccary snuffling up chopped coconut about 5 meters away from my right foot, and an agouti hovers in the background. When Paul Richards first sent me a copy of *The Naturalist in Nicaragua* in the late 1960s, I read it and learned many things. Today I read it again and find that Belt exposed the outlines of phenomena we are just now noticing and studying in tropical biology. Reading Belt again is like going for a long walk through the tropics with a friendly colleague, moving through a habitat that we both know well but taking a careful look for that factual tidbit neither of us will see or appreciate without the synergy of our combined experience. Seasonal tropical biologists would do well to re-read Belt about every ten years or so.

Just as Belt exposed some of the outlines of tropical biology, today we have by comparison an army of workers observing and recording the natural history of the tropics. But Belt was working amidst an ocean of nature, while all that remains to us are small and rapidly shrinking ponds. The consuming tragedy is that for those just coming to the tropics, or those who know the tropics well, Belt's book is a litany of habitat destruction. Contemporary residents of small Central American towns are less likely to see an agouti, peccary, or toucan than someone who is within commuting distance of a large urban zoo in North America. Visitors to the tropics can still see many of the natural wonders Belt describes in small parks and preserves, but these marvelous plants and animals could be far more widespread with only a few alterations in the direction of "tropical development."

Belt's book is a wonderful record of the tropics of more than 100 years ago, and those of us who are privileged to visit or work in the tropics now are indebted to him for his painstaking and pleasurable account. As we write our own papers and books, we would do well to emulate the care Belt took in making his records and ask ourselves if we are recording what

readers in the next century would want to know about
what we have seen and wondered about. Thomas Belt
was thirty-six when he began his four years in Nicaragua, and he died at the age of forty-five in Colorado. If he had waited until a normal retirement age to
write *The Naturalist in Nicaragua*, we would not
have had this book. If we do not act now, the remaining small bits of tropical forest that Belt describes and
celebrates will be lost to us and to the future, and *The
Naturalist in Nicaragua* will cease to be an introduction to the splendors of the tropics and will become
an obituary for them instead.

DANIEL H. JANZEN
Parque Nacional Santa Rosa
Guanacaste, Costa Rica, 1985

THE

NATURALIST IN NICARAGUA.

A Narrative of

A RESIDENCE AT THE GOLD MINES OF CHONTALES;

JOURNEYS IN THE SAVANNAHS AND FORESTS;

With Observations on Animals and Plants in Reference to
the Theory of Evolution of Living Forms.

By THOMAS BELT, F.G.S.

AUTHOR OF
"MINERAL VEINS," "THE GLACIAL PERIOD IN NORTH AMERICA," ETC. ETC.

SECOND EDITION, REVISED AND CORRECTED.

" It was his faith—perhaps is mine—
That life in all its forms is one,
And that its secret conduits run
Unseen, but in unbroken line,
From the great fountain-head divine,
Through man and beast, through grain and grass."
LONGFELLOW.

With Map and Illustrations.

LONDON:
EDWARD BUMPUS, 5 & 6 HOLBORN BARS, E.C.
1888.

PREFACE TO THE SECOND EDITION.

—————

IN the recently published "Life and Letters of Charles Darwin," edited by his son Mr. Francis Darwin (vol. iii. p, 188), the following passage occurs :—

"In the spring of this year (1874) he (Mr. Darwin) read a book which gave him great pleasure, and of which he often spoke with admiration, 'The Naturalist in Nicaragua,' by the late Thomas Belt. Mr. Belt, whose untimely death may well be deplored by naturalists, was by profession an engineer, so that all his admirable observations in natural history in Nicaragua and elsewhere, were the fruit of his leisure. The book is direct and vivid in style, and is full of description and suggestive discussions. With reference to it, my father wrote to Sir J. D. Hooker :—'Belt I have read, and I am delighted that you like it so much ; it appears to me the best of all natural history journals which have ever been published.' "

Praise so high, from a critic so competent, renders any apology for the publication of a second edition of the work referred to by Mr. Darwin, needless.

Moreover, apart from the intrinsic merits of the book, the great interest which is now generally displayed on all subjects connected with Central America and the circumstance that this book has now for some time been out of print—render it desirable that a new

edition should be issued from the press. In so doing
it seems fitting to say something of the life and work
of the author, whose death occurred only four years
after the first publication of this book. The following account is reprinted from the *Quarterly Journal of
Science* of January 1879 :—

"THOMAS BELT, F.G.S.

"In the obituary of the year, and amongst the list of
scientific men who have loved science for itself, and sought
truth for truth's sake, few will leave a brighter or happier
memory with their friends than Thomas Belt.

"Born in Newcastle in 1832, he was an early member of
the Tyneside Naturalists' Club, and there began that love of
nature and nature's ways that ever remained fresh with him
throughout his life.

"In 1852 his adventurous nature took him to the
Australian gold diggings, and there (the leading spirit of a
family of four brothers located in the colony) from 1853 to
1860 he successively visited, as a miner, the districts of
Friars and Forest Creeks, Maryborough, Mount Molingul,
Kingower, Korong, Mount Egerton.

"In this rough 'school of mines' he acquired that
practical knowledge which not only served him so well in
after-life in his profession, but gave him that insight into
the building-up of the earth's crust which enabled him, not
seldom, to put forth novel theories in geology and natural
phenomena. Unorthodox as they were when first promul-
gated, yet, silently and solidly, they commended themselves
to those who studied the facts and the inferences he drew
from them. Amid real hard work in Australia, he found
time to speculate on the flight of birds, and to show that

the mechanical action of the birds' wings is not always the prime mover, but that the force of the wind, particularly in the albatross, is the real agent that carries them sweeping over the ocean with the rapidity of the wind itself. Further, that this force is utilised by the faculty the bird has of balancing itself against the power of the wind. It is the equivalent of the string of the boy's kite, and almost overwhelming proof of this theory is afforded by the fact that the albatross is helpless in a calm, and cannot—from a level surface, as the deck of a ship—raise itself or fly so well as a domestic goose.

"His theory of whirlwinds—viz., that the upper strata of air pressed upon the lower rarefied and lighter strata, till a casual opening or thinning out in the upper layer leaves the lower strata free to fly upwards, and to form the circular whirlwinds common even in this country—was an outcome of his actual experience acquired in the dreadful dust storms of Australia. It is a curious fact that the paper on this subject, sent to a Melbourne scientific society, and put aside as unworthy of notice, was sent by Mr. Belt to the present Astronomer-Royal, and then, as communicated by the Astronomer-Royal to the Philosophical Institute of Victoria, was accepted and read in Melbourne, in December 1857. The paper itself will be found in the *London, Edinburgh, and Dublin Philosophical Magazine* for January 1859.

"The boldest of his speculations, and one of the soundest, as after-events proved, was his plan for crossing the Australian continent. He proposed, at the time the Government expedition was mooted, to replace the costly plans of the Government by the following scheme :—That he and his brother Anthony (who was unfortunately lost in the *Royal Charter*), should be conveyed to the Gulf of Carpentaria, with about twenty pack-horses loaded with provisions and water ; that an escort should protect them for some twenty miles from the coast, and that then the two voyagers only, with their pack-horses, should make their way to Cooper's Creek, the farthest known accessible point from the Victorian settled districts. Belt argued justly : ' If we fail, only two lives will be lost, but all the chances are in our favour; we are provided with water and food more than ample to cover the distance we have to travel. Every step of our road carries us homewards and to safety. If we never find a drop of water on the road, our animals have enough to carry those who have to bear the whole journey to their goal, and as the animals succumb they will be shot or turned adrift.' The event showed Belt's sagacity. The unfortunate Government expedition left Melbourne loaded with camp followers and *impedimenta*, and by the time they reached a few stages beyond Cooper's Creek were well-nigh exhausted. Burke, the leader of the expedition, in desperation started with his two men, Wills and King, and bravely struck out for the Gulf of Carpentaria. Through desert and fertile plains, not altogether destitute of water, they reached in safety the northern shore of Australia ; but the energy, the courage, and the strength that took them this long, weary journey did not suffice to carry them back over double the distance to their camp. Brave hearts ! they struggled on ; but King only, and as a worn-out man, ever saw Cooper's Creek again. Belt's plan would have solved the problem without loss of life, and at a tenth of the cost. His ideas were in advance of his time, and he had that belief in his own powers which should have won his plan the attention its merits deserved. The writer knows the fact, that had Belt then possessed the means, he would have spent them all in his endeavour to carry out this scheme of crossing the Australian continent.

"In 1862 Belt returned to England, and his professional engagements led him to North Wales, Nova Scotia, Central America, and Chontales, Nicaragua. At the latter place his entomological collection has made him famous. Many

hundred species of coleoptera and lepidoptera attest his
energy and labour; and his charming book, 'The Naturalist
in Nicaragua,' whilst illustrating his great powers of observation, has endeared him to every lover of nature, and
proved the painstaking truth with which he collected his
facts.

"The succeeding years of his life were spent in almost
continued travel : to North and South Russia, Siberia, the
Kirghese Steppes, and many times to the United States.
In these journeys he, from time to time, made those observations upon glacial action, upon which he built up his theories
of the ice age.   These became the ruling passion of his
later years.   Much of this work will be found in the
Quarterly Journal of Science and in the *Quarterly Journal
of the Geological Society*.   How much of it will stand
the test of time the future only can tell; but all this
special work of his is, at least, a careful and elaborate
argument, advocating the theory that the extraordinary
changes of climate in past ages, over large areas of the
earth's surface which are now temperate regions, during the
period called by geologists the glacial epoch, may have been
brought about by other causes of less intensity than the
submergences and emergences of the land, even than by
the displacement of whole continents, which theories have
been advanced by some to account for the phenomena in
question.

"Mr. Belt advocates the agency of ice, and ice-dams, and
great lakes—to use his own words—in place of 'great up-
heavals and depressions of the earth's surface within a comparatively short period;' and he questions the hypothesis by
which 'we are taught that an immense area in Europe and
America has been a sea bottom, and every part of it a sea
beach as the land rose again, without any evidence of marine
life having been left behind;' and he claims that his theory
of glacial action 'explains all the phenomena by one great

advance southwards of the ice of a single glacial period.'—
Quarterly Journal of Science, 'Loess of the Rhine and the
Danube,' January 1877.

" The immediate cause of his death was brain fever, following a long attack of mountain fever."

In the " Natural History Transactions of North-
umberland, Durham, and Newcastle-on-Tyne," vol. vii.,
1879, the following short memoir, by Mr. Joseph
Wright, giving some further details of Mr. Belt's
career, appears—

"'Died at Denver, Colorado, U.S.A., September 22nd,
1878, Mr. Thomas Belt, F.G.S., aged forty-five.' Such was
the brief announcement by telegram which appeared in
the newspapers, and· told to his astonished friends in this
district that he had passed away from their midst.

"His attainments, and the high position he had won for
himself in the scientific world, render it only fitting that
some record of his life and labours should appear in the
'Transactions of the Tyneside Naturalists' Field Club,' of
which he was a member for many years.

" Mr. Belt was born in Newcastle-upon-Tyne, in 1832, and
received his education at the school of the late Mr. John
Storey, one of the first secretaries of our Club.

" He early evinced a taste for natural history pursuits, the
departments of botany and entomology being his favourite
studies. In June 1850, he became a member of the Club,
and in the second 'volume of the 'Transactions' his name
several times appears as the authority for the habitats of
some of the rarer plants of the district. On more than
one occasion, his old master, Mr. Storey, acknowledges his
obligations to him for help on these points.

"In October 1851, he discovered at Ryton a plant new to
the district, the Frog-Bit, *Hydrocharus Morsus-rance.* We

also find him communicating lists of his captures amongst the lepidoptera to the Club.

"About this time the discovery of gold had been made in Australia, and, like a great many more, Mr. Belt left Tyneside for the new El Dorado.

"This step, we may say, was the turning-point in his life, and had a great influence on his future career. During his residence in Australia, although at a time when the whole colony was moved by the gold-fever, the same quiet habits of observation which marked him on Tyneside are seen. The new aspects of nature with which he was brought into contact in Australia aroused his spirit of investigation, and in 1857 he was reading before the Philosophical Institute of Victoria a paper on 'The Origin of Whirlwinds.' This paper is printed in the *Philosophical Magazine* for 1859, to which periodical it was communicated by the Astronomer-Royal.

"The auriferous quartz veins of Australia he made his peculiar study, the results of which he embodied in a work on 'Mineral Veins : an Inquiry into their Origin.' This book he published in 1861, and it at once lifted him into the position of an authority on the subject.

"On his return to England, his services were greatly in request as a mining engineer, to which profession he now devoted himself, with an establishment in London. In the prosecution of his labours he travelled over both Asia and America ; and in his long wanderings his keen powers of observation were ever on the alert to enlarge the domain of human knowledge.

"In 1863 Mr. Belt went to Nova Scotia, where he had the superintendence of the Nova-Scotian Gold Company's Mines. Here the great glacial phenomena of North America were unfolded to his view, and to the study of them he devoted himself with enthusiasm. In his investigations into glacial phenomena, careful observations were made at the great lakes of the American continent, the gorge of the Niagara,

and the valley of the St. Lawrence, followed afterwards by
an examination of the steppes of Siberia and Southern
Russia, and among the drifts and gravels of our own country.
These results were from time to time communicated to the
various learned societies and scientific periodicals. It was
his intention to embody his accumulated facts and observations in this department of geological inquiry in a work on
Glacial Phenomena; but this purpose of his life his early
death has prevented.

"Whilst in Nova Scotia, where he sojourned for two or
three years, he took an active part in the Proceedings of
the Nova-Scotian Institute of Natural Science; and the
first geological paper printed in their Transactions is from
his pen; it is also in these Transactions that his paper on
the Glacial Period in North America appeared.

"After his return from Nova Scotia, he was engaged for
some time in examining the quartz rocks of North Wales,
a project having been at that time started to seek for gold
in these rocks. Whilst so engaged he examined carefully the
geology and palæontology of the district of Dolgelly, where
he resided, and the results of which he published in two
papers in the *Geological Magazine*, vols. iv., v., 1867–8.

"In 1868 Mr. Belt went to Nicaragua to superintend the
mining operations of the Chontales Gold-Mining Company.
Here he remained until 1872, and to his residence in that
district we owe the work by which his name will be best
known. This work, 'The Naturalist in Nicaragua,' he
published in 1874, and we have in it one of the most
interesting volumes of travel and natural history in the
English language. His observations on the various departments of zoology, botany, and geology, which came under
his notice in that district, show the eye and the pen of a
competent investigator, and render the book truly a classic
one amongst our natural history literature. In 1873, and
again in 1875 and 1876, he was in Russia, and travelled

over a large portion of that great empire. The steppes of Siberia, and also those of Southern Russia, he made his peculiar study; and the results of his observations on these vast plains he embodied in two papers, which he read before the Geological Society of London in 1874 and 1877, and which are published in their *Journal*.

"In the early part of the summer of 1878 he was down in his native north, revisiting his old acquaintances and the scenes of his youth; for always, in all his wanderings, he turned lovingly to Tyneside. He at this time was in his usual health and genial spirits; and little did his friends think that it was to be his last visit to the place of his birth, and that they should see his face no more.

"He shortly afterwards left England for Colorado, to fulfil a professional engagement. Here he was struck down with fever, which terminated fatally on the 21st of September. To the last he was an earnest student, and the latest record we have of him shows him still accumulating facts in further-ance of the work on glacial phenomena to which he had devoted himself. The letter of the Denver correspondent of the *Times*, published in that paper September 25th, 1878, announces the discovery by Mr. Belt of a human skull that might prove to be the oldest in existence, the deposits in which it was found being in his belief of the glacial age.

"It may be said of him 'that his sun went down while it was yet day,' and that the work to which he had dedicated so much of his life remains unaccomplished. Yet the name of Thomas Belt will not be forgotten. Though he has passed away from us in the flower of his age, the work that he has done has gained for him a position in the scientific world to which few of greater years attain.

"He was a careful and accurate observer, and able with his pen to lay before the world the results of his observations clearly and temperately. Whatever he undertook he did it well, and in the departments of natural science to which he applied himself his name stands as an authority, and his work is quoted as that of a master.

"Residing as he did at a distance from Tyneside, and actively engaged in the duties of his profession (a profession which at one time took him to North America, at another to South America, and to Siberia), he could not take any active part in the work of the Club, which undoubtedly he would have done had he lived among us. Yet he took a warm interest in its welfare, and was always glad to hear of its progress. Our local natural history may have lost somewhat by his long absence, but that of the world at large has the more benefited by his labours, and he adds another bright name to the roll of those who have so well upheld the natural history fame of the Newcastle district."

LIST OF WORKS AND PAPERS, BY MR. THOMAS BELT.

An Inquiry into the Origin of Whirlwinds. Read before the Philosophical Institute, and published in the *Philosophical Magazine*, vol. xvii., p. 47.

Mineral Veins. An Inquiry into their Origin. Founded on a Study of the Auriferous Quartz Veins of Australia. 1861. London : John Weale.

The Naturalist in Nicaragua. A Narrative of a Residence at the Gold Mines of Chontales, and Journeys in the Savannahs and Forests. 1874. London : John Murray.

Note on the Discovery of a Human Skull in the Drift near Denver, Colorado. Read before the American Association for the Advancement of Science at St. Louis, Mo., August 1878.

Transactions of the Nova-Scotian Institute.

On some Recent Movements of the Earth's Surface. Vol. i., pt. 1, p. 19.

List of Butterflies observed in the neighbourhood of Halifax, Nova Scotia. Vol. ii., pt. 1, p. 97.

The Production and Preservation of Lakes by Ice Action. Vol. ii., pt. 3, p. 70.

The Glacial Period in North America. Vol. ii., pt. 4, p. 91.

Geological Magazine.

On some new Trilobites from the Upper Cambrian of North Wales. Vol. iv., p. 294.

On the Lingula Flags, or Festiniog Group of the Dolgelly District. Vol. iv., pp. 493–536, and vol. v., p. 5.

On the First Stages of the Glacial Period in Norfolk and Suffolk. Vol. xiv., p. 156.

Quarterly Journal of the Geological Society.

On the Steppes of Siberia. Vol. xxx., p. 463.

On the Steppes of Southern Russia. Vol. xxx., p. 843.

On the Drift of Devon and Cornwall : its Origin, Correlation with that of the South-West of England, and Place in the Glacial Series. Vol. xxxii., p. 80.

Quarterly Journal of Science.

An Examination of the Theories that have been proposed to account for the Climate of the Glacial Period. Vol. xi., 1874, p. 421.

Niagara : Glacial and Post-Glacial Phenomena. Vol. xii., 1875, p. 135.

On the Geological Age of the Deposits containing Flint Implements at Hoxne, in Suffolk, and the relation that Palæolithic Man bore to the Glacial Period. Vol. xiii., 1876, p. 289.

On the Loess of the Rhine and the Danube. Vol. xiv., 1877, p. 67.

On the Glacial Period in the Southern Hemisphere. Vol. xiv., 1877, p. 326.

On the Discovery of Stone Implements in Glacial Drift in North America. Vol. xv., 1878, p. 55.
On the Superficial Gravels and Clays around Finchley, Ealing, and Brentford. Vol. xv., 1878, p. 316.

It needs not to add more. It would be easy for the writer, who looks back with recollections of infinite pleasure upon a journey made to Mexico with Mr. Belt in 1876, and to numerous expeditions undertaken with him in Great Britain, to dwell on many incidents of personal travel, and to say much of his pleasant and genial qualities as a companion. With a mind keenly alive to all things natural he brought to bear, on everything that came under his notice, a wide and varied knowledge. Singularly modest and even-tempered by nature, he was only roused to anger by any sense of oppression or by wanton cruelty. But, indeed, his character may be read in his book. Those who knew him, loved him. Nor was he ever happier than when assisting others in the cultivation and enjoyment of those pursuits which occupied his own leisure.

Only a few days before the fever seized him he wrote from Georgetown, Colorado :—

"I am expecting to start East in about ten days' time, but shall not leave America until about the middle of September. The heat here has been very great, or rather it has been in the States eastward. Up at this height (over 8000 feet) it is never too hot. We had many astronomers at Denver to see the eclipse, which was a great success. The opinion is very general amongst them that the sun's heat has not been constant in long periods of time, and they refer the cause of the variation in geological climates to such fluctuations."

He rests in the Riverside Cemetery near Denver, Colorado ; nor should this short notice close without reference to the kind attention which he received from Mr. and Mrs. James Duff of Denver, during his fatal illness.

LONDON, *February* 1888.

PREFACE TO THE FIRST EDITION.

THE following pages have been written in the intervals between arduous professional engagements. Begun on the Atlantic during my voyage home from Central America, the first half relieved the tedium of a long and slow recovery from the effects of an accident on board ship. The middle of the manuscript found me traversing the high passes of the snow-clad Caucasus, where I made acquaintance with the Abkassians, in whose language Mr. Hyde Clarke finds analogies with those of my old friends the Brazilian Indians. I now write this brief preface and the last chapter of my book on my way across the continent to the Urals, and beyond, to the country of the nomad Kirghiz and the far Altai mountains on the borders of Thibet; and when readers receive my work I shall probably have turned my face homewards again, and for weeks be travelling across the frozen Siberian steppes, wrapped in furs, listening to the sleigh bells, and wondering how my book has sped. It is full of theories—I trust not unsupported by facts: some thought out on the plains of Southern Australia;

some during many a solitary sleigh drive over frozen
lakes in North America ; some in the great forests of
Central and South America ; some on the wide ocean ;
and some, again, in the bowels of the earth when
seeking for her hidden riches. The thoughts are
those of a lifetime compressed into a little book ; and,
like the genie of the Arabian tale, imprisoned in an
urn, they may, when it is opened, grow and magnify,
or, on the contrary, be kicked back into the sea of
oblivion.

This much is necessary ; not to disarm criticism, but
to excuse myself to those authors whose labours on
some of the subjects I have treated of I may not have
mentioned. I have, during my sojourns in England,
worked hard to read up the literature of the various
questions discussed, but I know there must be many
oversights and omissions in referring to what others
have done ; especially with regard to continental
writers, for I know no language but my mother-
tongue, and their works, excepting where I have had
access to translations, have been sealed books to me.

I am indebted to Mr. H. W. Bates for much assistance, and especially for undertaking the superintendence of these sheets in their passage through the
press ; to Mr. W. C. Hewitson, of Oatlands Park, I
am under many obligations, for taking charge of my
entomological collections, for naming many of my
butterflies, and for access to his magnificent collection
of Diurnal Lepidoptera. Mrs. Osbert Salvin and Dr.

P. L. Sclater have named for me my collection of birds; and for much entomological information I am indebted to Professor Westwood, Mr. F. Smith, and Dr. D. Sharp; whilst, in botany, Professor D. Oliver, of Kew, has kindly named for me some of the plants. Through the assistance of these eminent authorities, I trust that the scientific names scattered throughout the book may be depended upon as correct.

NIJNI NOVGOROD,
October 9th, 1873.

CONTENTS.

—✠—

LIST OF ILLUSTRATIONS.

—⋈—

THE

NATURALIST IN NICARAGUA.

CHAPTER I.

Arrival at Greytown — The river San Juan—Silting up of the harbour—Crossing the bar—Lives lost on it—Sharks—Christopher Columbus—Appearance of the town—Trade—Healthiness of the town and its probable cause—Comparison between Greytown, Pernambuco, and Maceio—Wild fruits—Plants—Parrots, toucans, and tanagers—Butterflies and beetles—Mimetic forms —Alligators — Boy drowned at Blewfields by an alligator— Their method of catching wild pigs.

AT noon on the 15th February 1868, the R.M.S.S. *Solent*, in which I was a passenger, anchored off Greytown, or San Juan del Norte, the Atlantic port of Nicaragua in Central America. We lay about a mile from the shore, and saw a low flat coast stretching before us. It was the delta of the river San Juan, into which flows the drainage of a great part of Nicaragua and Costa Rica, and which is the outlet for the waters of the great lake of Nicaragua. Its water-shed extends to within a few miles of the Pacific, for here the isthmus of Central America, as in the great continents to the north and south of it, sends off by far the largest portion of its drainage to the Atlantic. In the rainy season the San Juan is a noble river, and even in the dry

A

months, from March to June, there is sufficient water coming down from the lake to keep open a fine harbour, if it were not that about twenty miles above its mouth it begins to dissipate its force by sending off a large branch called the Colorado river, and lower down parts with more of its waters by side channels. Twenty years ago the main body of water ran past Greytown; there was then a magnificent port, and large ships sailed up to the town, but for several years past the Colorado branch has been taking away more and more of its waters, and the port of Greytown has in consequence silted up. All ships now have to lie off outside, and a shallow and, in heavy weather, dangerous bar has to be crossed.

All we could see from the steamer was the sandy beach on which the white surf was breaking, a fringe of bushes with a few coco-nut palms holding up their feathery crowns, and in the distance a low background of dark foliage. Before we anchored a gun was fired, and in quick answer to the signal some canoes, paddled by negroes of the Mosquito coast, here called "Caribs," were seen crossing the bar, and in a few minutes were alongside. Getting into one of the canoes with my boxes, I was rapidly paddled towards the shore. When we reached the bar we were dexterously taken over it— the Caribs waited just outside until a higher wave than usual came rolling in, then paddling with all their might we were carried over on its crest, and found ourselves in the smooth water of the river.

Many lives have been lost on this bar. In 1872 the commander of the United States surveying expedition and six of his men were drowned in trying to cross it in heavy weather. Only a few mangled remnants of their bodies were ever found; for what adds to the horror of an upset at this place, and perhaps has unnerved many a man at a critical moment, is that large sharks swarm about the entrance to the river. We saw the fin of one rising above the surface of the water as it swam lazily about, and the sailors of the mail steamers when lying off the port often amuse themselves by catching them with large hooks baited with pieces of meat. It is probable that it was at one of the mouths of the San Juan that Columbus, in his fourth voyage, lost a boat's crew who had been sent for wood and fresh water, and when returning were swamped on the bar. Columbus had rounded Cape Gracias a Dios four days before, and had sailed down the coast with a fair wind and tide, so that he might easily have reached the San Juan.

Inside the bar we were in smooth water, for but a small stream is discharged by this channel. On our right was a sandy beach, on our left great beds of grass growing out of the shoal water—weedy banks filled up the once spacious harbour, and cattle waded amongst the long grass, where within the last twenty years a frigate has lain at anchor. Wading and aquatic birds were abundant in the marshes, amongst which white cranes and a chocolate-brown jacana, with lemon-yellow underwing, were the most conspicuous. A large alligator lazily crawled off a mud-spit into the water, where he floated, showing only his eyes and the pointed scales of his back above the surface. The town was now in full view—neat, white-painted houses, with plume-crowned palms rising amongst and over them, and we landed at one of several wooden wharves that jut into the river.

Greytown, though only a small place, is one of the

neatest tropical towns that I have visited. The houses, especially in the business portion of the town, are well built of wood, and painted white with brown roofs. Pretty flower gardens surround or front many of them. Others are nearly hidden amongst palms and bread-fruit, orange, mango, and other tropical fruit trees. A lovely creeper (*Antigonon leptopus*), with festoons of pink and rose-coloured flowers, adorns some of the gardens. It is called *la vegessima*, "the beautiful," by the natives, and I found it afterwards growing wild in the provinces of Matagalpa and Segovia, where it was one of the great favourites of the flower-loving Indians. The land at and around Greytown is perfectly level. The square, the open spaces, and many of the streets are covered with short grass that makes a beautful sward to walk on.

The trade in the town is almost entirely in the hands of foreign residents, amongst whom Mr. Hollenbeck, a citizen of the United States, is one of the most enter-prising. A considerable import trade is done with the States and England. Coffee, indigo, hides, cacao, sugar, logwood, and india-rubber are the principal exports. I called on Dr. Green, the British Consul, and found him a most courteous and amiable gentleman, ready to afford protection or advice to his countrymen, and on very friendly terms with the native authorities. He has lived for many years in Nicaragua, and his many charitable kindnesses, and especially the medical assist-ance that he renders in all cases of emergency, free of charge, have made him very popular at Greytown. His beautiful house and grounds, with a fine avenue of coco-nut trees in full bearing, form one of the most attractive sights in Greytown. I found Mr. Paton, the vice-consul,

equally obliging, and I am indebted to him for much
information respecting the trade of the port, particularly
with regard to the export of india-rubber, the development of which trade he was one of the first to encourage.

Behind the town there is a long lagoon, and for several
miles back the land is quite level, and interspersed with
lakes and ponds with much marshy ground. Perfectly
level, surrounded by swamps, and without any system
of drainage, either natural or artificial, excepting such
as the sandy soil affords, Greytown might be thought a
very unhealthy site for a town. Notwithstanding, however, its apparent disadvantages, and that for nine
months of the year it is subject to heavy tropical rains,
it is comparatively healthy, and freer from fever than
many places that appear at first sight better situated.
Much is due to the porous sandy soil, but more I believe
to what appears at first sight an element of danger, the
perfect flatness of the ground. Where there are hills
there must be hollows, and in these the air stagnates;
whilst here, where the land is quite level, the trade
winds that blow pretty constantly find their way to
every part, and carry off the emanations from the soil.
As a similar instance I may mention the city of Pernambuco, on the eastern coast of Brazil, containing
80,000 inhabitants. It is perfectly level like Greytown,
surrounded and intersected with channels of water,
above the level of which it only stands a few feet. The
crowded parts of the town are noted for their evil
smells and filth, but, though entirely without drainage,
it is celebrated for its healthiness; whilst a little lower
down the coast, the town of Maceio, situated about
sixty feet above the sea, surrounded by undulating ranges

and with a good natural drainage, is much more unhealthy, fevers being very prevalent.   As at Greytown
so at Pernambuco, the trade winds blow with much regularity, and there are neither hills nor hollows to interfere with the movements of the air, so that miasmatic
exhalations cannot accumulate.

Surrounding the cleared portions around Greytown is
a scrubby bush, amongst which are many guayava trees
(*Psidium sp.*) having a fruit like a small apple filled
with seeds, of a sub-acid flavour, from which the celebrated guava jelly is made.   The fruit itself often
occasions severe fits of indigestion, and many of the
natives will not swallow the small seeds, but only the
pulpy portion, which is said to be harmless.   I saw
another fruit growing here, a yellow berry about the
size of a cherry, called " Nancito " by the natives.   It
is often preserved by them with spirit and eaten like
olives.   Beyond the brushwood, which grows where the
original forest has been cut down, there are large trees
covered with numerous epiphytes—Tillandsias, orchids,
ferns, and a hundred others, that make every big tree
an aërial garden.   Great arums perch on the forks and
send down roots like cords to the ground, whilst lianas
run from tree to tree or hang in loops and folds like the
disordered tackle of a ship.

Green parrots fly over in screaming flocks, or nestle
in loving couples amidst the foliage, toucans hop along
the branches, turning their long, highly-coloured beaks
from side to side with an old-fashioned look, and beautiful tanagers (*Ramphocœlus passerinii*) frequent the outskirts of the forest, all velvety black, excepting a large
patch of fiery-red above the tail, which renders the bird

very conspicuous.   It is only the male that is thus
coloured, the female being clothed in a sober suit of
greenish-brown.   I think this bird is polygamous, for
several of the brown ones were always seen with one of
the red-and-black ones.   The bright colours of the male
must make it very conspicuous to birds of prey, and,
probably in consequence, it is not nearly so bold as the
obscurely-coloured females.   When a clear space in the
brushwood is to be crossed, such as a road, two or three
of the females will fly across first, before the male will
venture to do so, and he is always more careful to get
himself concealed amongst the foliage than his mates.

I walked some distance into the forest along swampy
paths cut by charcoal burners, and saw many beautiful
and curious insects.   Amongst the numerous butterflies, large blue Morphos and narrow, weak-winged
Heliconidæ, striped and spotted with yellow, red, and
black, were the most conspicuous and most characteristic of tropical America.   Amongst the beetles I found
a curious longicorn (*Desmiphora fasciculata*), covered
with long brown and black hairs, and closely resembling
some of the short, thick, hairy caterpillars that are
common on the bushes.   Other closely allied species
hide under fallen branches and logs, but this one clung
exposed amongst the leaves, its antennæ concealed
against its body, and it resemblance to a caterpillar so
great, that I was at first deceived by it.   It is well
known that insectivorous birds will not touch a hairy
caterpillar, and this is only one of numberless instances
where insects, that have some special protection against
their enemies, are closely imitated by others belonging
to different genera, and even different orders.   Thus,

wasps and stinging ants have hosts of imitators amongst moths, beetles, and bugs, and I shall have many curious facts to relate concerning these mimetic resemblances. To those not acquainted with Mr. Bates's admirable remarks on mimetic forms, I must explain that we have to speak of one species imitating another, as if it were a conscious act, only on account of the poverty of our language. No such idea is entertained, and it would have been well if some new term had been adopted to express what is meant. These deceptive resemblances are supposed, by the advocates of the origin of species by natural selection, to have been brought about by varieties of one species somewhat resembling another having special means of protection, and preserved from their enemies in consequence of that unconscious imitation. The resemblance, which was perhaps at first only remote, is supposed to have been increased in the course of ages by the varieties being protected that more and more closely approached the species imitated, in form, colour, and movements. These resemblances are not only between insects of different genera and orders, but between insects and flowers, leaves, twigs, and bark of trees, and between insects and inanimate nature. They serve often for concealment, as when leaves are imitated by leaf-insects and many butterflies, or for a disguise that enables predatory species to get within reach of their prey, as in those spiders that resemble the petals of flowers amongst which they hide.

That I may not travel over the same ground twice, I may here mention that on a subsequent visit to Greytown I rode a few miles northward along the beach. On my return, I tied up the horse and walked about a mile

ALLIGATORS IN SAN JUAN RIVER.

over the sand-bank that extends down to the mouth of
the river. A long, deep branch forms a favourite resort
for alligators. At the far end of a sand-spit, near where
some low trees grew, I saw several dark objects lying
close to the water on the shelving banks. They were
alligators basking in the sun. As I approached, most of
them crawled into the water. Mr. Hollenbeck had been
down a few days before shooting at them with a rifle, to
try to get a skull of one of the monsters, and I passed a
dead one that he had shot. As I walked up the beach,
I saw many that were not less than fifteen feet in length.
One lay motionless, and thinking it was another dead
one, I was walking up to it, and had got within three
yards, when I saw the film over its eye moving ; otherwise it was quite still, and its teeth projecting beyond
its lips added to its intense ugliness and appearance of
death. There was no doubt, however, about the movement of the eye-covers, and I went back a short distance
to look for a stick to throw at it; but when I turned
again, the creature was just disappearing into the water.
It is their habit to lie quite still, and catch animals
that come near them. Whether or not it was waiting
until I came within the swoop of its mighty tail I know
not, but I had the feeling that I had escaped a great
danger. It was curious that it should have been so
bold only a few days after Mr. Hollenbeck had been
down shooting at them. There were not less than
twenty altogether, and they swam out into the middle
of the inlet and floated about, looking like logs in the
water, excepting that one stretched up its head and gave
a bellow like a bull. They sometimes kill calves and
young horses, and I was told of one that had seized a

full-grown horse, but its struggles being observed, some natives ran down and saved it from being pulled into the water and drowned. I heard several stories of people being killed by them, but only one was well authenticated. This was told me by the head of the excellent Moravian Mission at Blewfields, who was a witness of the occurrence. He said that one Sunday, after service at their chapel at Blewfields, several of the youths went to bathe in the river, which was rather muddy at the time ; the first to plunge in was a boy of twelve years of age, and he was immediately seized by a large alligator, and carried along under water. My informant and others followed in a canoe, and ultimately recovered the body, but life was extinct. The alligator cannot devour its prey beneath the water, but crawls on land with it after he has drowned it. They are said to catch wild pigs in the forest near the river by half burying themselves in the ground. The pigs come rooting amongst the soil, the alligator never moves until one gets within its reach, when it seizes it and hurries off to the river with it. They are often seen in hot weather on logs or sand-spits lying with their mouths wide open. The natives say they are catching flies, that numbers are attracted by the saliva of the mouth, and that when sufficient are collected, the alligator closes its jaws upon them, but I do not know that any reliance can be placed on the story. Probably it is an invention to account for the animals lying with their mouths open ; as in all half-civilised countries I have visited I have found the natives seldom admit they do not know the reason of anything, but will invent an explanation rather than acknowledge their ignorance.

CHAPTER II.

I FOUND at Greytown the mail-boat of the Chontales
Gold-Mining Company, which came down monthly in
charge of Captain Anderson, an Englishman who had
knocked about all over the world. The crew consisted
of four Mosquito negroes, who are celebrated on this
coast for their skill as boatmen. Besides the crew, we
were taking three other negroes up to the mines, and
with my boxes we were rather uncomfortably crowded
for a long journey. The canoe itself was made from the
trunk of a cedar-tree (*Cedrela odorata*). It had been
hollowed out of a single log, and the sides afterwards
built up higher with planking. This makes a very
strong boat, the strength and thickness being where it
is most required, at the bottom, to withstand the
thumping about amongst the rocks of the rapids. I
was once in one, coming down a dangerous rapid on the
river Gurupy, in Northern Brazil, when we were driven
with the full force of the boiling stream broadside upon

a rock, with such force that we were nearly all thrown down, but the strong canoe was uninjured, although no common boat could have withstood the shock.

Having determined to go up the river in this boat, we took provisions with us for the voyage, and one of the negroes agreed to act as cook. Having arranged everything, and breakfasted with my kind friends, Mr. and Mrs. Hollenbeck, I bade them adieu, and settled myself into the small space in the canoe that I expected to occupy for six days. Captain Anderson took the helm, the " Caribs " dipped their paddles into the water, and away we glided into a narrow channel amongst long grass and rushes that almost touched us on either side. Greytown, with its neat white houses, and feathery palms, and large-leaved bread-fruit trees, was soon shut out from our view, and our boatmen plying their paddles with the greatest dexterity and force, made the canoe shoot along through the still water. Soon we emerged into a wider channel where a stronger stream was running, and then we coasted along close to the shore to avoid the strength of the current. The banks at first were low and marshy and intersected by numerous channels; the principal tree was a long, coarse-leaved palm, and there were great beds of wild cane and grass, amongst which we occasionally saw curious green lizards, with leaf-like expansions (like those on the leaf-insects), assimilating them in appearance to the vegetation amongst which they sought their prey. As we proceeded up the river, the banks gradually became higher and drier, and we passed some small plantations of bananas and plantains made in clearings in the forest, which now consisted of a great variety of dicotyledonous trees with many tall, graceful palms; the undergrowth being ferns, small palms, Melastomæ, Heliconiæ, &c. The houses at the plantations were mostly miserable thatched huts with scarcely any furniture, the owners passing their time swinging in dirty hammocks, and occasionally taking down a canoe-load of plantains to Greytown for sale. It is one of the rarest sights to see any of these squatters at work. Their plantain patch and occasionally some fish from the river suffice to keep them alive and indolent.

At seven o'clock we reached the Colorado branch, which carries off the greater part of the waters of the San Juan to the sea. This is about twenty miles above Greytown, but only eighteen by the Colorado to the sea, and is near the head of the delta, as I have already mentioned. The main body of water formerly flowed down past Greytown, and kept the harbour there open, but a few years ago, during a heavy flood, the river greatly enlarged and deepened the entrance to the Colorado Channel, and since then year by year the Greytown harbour has been silting up. Now (I am writing in 1873) there is twelve feet of water on the bar at the Colorado in the height of the dry season, whilst at Greytown the outlet of the river is sometimes closed altogether. The merchants at Greytown have entertained the project of dredging out the channel again, but now that the river has found a nearer way to the sea by the Colorado this would be a herculean task, and it would cost much less money to move the whole town to the Colorado, where by dredging the bar a fine harbour might easily be made, but unfortunately the Colorado is in Costa Rica, the Greytown branch in

Nicaragua, and there are constant bickerings between the two states respecting the outlet of this fine river, which make any well-considered scheme for the improvement of it impracticable at present. A sensible solution of the difficulty, would be a federation of the two small republics. The heads of the political parties in the two countries see, however, in this a danger to their petty ambitions, and will not risk the step, and so the boundary question remains an open one, threatening at any moment to plunge the two countries into an impoverishing war.

If the Colorado were not to be interfered with by man, it would, in the course of ages, carry down great quantities of mud, sand, and trunks of trees, and gradually form sand-banks at its mouth, pushing out the delta further and further at this point, until it was greatly in advance of the rest of the coast; the river would then break through again by some nearer channel, and the Colorado would be silted up as the Lower San Juan is being at present. The numerous half-filled-up channels and long lagoons throughout the delta show the various courses the river has at different times taken.

Our boatmen paddled on until nine o'clock, when we anchored in the middle of the stream, which was here about one hundred yards wide. Distant as we were from the shores, we were not too far for the mosquitoes, which came off in myriads to the banquet upon our blood. Sleep for me was impossible, and to add to the discomfort, the rain came down in torrents. We had an old tarpaulin with us, but it was full of holes, and let in the water in little streams, so that I was soon soaked to the skin. Altogether, with the streaming wet and the mosquitoes, it was one of the most uncomfortable nights I have ever passed.

The waning moon was sufficiently high at four o'clock to allow us to bring the long dreary night to an end, and to commence paddling up the river again. As the day broke the rain ceased, the mists cleared away, our spirits revived, and we forgot our discomforts of the night in admiration of the beauties of the river. The banks were hidden by a curtain of creeping and twining plants, many of which bore beautiful flowers, and the green was further varied here and there by the white stems of the cecropia trees. Now and then we passed more open spots, affording glimpses into the forest, where grew, in the dark shade, slender-stemmed palms and beautiful tree-ferns, contrasting with the great leaves of the Heliconiæ. At seven we breakfasted on a sand-bank, and got our clothes and blankets dried. There were numerous tracks of alligators, but it was too early to look for their eggs in the sand ; a month later, in March, when the river falls, they are found in abundance, and eaten by the canoe-men. At noon we reached the point where the Seripiqui, a river coming down from the interior of Costa Rica, joins the San Juan about thirty miles above Greytown. The Seripiqui is navigable by canoes for about twenty miles from this point, and then commences a rough mountain mule-track to San José, the capital of Costa Rica. We paddled on all the afternoon with little change in the river. At eight we anchored for the night, and although it rained heavily again, I was better prepared for it, and, coiling myself up under an umbrella beneath the tarpaulin, managed to sleep a little.

We started again before daylight, and at ten stopped at a small clearing for breakfast. I strolled back a little way into the gloomy forest, but it was not easy to get along on account of the undergrowth and numerous climbing plants that bound it together. I saw one of the large olive-green and brown mot-mots (*Momotus martii*), sitting upon a branch of a tree, moving its

HEADS OF MOT-MOTS.

long curious tail from side to side, until it was nearly at right angles to its body. I afterwards saw other species in the forests and savannahs of Chontales. They all have several characters in common, linked together in a series of gradations. One of these features is a spot of black feathers on the breast. In some species this is edged with blue, in others, as in the one mentioned above, these black feathers form only a small black spot nearly hidden amongst the rust-coloured feathers of the breast. Characters such as these, very conspicuous in some species, shading off in others through various gradations to insignificance, if not extinction, are known by naturalists to occur in numerous genera; and so far they have only been explained on the supposition of the descent of the different species from a common progenitor.

As I returned to the boat, I crossed a column of the army or foraging ants, many of them dragging along the legs and mangled bodies of insects that they had captured in their foray. I afterwards often encountered these ants in the forests, and it may be convenient to place together all the facts I learnt respecting them.

ECITONS, OR FORAGING ANTS.—The Ecitons, or foraging ants, are very numerous throughout Central America. Whilst the leaf-cutting ants are entirely vegetable feeders, the foraging ants are hunters, and live solely on insects or other prey; and it is a curious analogy that, like the hunting races of mankind, they have to change their hunting-grounds when one is exhausted, and move on to another. In Nicaragua they are generally called "Army Ants." One of the smaller species (*Eciton predator*) used occasionally to visit our house, swarm over the floors and walls, searching every cranny, and driving out the cockroaches and spiders, many of which were caught, pulled, or bitten to pieces and carried off. The individuals of this species are of various sizes; the smallest measuring one and a quarter lines, and the largest three lines, or a quarter of an inch.

B

I saw many large armies of this, or a closely allied species, in the forest. My attention was generally first called to them by the twittering of some small birds, belonging to several different species, that follow the ants in the woods. On approaching to ascertain the cause of this disturbance, a dense body of the ants, three or four yards wide, and so numerous as to blacken the ground, would be seen moving rapidly in one direction, examining every cranny, and underneath every fallen leaf. On the flanks, and in advance of the main body, smaller columns would be pushed out. These smaller columns would generally first flush the cockroaches, grasshoppers, and spiders. The pursued insects would rapidly make off, but many, in their confusion and terror, would bound right into the midst of the main body of ants. A grasshopper, finding itself in the midst of its enemies, would give vigorous leaps, with perhaps two or three of the ants clinging to its legs. Then it would stop a moment to rest, and that moment would be fatal, for the tiny foes would swarm over the prey, and after a few more ineffectual struggles it would succumb to its fate, and soon be bitten to pieces and carried off to the rear. The greatest catch of the ants was, however, when they got amongst some fallen brushwood. The cockroaches, spiders, and other insects, instead of running right away, would ascend the fallen branches and remain there, whilst the host of ants were occupying all the ground below. By-and-by up would come some of the ants, following every branch, and driving before them their prey to the ends of the small twigs, when nothing remained for them but to leap, and they would alight in the very throng of their foes, with

the result of being certainly caught and pulled to pieces.
Many of the spiders would escape by hanging suspended
by a thread of silk from the branches, safe from the foes
that swarmed both above and below.

I noticed that spiders were generally most intelligent
in escaping, and did not, like the cockroaches and other
insects, take shelter in the first hiding-place they found,
only to be driven out again, or perhaps caught by the
advancing army of ants. I have often seen large spiders
making off many yards in advance, and apparently
determined to put a good distance between themselves
and their foe. I once saw one of the false spiders, or
harvest-men (*Phalangidæ*), standing in the midst of an
army of ants, and with the greatest circumspection and
coolness lifting, one after the other, its long legs, which
supported its body above their reach. Sometimes as
many as five out of its eight legs would be lifted at
once, and whenever an ant approached one of those on
which it stood, there was always a clear space within
reach to put down another, so as to be able to hold up
the threatened one out of danger.

I was much more surprised with the behaviour of a
green, leaf-like locust. This insect stood immovably
amongst a host of ants, many of which ran over its
legs, without ever discovering there was food within
their reach. So fixed was its instinctive knowledge
that its safety depended on its immovability, that it
allowed me to pick it up and replace it amongst the
ants without making a single effort to escape. This
species closely resembles a green leaf, and the other
senses, which in the Ecitons appear to be more acute
than that of sight, must have been completely deceived.

It might easily have escaped from the ants by using its wings, but it would only have fallen into as great a danger, for the numerous birds that accompany the army ants are ever on the outlook for any insect that may fly up, and the heavy flying locusts, grasshoppers, and cockroaches have no chance of escape. Several species of ant-thrushes always accompany the army ants in the forest. They do not, however, feed on the ants, but on the insects they disturb. Besides the ant-thrushes, trogons, creepers, and a variety of other birds, are often seen on the branches of trees above where an ant army is foraging below, pursuing and catching the insects that fly up.

The insects caught by the ants are dismembered, and their too bulky bodies bitten to pieces and carried off to the rear. Behind the army there are always small columns engaged on this duty. I have followed up these columns often ; generally they led to dense masses of impenetrable brushwood, but twice they led me to cracks in the ground, down which the ants dragged their prey. These habitations are only temporary, for in a few days not an ant would be seen in the neighbourhood ; all would have moved off to fresh hunting-grounds.

Another much larger species of foraging ant (*Eciton hamata*) hunts sometimes in dense armies, sometimes in columns, according to the prey it may be after. When in columns, I found that it was generally, if not always, in search of the nests of another ant (*Hypoclinea sp.*), which rear their young in holes in rotten trunks of fallen timber, and are very common in cleared places. The Ecitons hunt about in columns, which branch off in various directions. When a fallen log is reached, the column spreads out over it, searching through all the holes and cracks. The workers are of various sizes, and the smallest are here of use, for they squeeze themselves into the narrowest holes, and search out their prey in the furthest ramifications of the nests. When a nest of the *Hypoclinea* is attacked, the ants rush out, carrying the larvæ and pupæ in their jaws, only to be immediately despoiled of them by the Ecitons, which are running about in every direction with great swiftness. Whenever they come across a *Hypoclinea* carrying a larva or pupa, they capture the burden so quickly, that I could never ascertain exactly how it was done.

As soon as an Eciton gets hold of its prey, it rushes off back along the advancing column, which is composed of two sets, one hurrying forward, the other returning laden with their booty, but all and always in the greatest haste and apparent hurry. About the nest which they are harrying, everything is confusion, Ecitons run here and there and everywhere in the greatest haste and disorder; but the result of all this apparent confusion is that scarcely a single *Hypoclinea* gets away with a pupa or larva. I never saw the Ecitons injure the Hypoclineas themselves, they were always contented with despoiling them of their young. The ant that is attacked is a very cowardly species, and never shows fight. I often found it running about sipping at the glands of leaves, or milking aphides, leaf-hoppers, or scale-insects that it found unattended by other ants. On the approach of another, though of a much smaller, species, it would immediately run away. Probably this cowardly and unantly disposition has caused it to become the prey of the Eciton. At any rate, I never saw the Ecitons attack the nest of other species.

The moving columns of Ecitons are composed almost entirely of workers of different sizes, but at intervals of two or three yards there are larger and lighter-coloured individuals that will often stop, and sometimes run a little backward, halting and touching some of the ants with their antennæ. They look like officers giving orders and directing the march of the column.

This species is often met with in the forest, not in quest of one particular form of prey, but hunting, like *Eciton predator*, only spread out over a much greater space of ground. Crickets, grasshoppers, scorpions, centipedes, wood-lice, cockroaches, and spiders are driven out from below the fallen leaves and branches. Many of them are caught by the ants; others that get away are picked up by the numerous birds that accompany the ants, as vultures follow the armies of the East. The ants send off exploring parties up the trees, which hunt for nests of wasps, bees, and probably birds. If they find any, they soon communicate the intelligence to the army below, and a column is sent up immediately to take possession of the prize. I have seen them pulling out the larvæ and pupæ from the cells of a large wasp's nest, whilst the wasps hovered about, powerless, before the multitude of the invaders, to render any protection to their young.

I have no doubt that many birds have acquired instincts to combat or avoid the great danger to which their young are exposed by the attacks of these and other ants. Trogons, parrots, toucans, mot-mots, and many other birds build in holes of trees or in the ground, and these, with their heads ever turned to the only entrance, are in the best possible position to pick off singly the scouts when they approach, thus effectually preventing them from carrying to the main army intelligence about the nest. Some of these birds, and especially the toucans, have bills beautifully adapted for picking up the ants before they reach the nest. Many of the smaller birds build on the branches of the bull's-horn thorn, which is always thickly covered with small stinging honey-eating ants, that would not allow the Ecitons to ascend these trees.

Amongst the mammalia the opossums can convey their young out of danger in their pouches, and the females of many of the tree-rats and mice have a hard callosity near the teats, to which the young cling with their milk teeth, and can be dragged away by the mother to a place of safety.

The eyes in the Ecitons are very small, in some of the species imperfect, and in others entirely absent; in this they differ greatly from those ants which hunt singly, and which have the eyes greatly developed. The imperfection of eyesight in the Ecitons is an advantage to the community, and to their particular mode of hunting. It keeps them together, and prevents individual ants from starting off alone after objects that, if their eyesight were better, they might discover at a distance. The Ecitons and most other ants follow each other by scent, and, I believe, they can communicate the presence of danger, of booty, or other intelligence, to a distance by the different intensity or qualities of the odours given off. I one day saw a column of *Eciton hamata* running along the foot of a nearly perpendicular tramway cutting, the side of which was about six feet high. At one point I noticed a sort of assembly of about a dozen individuals that appeared in consultation. Suddenly one ant left the conclave, and ran with great speed up the perpendicular face of the cutting without stopping. It was followed by others, which, however, did not keep straight on like the first, but ran a short way, then returned, then again followed a little further than the first time. They were evidently scenting the trail of the pioneer, and making it permanently recognisable. These ants followed the exact line taken by the first one, although it was far out of sight. Wherever it had made a slight detour they did so likewise. I scraped with my knife a small portion of the clay on the trail, and the ants were completely at fault for a time which way to go. Those ascending and those descending stopped at the scraped portion, and made short circuits until they hit the scented trail again, when all their hesitation vanished, and they ran up and down it with the greatest confidence. On gaining the top of the cutting, the ants entered some brushwood suitable for hunting. In a very short space of time the information was communicated to the ants below, and a dense column rushed up to search for their prey.

The Ecitons are singular amongst the ants in this respect, that they have no fixed habitations, but move on from one place to another, as they exhaust the hunting grounds around them. I think *Eciton hamata* does not stay more than four or five days in one place. I have sometimes come across the migratory columns. They may easily be known by all the common workers

moving in one direction, many of them carrying the
larvæ and pupæ carefully in their jaws.   Here and
there one of the light-coloured officers moves backwards
and forwards directing the columns.   Such a column
is of enormous length, and contains many thousands,
if not millions of individuals.   I have sometimes followed them up for two or three hundred yards without
getting to the end.

They make their temporary habitations in hollow
trees, and sometimes underneath large fallen trunks
that offer suitable hollows.   A nest that I came across
in the latter situation was open at one side.   The ants
were clustered together in a dense mass, like a great
swarm of bees, hanging from the roof, but reaching to
the ground below.   Their innumerable long legs looked
like brown threads binding together the mass, which
must have been at least a cubic yard in bulk, and contained hundreds of thousands of individuals, although
many columns were outside, some bringing in the pupæ
of ants, others the legs and dissected bodies of various
insects.   I was surprised to see in this living nest
tubular passages leading down to the centre of the
mass, kept open just as if it had been formed of inor-
ganic materials.   Down these holes the ants who were
bringing in booty passed with their prey.   I thrust a
long stick down to the centre of the cluster, and brought
out clinging to it many ants holding larvæ and pupæ,
which probably were kept warm by the crowding together of the ants.   Besides the common dark-coloured
workers and light-coloured officers, I saw here many
still larger individuals with enormous jaws.   These
they go about holding wide open in a threatening

manner, and I found, contrary to my expectation, that
they could give a severe bite with them, and that it
was difficult to withdraw the jaws from the skin again.

One day when watching a small column of these ants,
I placed a little stone on one of the ants to secure it.
The next that approached, as soon as it discovered the
situation of the prisoner, ran backwards in an agitated
manner, and communicated the intelligence to the
others.   They rushed to the rescue, some bit at the
stone and tried to move it, others seized the captive by
the legs, and tugged with such force that I thought the
legs would be pulled off, but they persevered until they
freed it.   I next covered one up with a piece of clay,
leaving only the ends of its antennæ projecting.   It
was soon discovered by its fellows, which set to work
immediately, and by biting off pieces of the clay, soon
liberated it.   Another time I found a very few of them
passing along at intervals.   I confined one of these under
a piece of clay, at a little distance from the line, with
his head projecting.   Several ants passed it, but at last
one discovered it and tried to pull it out, but could not.
It immediately set off at a great rate, and I thought it
had deserted its comrade, but it had only gone for
assistance, for in a short time about a dozen ants came
hurrying up, evidently fully informed of the circumstances of the case, for they made directly for their
imprisoned comrade, and soon set him free.   I do not
see how this action could be instinctive.   It was sympathetic help, such as man only among the higher mammalia shows.   The excitement and ardour with which
they carried on their unflagging exertions for the rescue
of their comrade could not have been greater if they had

been human beings, and this to meet a danger that can be only of the rarest occurrence.   Amongst the ants of Central America I place the Eciton as the first in intelligence, and as such at the head of the Articulata. Wasps and bees come next to ants, and then others of the Hymenoptera.   Between ants and the lower forms of insects there is a greater difference in reasoning powers than there is between man and the lowest mammalian. A recent writer has argued that of all animals ants approach nearest to man in their social condition.* Perhaps if we could learn their wonderful language we should find that even in their mental condition they also rank next to humanity.

I shall relate two more instances of the use of a reasoning faculty in these ants.   I once saw a wide column trying to pass along a crumbling, nearly perpendicular, slope.   They would have got very slowly over it, and many of them would have fallen, but a number having secured their hold, and reaching to each other, remained stationary, and over them the main column passed.   Another time they were crossing a watercourse along a small branch, not thicker than a goosequill.   They widened this natural bridge to three times its width by a number of ants clinging to it and to each other on each side, over which the column passed three or four deep.   Except for this expedient they would have had to pass over in single file, and treble the time would have been consumed.   Can it not be contended that such insects are able to determine by reasoning powers which is the best way of doing a thing, and that

* Houzeau, Etudes sur les Facultés mentales des Animaux comparées à celles de l'Homme.

their actions are guided by thought and reflection?
This view is much strengthened by the fact that the
cerebral ganglia in ants are more developed than in
any other insect, and that in all the Hymenoptera, at
the head of which they stand, " they are many times
larger than in the less intelligent orders, such as
beetles." *

The Hymenoptera standing at the head of the Articulata, and the Mammalia at the head of the Vertebrata,
it is curious to mark how, in geological history, the appearance and development of these two orders (culminating, one in the Ants; the other in the Primates) run
parallel. The Hymenoptera and the Mammalia both
make their first appearance early in the secondary period,
and it is not until the commencement of the tertiary epoch
that ants and monkeys appear upon the scene. There
the parallel ends. No one species of ant has attained any
great superiority above all its fellows, whilst man is
very far in advance of all the other Primates.

When we see these intelligent insects dwelling together in orderly communities of many thousands of
individuals, their social instincts developed to a high
degree of perfection, making their marches with the
regularity of disciplined troops, showing ingenuity in
the crossing of difficult places, assisting each other in
danger, defending their nests at the risk of their own
lives, communicating information rapidly to a great
distance, making a regular division of work, the whole
community taking charge of the rearing of the young,
and all imbued with the strongest sense of industry, each
individual labouring not for itself alone but also for its

* Darwin, Descent of Man, vol. i. p. 145.

fellows—we may imagine that Sir Thomas More's description of Utopia might have been applied with greater justice to such a community than to any human society. " But in Utopia, where every man has a right to everything, they do all know that if care is taken to keep the public stores full, no private man can want anything; for among them there is no unequal distribution, so that no man is poor, nor in any necessity, and though no man has anything, yet they are all rich; for what can make a man so rich as to lead a serene and cheerful life, free from anxieties, neither apprehending want himself, nor vexed with the endless complaints of his wife ? He is not afraid of the misery of his children, nor is he contriving how to raise a portion for his daughters, but is secure in this, that both he and his wife, his children and grandchildren, to as many generations as he can fancy, will all live both plentifully and happily."

CHAPTER III.

AFTER breakfast we again continued our voyage up the river, and passed the mouth of the San Carlos, another large stream running down from the interior of Costa Rica. Soon after we heard some wild pigs (*Dicoteles tajaçu*) or Wari, as they are called by the natives, striking their teeth together in the wood, and one of the boatmen leaping on shore soon shot one, which he brought on board after cutting out a gland on its back that emits a musky odour, and we afterwards had it cooked for our dinner. These Wari go in herds of from fifty to one hundred. They are said to assist each other against the attacks of the jaguar, but that wary animal is too intelligent for them. He sits quietly upon a branch of a tree until the Wari come underneath ; then jumping down kills one by breaking its neck ; leaps up into the tree again and waits there until the herd depart, when he comes down and feeds on the slaughtered Wari in quietness. We shortly afterwards passed one

of the large boats called *bungos*, that carry down to
Greytown the produce of the country and take up mer-
chandise and flour. This one was laden with cattle and
india-rubber. The bungos are flat-bottomed boats, about
forty feet long and nine feet wide. There is generally
a little cabin, roofed over at the stern, in which the
wife of the captain lives. The bungo is poled along by
twelve bungo-men, who have usually only one suit of
clothes each, which they do not wear during the day,
but keep stowed away under the cargo that it may be
dry to put on at night. Their bronzed, glistening,
naked bodies, as they ply their long poles together in
unison, and chant some Spanish boat-song, is one of the
things that linger in the memory of the traveller up
the San Juan. Our boatmen paddled and poled until
eleven at night, when we reached Machuca, a settlement consisting of a single house, just below the rapids
of the same name, seventy-seven miles above Greytown.

We breakfasted at Machuca before starting next
morning, and I walked up round the rapids and met the
canoe above them. About five o'clock, after paddling
all day, we came in sight of Castillo, where there is an
old ruined Spanish fort perched on the top of a hill
overlooking the little town, which lies along the foot
of the steep hill; hemmed in between it and the river,
so that there is only room for one narrow street. It was
near Castillo that Nelson lost his eye. He took the
fort by landing about half a mile lower down the river,
and dragging his guns round to a hill behind it by
which it was commanded. This hill is now cleared of
timber and covered with grass, supporting a few cows
and a great many goats. In front of the town run the

rapids of Castillo, which are difficult to ascend, and as there is no road round them excepting through the town of Castillo, advantage has been taken of the situation to fix the custom-house there, where are collected the duties on all articles going up to the interior. The first view of Castillo when coming up the river is a fine one. The fort-crowned hill and the little town clinging to its foot form the centre of the picture. The clear, sparkling, dancing rapids on one side contrast with the still, dark forest on the other, whilst the whole is relieved by the bright green grassy hills in the background. This view is the only pleasant recollection I have carried away of the place. The single street is narrow, dirty, and rugged, and when the shades of evening begin to creep up, swarms of mosquitoes issue forth to buzz and bite.

I here made the acquaintance of Colonel M'Crae, who was largely concerned in the india-rubber trade. He afterwards distinguished himself during the revolutionary outbreak of 1869. He collected the rubber men and came to the assistance of the government, helping greatly to put down the insurrection. Originally a British subject, but now a naturalised Nicaraguan, he has filled with great credit for some time the post of deputy-governor of Greytown, and I always heard him spoken of with great esteem both by Nicaraguans and foreigners. He showed to me pieces of cordage, pottery, and stone implements brought down by the rubber men from the wild Indians of the Rio Frio. Castillo is one of the centres of the rubber trade. Parties of men are here fitted out with canoes and provisions, and proceed up the rivers, far into the uninhabited forests of the Atlantic slope. They remain for several months away, and are expected to bring the rubber they obtain to the merchants who have fitted them out, but very many prove faithless, and carry off their produce to other towns, where they have no difficulty in finding purchasers. Notwithstanding these losses, the merchants engaged in the rubber trade have done well; its steadily increasing value during the last few years having made the business a highly remunerative one. According to the information supplied to me at Greytown by Mr. Paton, the exports of rubber from that port had increased from 401,475 lbs., valued at 112,413 dollars, in 1867, to 754,886 lbs., valued at 226,465 dollars, in 1871. India-rubber was well known to the ancient inhabitants of Central America. Before the Spanish conquest the Mexicans played with balls made from it, and it still bears its Aztec name of *Ulli*, from which the Spaniards call the collectors of it *Ulleros*. It is obtained from quite a different tree, and prepared in a different manner, from the rubber of the Amazons. The latter is taken from the *Siphonia elastica*, a Euphorbiaceous tree; but in Central America the tree that yields it is a species of wild fig (*Castilloa elastica*). It is easily known by its large leaves, and I saw several whilst ascending the river. When the collectors find an untapped one in the forest, they first make a ladder out of the lianas or " vejuccos " that hang from every tree ; this they do by tying short pieces of wood across them with small lianas, many of which are as tough as cord. They then proceed to score the bark, with cuts which extend nearly round the tree like the letter V, the point being downwards. A cut like this is made about every three feet all the way up the trunk. The milk will all run out of a tree in about an hour after it is cut, and is

C

collected into a large tin bottle made flat on one side
and furnished with straps to fix on to a man's back.
A decoction is made from a liana (*Calonyction speci-
osum*), and this on being added to the milk, in the
proportion of one pint to a gallon, coagulates it to rubber,
which is made into round flat cakes.   A large tree, five
feet in diameter, will yield when first cut about twenty
gallons of milk, each gallon of which makes two and a
half pounds of rubber.   I was told that the tree recovers
from the wounds and may be cut again after the lapse of
a few months ; but several that I saw were killed through
the large Harlequin beetle (*Acrocinus longimanus*) laying
its eggs in the cuts, and the grubs that are hatched boring
great holes all through the trunk.   When these grubs
are at work you can hear their rasping by standing at
the bottom of the tree, and the wood-dust thrown out of
their burrows accumulates in heaps on the ground below.
The Government attempts no supervision of the forests :
any one may cut the trees, and great destruction is going
on amongst them through the young ones being tapped
as well as the full-grown ones.   The tree grows very
quickly, and plantations of it might easily be made, which
would in the course of ten or twelve years become highly
remunerative.

We left Castillo at daylight the next morning, and
continued our journey up the river.   Its banks presented but little change.   We saw many tall graceful
palms and tree ferns, but most of the trees were dicoty-
ledons.   Amongst these the mahogany (*Swietonia maho-
gani*) and the cedar (*Cedrela odorata*) are now rare near
the river, but a few such trees were pointed out to me.
High up in one tree, underneath which we passed, were

seated some of the black Congo monkeys (*Mycetes palli-atus*) which at times, especially before rain and at night-fall, make a fearful howling, though not so loud as the Brazilian species. Screaming macaws, in their gorgeous livery of blue, yellow, and scarlet, occasionally flew over-head, and tanagers and toucans were not uncommon.

Twelve miles above Castillo we reached the mouth of the Savallo, and stayed at a house there to breakfast, the owner, a German, giving us roast wari, fowls, and eggs. He told me that there was a hot spring up the Savallo, but I had not time to go and see it. Above Savallo the San Juan is deep and sluggish, the banks low and swampy. The large palm, so common in the delta of the river, here reappeared with its great coarse leaves twenty feet in length, springing from near the ground.

Our boatmen continued to paddle all day, and as night approached redoubled their exertions, singing to the stroke of their paddles. I was astonished at their endurance. They kept on until eleven o'clock at night, when we reached San Carlos, having accomplished about thirty-five miles during the day against the current. San Carlos is at the head of the river, where it issues from the great lake of Nicaragua, about one hundred and twenty miles from Greytown. The mean level of the waters of the lake, according to the survey of Colonel O. W. Childs, in 1851, is 107½ feet, so that the river falls on an average a little less than one foot per mile. The height of the lowest pass between the lake and the Pacific is said to be twenty-six feet above the lake, therefore at that point the highest elevation between the two oceans is only about 133 feet; but even allowing that an error of a few feet may be discovered when a thorough

survey is made across from sea to sea, there can be no
doubt that at this point occurs the lowest pass between
the Atlantic and the Pacific in Central America.   This
fact, and the immense natural reservoir of water near the
head of the navigation, point out the route as a practi-
cable one for a ship canal between the two oceans.

Instead of cutting a canal from the head of the delta
of the San Juan to the sea, as has been proposed, the
Colorado branch might be straightened, and dredged to
the required depth.   Higher up, the Torre, Castillo and
Machuca Rapids form natural dams across the river.
These might be raised, locks formed round them, and the
water deepened by dredging between them.   In this way
the great expense of cutting a canal, and the fearful
mortality that always arises amongst the labourers when
excavations are made in the virgin soil of the tropics,
especially in marshy lands, would be greatly lessened
between the lake and the Atlantic.   Another great advantage would be that the deepening of the river could
be effected by steam power, so that it would not be
necessary to bring such a multitude of labourers to the
isthmus as would be required if a canal were cut from
the river; the whole track, moreover, passes through
virgin forests rich in inexhaustible supplies of fuel.*

San Carlos is a small town at the foot of the great
lake, where it empties its waters into the San Juan
river, its only outlet to the ocean.   On a hill behind the
town, and commanding the entrance to the river, are the

* Since the publication of the first edition of this work the com-
missioners, appointed by the Government of the United States to
examine into the practicability of making a canal across the isthmus,
have reported in favour of the Nicaraguan route.   The total cost is
estimated at £12,250,000 sterling.

ruins of a once strong fort built by the Spaniards, the
crumbling walls now green with the delicate fronds of a
maidenhair fern (*Adiantum*).   The little town consists of
a single rugged street leading up from the lake.   The
houses are mostly palm-thatched huts, with the bare
earth floors seldom or never swept.   The people are of
mixed origin, Indian, Spanish, and Negro, the Indian
element predominating.   Two or three better built
stores, and the quarters of the military governor, redeem
the place from an appearance of utter squalor.   Behind
the town there are a few small clearings in the forest,
where maize is grown.   Some orange, banana, and plantain trees exhaust the list of the productions of San
Carlos, which is supported by being a calling place for
all vessels proceeding up and down the river, and by the
Ulleros or rubber-men who start from it for expeditions
up the Rio Frio and other rivers.   We found there two
men who had just been brought down the Rio Frio
by their companions, greatly injured, by the lianas up
which they had made their ladder to ascend one of the
rubber trees, having broken and precipitated them to the
ground.   I learnt that this was a very unusual accident,
the lianas generally being very tough and strong, like
great cables.

Most fabulous stories have been told about the Rio
Frio and its inhabitants ; stories of great cities, golden
ornaments, and light-haired people, and it may be
useful to relate what is known about it.

The Rio Frio comes down from the interior of Costa
Rica, and joins the San Juan, near where the latter
issues from the lake.   The banks of its upper waters are
inhabited by a race of Indians who have never been

subjugated by the Spaniards, and about whom very little is known. They are called Guatuses, and have been said to have red or light-coloured hair and European features, to account for which various ingenious theories have been advanced; but, unfortunately for these specula-tions, some children, and even adults, have been captured and brought down the river by the Ulleros, and all these have the usual features and coarse black hair of the Indians. One little child that Dr. Seemann and I saw at San Carlos, in 1870, had a few brownish hairs amongst the great mass of black ones; but this character may be found amongst many of the indigenes, and may result from a very slight admixture of foreign blood. I have seen altogether five children from the Rio Frio, and a boy about sixteen years of age, and they had all the common Indian features and hair; though it struck me that they appeared rather more intelligent than the generality of Indians. Besides these, an adult woman was captured by the rubber-men and brought down to Castillo, and I was told by several who had seen her that she did not differ in any way from the usual Indian type.

The Guatuse (pronounced Watúsa) is an animal about the size of a hare, very common in Central America, and good eating. It has reddish-brown fur, and the usual explanation of the Nicaraguans is that the Indians of the Rio Frio were called "Guatuses" because they had red hair. It is very common to find the Indian tribes of America called after wild animals, and my own opinion is that the origin of the fable about the red hair was a theory to explain why they were called Guatuses; for the natives of Nicaragua, and of parts much nearer

home, are fond of giving fanciful explanations of the
names of places and things : thus, I have been assured
by an intelligent and educated Nicaraguan, that Guatemala was so called by the Spaniards because they found
the guaté (a kind of grass) in that country bad, hence
" guaté malo," " bad guaté,"—whereas every student of
Mexican history knows that the name was the Spanish
attempt to pronounce the old Aztec one of Quauhte-
mallan, which meant the Land of the Eagle. I shall
have other occasions, in the course of my narrative, to
show how careful a traveller in Central America must
be not to accept the explanations of the natives of the
names of places and things.

The first people who ascended the Rio Frio were
attacked by the Indians, who killed several with their
arrows. Exaggerated opinions of their ferocity and
courage were in consequence for a long time prevalent,
and the river remained unknown and unexplored, and
probably would have done so to the present day, if it
had not been for the rubber-men. When the trade in
india-rubber became fully developed, the trees in the
more accessible parts of the forest were soon exhausted,
and the collectors were obliged to penetrate farther and
farther back into the untrodden wilds of the Atlantic
slope. Some more adventurous than others ascended
the Rio Frio, and being well provided with firearms,
which they mercilessly used, they were able to defy the
poor Indians, armed only with spears and bows and
arrows, and to drive them back into the woods. The
first Ulleros who ascended the river were so successful
in finding rubber, that various other parties were
organised, and now an ascent of the Rio Frio from San

Carlos is of common occurrence. The poor Indians are now in such dread of firearms, that on the first appearance of a boat coming up the river they desert their houses and run into the woods for shelter. The Ulleros rush on shore and seize everything that the poor fugitives have left behind them; and in some cases the latter have not been able to carry off their children, and these have been brought down in triumph to San Carlos. The excuse for stealing the children is that they may be baptized and made Christians; and I am sorry to say that this shameful treatment of the poor Indians is countenanced and connived at by the authorities. I was told of one commandante at San Carlos who had manned some canoes and proceeded up the river as far as the plantain grounds of the Indians, loaded his boats with the plantains, and brought them down to San Carlos, where the people appear to be too indolent to grow them themselves. All who have ascended the river speak of the great quantities of plantains that the Guatuses grow, and this fruit, and the abundant fish of the river, form their principal food. Their houses are large sheds open at the sides, and thatched with the " suiti " palm. As is often the case amongst the Indians, several families live in one house. The floor is kept well cleaned. I was amused with a lady in San Carlos who, in describing their well-kept houses to Dr. Seemann and myself, pointed to her own unswept and littered earth floor and said, " They keep their houses very, very clean— as clean as this." The lad and the woman who were captured and brought down the Rio Frio both ran away—the one from San Carlos, the other from Castillo; but neither could succeed in reaching home, on

account of the swamps and rivers in their way, and
after wandering about the woods for some time they
were recaptured. I saw the lad soon after he was taken
the second time. He had been a month in the woods,
living on roots and fruits, and had nearly died from
starvation. He had an intelligent, sharp, and independent look about him, and kept continually talking in
his own language, apparently surprised that the people
around him did not understand what he was saying.
He was taken to Castillo, and met there the woman
who had been captured a year before, and had learnt to
speak a little Spanish. Through her as an interpreter,
he tried to get permission to return to the Rio Frio,
saying that if they would let him go he would come
back and bring his father and mother with him. This
simple artifice of the poor boy was, of course, ineffectual.
He was afterwards taken to Granada, for the purpose,
they said, of being educated, that he might become the
means of opening up communication with his tribe.

The rubber-men bring down many little articles that
they pillage from the Indians. They consist of cordage,
made from the fibre of Bromeliaceous plants, bone
hooks, and stone implements. Amongst the latter, I
was fortunate enough to obtain a rude stone hatchet, set
in a stone-cut wooden handle : it was firmly fixed in a
hole made in the thick end of the handle.* It is a
singular fact, and one showing the persistence of particular ways of doing things through long ages amongst
people belonging to the same race, that, in the ancient
Mexican, Uxmal, and Palenque picture-writings, bronze

* Well figured in Evan's "Ancient Stone Implements," p. 140,
but erroneously stated in the text to be from Texas.

axes are represented fixed in this identical manner in holes at the thick ends of the handles.

We slept on board one of the steamers of the American Transit Company. It was too dark when we arrived at San Carlos to see anything that night of the great lake, but we heard the waves breaking on the beach as on a sea-shore, and from further away came that moaning sound that has from the earliest ages of history connected the idea of the sea with sorrow and sadness.* The steamer we stayed in was one of four river-boats belonging to the Transit Company, which was at this time in difficulties, and ultimately the boats were sold ; part of them being bought by Mr. Hollenbeck, and used by the navigation company which he established. These steamers are built expressly for shallow rivers, and are very different structures from anything we see in England. The bottom is made quite flat, and divided into compartments ; the first deck being only about eighteen inches above the water, from which it is divided by no bulwarks or other protection. Upon this deck are placed the cargo and the driving machinery. A vertical boiler is fixed at the bow, and two horizontal engines, driving a large paddle-wheel, at the stern. The second deck is for passengers, and is raised on light wooden pillars braced with iron rods about seven feet above the first. Above this is another deck, on which are the cabins of the officers and the steering apparatus. The appearance of such a structure is more like that of a house than a boat. The one we were in, the *Panaloya*, drew only three feet of water, when laden with 400 passengers and twenty tons of cargo.

* " There is sorrow on the sea ; it cannot be quiet " (Jer. xlix. 23).

CHAPTER IV.

As daylight broke next morning, I was up, anxious to see the great lake about which I had heard so much. To the north-west a great sheet of quiet water extended as far as the eye could reach, with islands here and there, and—the central figure in every view of the lake —the great conical peak of Ometépec towered up, 5050 feet above the sea, and 4922 feet above the surface of the lake. To the left, in the dim distance, were the cloud-capped mountains of Costa Rica; to the right, nearer at hand, low hills and ranges covered with dark forests. The lake is too large to be called beautiful, and its vast extent and the mere glimpses of its limits and cloud-capped peaks appeal to the imagination rather than to the eye. At this end of the lake the water is shallow, probably filled up by the mud brought down by the Rio Frio.

We had still a voyage of sixty miles before us up the lake, and this was to be accomplished not by paddling, but by sailing; so we now rigged two light masts, and soon after seven o'clock sailed slowly away from San Carlos before a light breeze, which in an hour's time freshened and carried us along at the rate of about six miles an hour. The sun rose higher and higher; the day waxed hotter and hotter. About noon the wind failed us again, and the sun right overhead, in a clear pitiless sky, scorched us with its rays, while our boat lay like a log upon the water, the pitch melting in the seams with the heat. The surface of the lake was motionless, save for a gentle heaving. We were almost broiled with the stifling heat, but at last saw a ripple on the water come up from the north-east; soon the breeze reached us, and our torment was over; our sails, no more idly flapping, filled out before the wind; the canoe dashed through the rising waves; our drooping spirits revived, and there was an opening out of provisions, and life again in the boat. The breeze continued all the afternoon, and at dark we were off the islands of Nancital, having been all day within a few miles of the north-eastern side of the lake, the banks of which are everywhere clothed with dark gloomy-looking forests. One of the islands was a favourite sleeping-place for the white egrets. From all sides they were flying across the lake towards it; and as night set in, the trees and bushes by the water-side were full of them, gleaming like great white flowers amongst the dark green foliage. Flocks of muscovy and whistling ducks also flew over to their evening feeding-places. Great masses of a floating plant, shaped like a cabbage, were abundant on the lake,

and on these the white egrets and other wading birds
often alighted. The boatmen told me—and the story is
likely enough to be true—that the alligators, floating
about like logs, with their eyes above the water, watch
these birds, and, moving quietly up until within a few
yards of them, sink down below the surface, come up
underneath them, catch them by the legs and drag them
under water. Besides the alligators, large freshwater
sharks appear to be common in the lake. Sometimes,
when in shallow water, we saw a pointed billow rapidly
moving away from the boat, produced by some large
fish below, and I was told it was a shark.

After dark the wind failed us again, and we got
slowly along, but finally reached our port, San Ubaldo,
about ten o'clock, and found an officer of the mining
company, living in a small thatched hut, stationed there
to send on the machinery and other goods that arrived
for the mines. A large tiled store had also just been
built by the owner of the estate there, Don Gregorio
Quadra, under the verandah of which I hung my hammock for the night. Mules were waiting at San Ubaldo
for us, and early next morning we set off, with our
luggage on pack mules. We crossed some rocky low
hills, with scanty vegetation, and, after passing the
cattle hacienda of San José, reached the plains of the
same name, about two leagues in width, now dry and
dusty, but in the wet season forming a great slough of
water and tenacious mud, through which the mules
have to wade and plunge.

In the midst of these plains there are some rocky
knolls, like islands, on which grow spiny cactuses, low
leathery-leaved trees, slender, spiny palms, with plum-

like fruit, prickly acacias, and thorny bromelias. This
spiny character of vegetation seems to be characteristic
of dry rocky places and tracts of country liable to great
drought. Probably it is as a protection from herbivorous
animals, to prevent them browsing upon the twigs and
small branches where herbaceous vegetation is dried up.
Small armadillos abound near these rocky knolls, and
are said to feed on ants and other insects. We had a
long chase after one, which we observed some distance
from the rock, over the cracked and dried-up plain:
though it could not run very fast, it doubled quickly,
and the rough cracked ground made odds in its favour;
but it was ultimately secured. Pigeons, brown coloured,
of various sizes, from that of a thrush to that of a common dove, were numerous and very tame. One of the
smallest species alights and seeks about in the streets
of small towns for seeds, like a sparrow, and more boldly
than that bird, for it is not molested by the children—
more perhaps from indolence than from any lack of the
element of cruelty in their dispositions. After crossing
the plains we rode over undulating hills, here called
savannahs, with patches of forest on the rising ground,
and small plains on which grows the ternate-leaved jicara
(pronounced hickory), a tree about as large as an apple-
tree, with fruit of the size, shape, and appearance of a
large green orange, but growing on the trunk and
branches, not amongst the leaves. The outside of the
fruit is a hard thin shell, packed full of seeds in a kind
of dry pulp, on which are fed fowls, and even horses and
cattle in the dry season ; the latter are said sometimes
to choke themselves with the fruit, whilst trying to eat
it. Of the bruised seeds is also made a cooling drink,

much used in Nicaragua. The jicara trees grow apart at equal distances, as if planted by man. The hard thin shell of the fruit, carved in various patterns on the outside, is made into cups and drinking-vessels by the natives, who also cultivate other species of jicara, with round fruit, as large as a man's head, from which the larger drinking-bowls are made. In the smaller jicaras chocolate is always made and served in Central America, and, being rounded at the bottom, little stands are made to set them in; these are sometimes shaped like egg-cups, sometimes like toy washhand-stands. In making their earthenware vessels, the Indians up to this day follow this natural form, and their water-jars and bowls are made rounded at the bottom, requiring stands to keep them upright.

The meals of Montezuma were served on thick cushions or pillows. This was probably on account of the rounded bases of the bowls and dishes used. The gourd forms of bowls possibly originated from the clay being moulded over gourds which were burnt out in the baking process. It is said that in the Southern States the kilns in which the ancient pottery was baked have been found, and in some the half-baked ware remained, retaining the rinds of the gourds over which they had been moulded. Afterwards, when the potter learned to make bowls without the aid of gourds, he still retained the shape of his ancient pattern.

The name, too, like the form, has had a wonderful vitality. It is the "xicalli" of the ancient Aztecs, changed to "jicara" by the Spaniards, by which they mean a chocolate-cup; and even in Italy a modification of the same word may be heard, a tea-cup being called a *chicchera*.

On the top of one of the hills we just got a glimpse of a small pack of wolves, or *coyotes*, as they are called, from the Aztec *coyotl*. They are smaller than the European wolf, and are cunning, like a fox, but hunt in packs. They looked down at us from the ridge of the hill for a few moments, then trotted off down the other side. Their howlings may often be heard in the early morning.

Cattle, horses, and mules are bred on these plains. Male asses are kept at some of the haciendas. They are not allowed to mix with any of their own kind, and are well fed and in good condition ; but they are only of small size, and the breed of mules might be greatly improved by the introduction of larger asses.

The vegetation on the plains was rapidly drying up. Many of the trees shed their leaves in the dry season, just as they do with us in autumn. The barrenness of the landscape is relieved in March by several kinds of trees bursting into flower when they have shed their leaves, and presenting great domes of brilliant colour —some pink, others red, blue, yellow, or white, like single-coloured bouquets. One looked like a gigantic rhododendron, with bunches of large pink flowers. The yellow-flowered ones belong to wild cotton-trees, from the pods of which the natives gather cotton to stuff pillows, &c. About one o'clock we reached rather a large river, and after crossing it came in sight of the town of Acoyapo, one of the principal towns of the province of Chontales. We stayed and had dinner with Señor Don Dolores Bermudez, a Nicaraguan gentleman

who had been educated in the States, and spoke English
fluently. He very kindly took me over the town, and
I always found him ready to give me information respecting the antiquities and natural products of the
country. Acoyapo and the district around it contains
about two thousand inhabitants. The store-keepers,
lawyers, and hacienderos are of Spanish and mixed
descent. Amongst the lower classes there is much
Indian and some negro blood; but there are many pure
Indians scattered through the district, living near the
rivers and brooks, and growing patches of maize and
beans. In the centre of the town is a large square or
plaza, with a stucco-fronted church occupying one side,
and the principal stores and houses ranging around the
other three sides. A couple of coco-palms grow in
front of the church, but do not thrive like those near
the sea-coast. It was Saturday, the 22nd of February,
when we arrived; this was a great feast-day, or festa, at
Acoyapo, and the town was full of country people, who
were amusing themselves with horse-races, cock-fights,
and drinking aguardiente. Their mode of cock-fighting
is very cruel, as the cocks are armed with long sickle-
shaped lancets, tied on to their natural spurs, with
which they give each other fearful gashes and wounds.
All classes of Nicaraguans are fond of this amusement;
in nearly every house a cock will be found, tied up in
a corner by the leg, but treated otherwise like one of
the family. The priests are generally great abettors
of the practice, which forms the usual amusement of
the towns on Sunday afternoons. I have heard many
stories of the padres after service hurrying off to the
cock-pit with a cock under each arm. Bets are made

D

on every fight, and much money is lost and won over
the sport.

Like most of the Nicaraguan towns, Acoyapo appears
to have been an Indian city before the Spanish conquest. The name is Indian, and in the plaza Señor
Bermudez pointed out to me some flat bared rock surfaces, on which were engraved circles and various
straight and curved characters, covering the whole face
of the rock. Some rude portions of stone statues that
have been found in the neighbourhood are also preserved
in the town. The Spaniards called the town San Sebas-
tian ; but the more ancient name is likely to prevail,
notwithstanding that in all official documents the
Spanish one is used. Acoyapo is a grazing district,
and there are some large cattle haciendas, especially
towards the lake. The town suffers from fever owing
to the neighbouring swamp. Much of the land around
is very fertile; but little of it is cultivated, as the people
are indolent, and content if they make a bare livelihood.
We left Acoyapo about three o'clock : our road lay up
the river, which we crossed three times. Excepting near
the river, the country was very thinly timbered ; and it
was pleasant, after riding across the open plains, exposed
to the hot rays of the sun, to reach the shady banks of
the stream, by which grew many high thick-foliaged
trees, with lianas hanging from them, and bromelias,
orchids, ferns, and many other epiphytes perched on
their branches. At these spots, too, were various beautiful birds, amongst which the *Sisitote*, a fine black and
orange songster, and a trogon (*Trogon melanocephalus*,
Gould), were the most conspicuous.

We reached and crossed a high range, from the

summit of which we had a splendid view over the plains and savannahs we had crossed, to the great lake, with its islands and peaked hills, and beyond the dark dim mountains of Costa Rica, amongst which dwell the Indians of the Rio Frio and other little-known tribes. Before us were spread out well-grassed savannahs, thinly timbered, excepting where dark winding lines of trees or light green thickets of bamboos marked the course of rivers or mountain brooks. Here and there were dotted thatched huts, in which dwelt the owners of the cattle, mules, and horses feeding on the meadows. Far in the distance the view was bounded by a line of dark, nearly black-looking forest, which, there commencing, extends unbroken to the Atlantic. Near its edge, a seven-peaked range marked the neighbourhood of Libertad—the beginning of the gold-mining district. Descending the slope of the range, we found the savannahs on its eastern side much more moist than those to the westward of it; and as we proceeded, the humidity of the ground increased, and the crossings of some of the valleys and swamps were difficult for the mules. The dry season had set in, and these places were rapidly drying up; but in many it had just reached that stage when the mud was most tenacious; at one very bad crossing, called an " *estero*," my mule fell, with my leg underneath him, pinning me in the mud. The poor beast was exhausted, and would not move. Night had set in—it was quite dark, and I had lagged some distance behind my companions: fortunately they heard my shouts, and, soon returning, extricated me from my awkward predicament. Without further mishap we reached Esquipula, a village inhabited mostly by half-breeds, and slung our hammocks for the night in a small thatched house belonging to the mining company, who kept many of their draught bullocks at this place on account of the excellent pasture around.   The village of Esquipula is built near the river Mico, which, rising in the forest-clad ranges to the eastward, runs for several miles through the savannahs, then again enters the forest and flows into the Atlantic at Blewfields, a broad and deep river.   This river must have had at one time a large Indian population dwelling in settled towns near its banks.   Their burial-places, marked with great heaps of stones, are frequent, and pieces of pottery, broken stone statues and pedestals are often met with.   Near Esquipula there are some artificial-looking mounds, with great stones set round them ; in fact, this and another village, a few miles to the south, called San Tomas, are, I believe, both built on the sites of old Indian towns.   The Indians of the Rio Mico gave the Spaniards some trouble on their first settlement of the country.   About two leagues from Acoyapo, the site of a small town was pointed out to me, now covered with low trees and brushwood.   Here the Spaniards were attacked in the night-time by the Rio Mico Indians, and all of them killed, excepting the young women, who were carried off into captivity, and the place has ever since lain desolate.

Many extravagant stories have been told of the great statues that are said to have been seen on the banks of the Mico, much lower down the river than where we crossed it ; but M. Etienne, of Libertad, who descended it to Blewfields, and some Ulleros of San Thomas, who had frequently been down it after india-rubber, assured me that the reported statues were merely rude carvings of faces and animals on the rocks. They appear to be similar to what are found on many rivers running into the Caribbean Sea, and to those which were examined by Schomburgk on the rocks of the Orinoco and Essequibo. As others like them, of un-doubted Carib workmanship, have been found in the Virgin Islands, it is possible that they are all the work of that once-powerful race, and not of the settled agri-cultural and statue-making Indians of the western part of the continent.

We started from Esquipula early next morning, and crossed low thinly-timbered hills and savannahs to Pital, a scattered settlement of many small thatched houses, close to the borders of the great forest; on the edge of which were clearings, made for growing maize, which is cultivated entirely on burnt forest land. At some parts they had already commenced cutting down trees for fresh clearings; these would be burnt in April, and the maize sown the following month, in the usual primitive way, just as it was in Mexico before and at the Spanish conquest. In commencing a clearing, the brushwood is first cut close to the ground, as it would be difficult to do so after the large trees are felled. The big timber is then cut down, and in April it is set fire to. All the small wood and leaves burn well; but most of the large trunks are left, and many of the branches. Most of the latter are cut up to form a fence round the clearing, this at Pital and Esquipula being made very close and high to keep out deer. In May, the maize is sown; the sower makes little holes with a pointed stick, a few feet apart, into each of which he drops two or three grains, and covers them with his foot. In a few days the green leaves shoot up, and grow very quickly. Numerous wild plants also spring up, and in June these are weeded out; the success of the crop greatly depending upon the thoroughness with which this is done. In July each plant has produced two or three ears; and before the grain is set these are pulled off, excepting one, as if more are left they do not mature well. The young ears are boiled whole, and make a tender and much-esteemed vegetable. They are called at this stage " *chilote*," from the Aztec *xilotl;* and the ancient Mexicans in their eighth month, which began on the 16th July, made a great festival, called the feast of *Xilonen.* The poor Indians now have often reason to rejoice when this stage is reached, as their stores of corn are generally exhausted before then, and the " chilote" is the first fruits of the new crop. In the beginning of August the grains are fully formed, though still tender and white; and it is eaten as green corn, now called " *elote.*" In September the maize is ripe, and is gathered when dry, and stowed away, generally over the rooms of the natives. A second crop is often sown in December.

Maize is very prolific, bearing a hundredfold, and ripening in April. From the most ancient times, maize has been the principal food of the inhabitants of the western side of tropical America. On the coast of Peru, Darwin found heads of it,* along with eighteen recent species of marine shells, in a raised beach eighty-five feet

* "Geological Observations in South America, 1846," p. 49; and " Animals and Plants under Domestication," vol. i. p. 320.

above the level of the sea ; and in the same country it
has been found in tombs apparently more ancient than
the earliest times of the Incas.*   In Mexico it was known
from the earliest times of which we have any record, in
the picture writings of the Toltecs ; and that ancient
people carried it with them in all their wanderings.   In
Central America the stone grinders, with which they
bruised it down, are almost invariably found in the
ancient graves, having been buried with the ashes of
the dead, as an indispensable article for their outfit for
another world.   When Florida and Louisiana were first
discovered, the native Indian tribes all cultivated maize
as their staple food ; and throughout Yucatan, Mexico,
and all the western side of Central America, and through
Peru to Chili, it was, and still is, the main sustenance
of the Indians.   The people that cultivated it were all
more or less advanced in civilisation ; they were settled
in towns ; their traders travelled from one country to
another with their wares ; they were of a docile and tract-
able disposition, easily frightened into submission.   It is
likely that these maize-eating peoples belonged to closely
affiliated races.   In the West India Islands they occupied
most of Cuba and Hayti ; but from Porto Rico southwards the islands were peopled by the warlike Caribs,
who harassed the more civilised tribes to the north.
From Cape Gracias á Dios southward, the eastern coast
of America was peopled on its first discovery by much
ruder tribes, who did not grow maize, but made bread
from the roots of the mandioca (*Manihot aipim*) ; and
still in British Guiana, on the Lower Amazon, and in
north-eastern Brazil, farina made from the roots of the

* Von Tschudi, " Travels in Peru," English edition, p. 177.

mandioca is the staple food. Maize has been introduced
by the Portuguese, but it has no native name, and is
used mostly for feeding cattle and fowls, scarcely at all
for the food of the people. This fundamental difference in the food of the indigenes points to a great
distinction between the peoples to which I shall have
in the sequel to revert. In the West India Islands,
Cuba and Hayti seem to have been peopled from
Yucatan, and Florida, Porto Rico, and all the islands
to the southwards, from Venezuela.

In Central America, the bread made from the maize
is prepared at the present day exactly as it was in
ancient Mexico. The grain is first of all boiled along
with wood ashes or a little lime : the alkali loosens the
outer skin of the grain, and this is rubbed off with the
hands in running water, a little of it at a time, placed
upon a slightly concave stone, called a *metlate*, from the
Aztec *metlatl*, on which it is rubbed with another stone
shaped like a rolling-pin. A little water is thrown on
it as it is bruised, and it is thus formed into paste. A
ball of the paste is taken and flattened out between the
hands into a cake about ten inches diameter and three-
sixteenths of an inch thick, which is baked on a slightly
concave earthenware pan. The cakes so made are called
tortillas, and are very nutritious. When travelling, I
preferred them myself to bread made from wheaten
flour. When well made and eaten warm, they are very
palatable.

There are a few small sugar plantations near Pital.
The juice is pressed out of the canes by rude wooden
rollers set upright in threes, the centre one driving the
one on each side of it by projecting cogs. The whole

are set in motion by oxen travelling round the same as
in a thrashing-mill.   The ungreased axles of the rollers,
squeaking and screeching like a score of tormented pigs,
generally inform the traveller of their vicinity long before
he reaches them.   The juice is boiled, and an impure
sugar made from it.   I do not think that the sugar-
cane was known to the ancient inhabitants of this
country : it is not mentioned by the historians of the
conquest of Mexico and Peru, nor has it, like maize and
cacao, any native name.

As soon as we passed Pital we entered the great forest,
the black margin of which we had seen for many miles,
that extends from this point to the Atlantic.   At first
the road lay through small trees and brushwood, a second
growth that had sprung up where the original forest had
been cut for maize plantations ; but after passing a brook
bordered by numerous plants of the *pita*, from which a
fine fibre is obtained, and which gives its name to Pital,
we entered the primeval forest.   On each side of the
road great trees towered up, carrying their crowns out
of sight amongst a canopy of foliage ; lianas wound round
every trunk and hung from every bough, passing from
tree to tree, and entangling the giants in a great network of coiling cables, as the serpents did Laocoon ; the
simile being strengthened by the fact that many of the
trees are really strangled in the winding folds.   Sometimes a tree appears covered with beautiful flowers,
which do not belong to it, but to one of the lianas
that twines through its branches and sends down great
rope-like stems to the ground.   Climbing ferns and
vanilla cling to the trunks, and a thousand epiphytes
perch themselves on the branches.   Amongst these are

large arums that send down aërial roots, tough and
strong, and universally used instead of cordage by the
natives. Amongst the undergrowth several small species
of palms, varying in height from two to fifteen feet, are
common; and now and then magnificent tree ferns,
sending off their feathery crowns twenty feet from the
ground, delight the sight with their graceful elegance.
Great broad-leaved heliconiæ, leathery melastomæ,
and succulent-stemmed, lop-sided leaved begonias are
abundant, and typical of tropical American forests.
Not less so are the cecropia trees, with their white
stems and large palmated leaves standing up like
great candelabra. Sometimes the ground is carpeted
with large flowers, yellow, pink, or white, that have
fallen from some invisible tree-top above, or the air is
filled with a delicious perfume, for the source of which
one seeks around in vain, as the flowers that cause it are
far overhead out of sight, lost in the great overshadowing
crown of verdure. Numerous babbling brooks intersect
the forest, with moss-covered stones and fern-clad nooks.
One's thoughts are led away to the green dells in English
denes, but are soon recalled; for the sparkling pools are
the favourite haunts of the fairy humming-birds, and like
an arrow one will dart up the brook, and, poised on wings
moving with almost invisible velocity, clothed in purple,
golden, or emerald glory, hang suspended in the air;
gazing with startled look at the intruder, with a sudden
jerk, turning round first one eye, then the other, and
suddenly disappear like a flash of light.

Unlike the plains and savannahs we crossed yesterday,
where the ground is parched up in the dry season, the
Atlantic forest, bathed in the rains distilled from the

north-east trades, is ever verdant.   Perennial moisture
reigns in the soil, perennial summer in the air, and
vegetation luxuriates in ceaseless activity and verdure,
all the year round.   Unknown are the autumn tints, the
bright browns and yellows of English woods, much less
the crimsons, purples, and yellows of Canada, where the
dying foliage rivals, nay, excels the expiring dolphin in
splendour.   Unknown the cold sleep of winter; unknown
the lovely awakening of vegetation at the first gentle
touch of spring.   A ceaseless round of ever-active life
weaves the forest scenery of the tropics into one mono-
tonous whole, of which the component parts exhibit in
detail untold variety and beauty.

To the genial influence of ever-present moisture and
heat we must ascribe the infinite variety of the trees of
these forests.   They do not grow in clusters or masses of
single species, like our oaks, beeches, and firs, but every
tree is different from its neighbour, and they crowd upon
each other in unsocial rivalry, each trying to overtop the
other.   For this reason we see the great straight trunks
rising a hundred feet without a branch, and carrying
their domes of foliage directly up to where the balmy
breezes blow and the sun's rays quicken.   Lianas hurry
up to the light and sunshine, and innumerable epiphytes
perch themselves high up on the branches.

The road through the forest was very bad, the mud
deep and tenacious, the hills steep and slippery, and the
mules had to struggle and plunge along through from
two to three feet of sticky clay.   One part, named the
Nispral, was especially steep and difficult to descend, the
road being worn into great ruts.   We crossed the ranges
and brooks nearly at right angles, and were always

ascending or descending. About two we reached a
clearing and hacienda, belonging to an enterprising
German, named Melzer, near a brook called Las Lajas,
who was cultivating plantains and vegetables, and had
also commenced brick and tile making, besides planting
some thousands of coffee trees. His large clearings
were a pleasant change from the forest through which
we had been toiling, and we stayed a few minutes at his
house. After riding over another league of forest-
covered ranges, we reached Pavon, one of the mines
of the Chontales Company, and passing the Javali mine
soon arrived at Santo Domingo, the headquarters of the
gold-mining company whose operations I had come out
to superintend.

CHAPTER V.

Geographical position of Santo Domingo—Physical geography—The inhabitants—Mixed races—Negroes and Indians compared—Women
—Establishment of the Chontales Gold-Mining Company—My
house and garden—Fruits—Plantains and bananas—Probably not
indigenous to America—Propagated from shoots—Do not generally mature their seeds—Fig-trees—Granadillos and Papaws—
Vegetables—Dependence of flowers on insects for their fertilisation
—Insect plagues—Leaf-cutting ants—Their method of defoliating
trees—Their nests—Some trees are not touched by the ants—
Foreign trees are very subject to their attack—Method of destroying the ants—Migration of the ants from a nest attacked—Corrosive sublimate causes a sort of madness amongst them—Indian
plan of preventing their ascending young trees—Leaf-cutting ants
are fungus growers and eaters—The sagacity of the ants.

THE gold-mining village of Santo Domingo is situated in the province of Chontales, Nicaragua, in lat.
12° 16′ N. and long. 84° 59′ W., nearly midway between
the Atlantic and the Pacific, where Central America
begins to widen out northward of the narrow isthmus of
Panama and Costa Rica. It is in the midst of the great
forest that covers most of the Atlantic slope of Central
America, and which continues unbroken from where we
had entered it, at Pital, eastward to the Atlantic; westward it terminates in a sinuous margin about seven miles
from the village, and there commence the lightly timbered and grassy plains and savannahs stretching to the
Lake of Nicaragua. The surface of the land in the

forest region forms a succession of ranges and steep valleys, covered with magnificent timber and much undergrowth. Santo Domingo lies about 2000 feet above the level of the sea, and the hills around it rise from 500 to 1000 feet higher. It is built in the bend of a small stream, the head waters of a branch of the Blewfields river, on a level, low piece of ground, with the brook winding almost round it, and, beyond that, encircled by an amphitheatre of low hills in the hollow of which it lies. The road to the mines runs through it, and forms the main street, having on each side thatched stores and irregularly built houses. The inhabitants, about three hundred in number, are entirely dependent on the mines around, there being no cultivation or any other employment in the immediate neighbourhood. The people are of a mixed descent, in which Indian blood predominates, then Spanish with a slight admixture of the Negro element, whilst amongst the rising generation many fair-haired children can claim paternity amongst the numerous German and English workmen that have been employed at the mines. The storekeepers form the aristocracy of the village. They are indolent; lounging about, or lying smoking in their hammocks the greater part of the day, but generally civil and polite. They are particular in their dress, and may often be seen in faultless European costume, silk umbrella in hand, in twos or threes, taking a short quiet walk up the valley. The lower class of miners are scantily and badly clothed, especially when they come first to the mines. They are bare-footed, with poor ragged cotton trousers and a thin jacket of the same material. Generally, after being a year or two at the mines, they begin to wear better clothing, and may often

be seen with a new shirt, which to show off is worn hanging down outside, like a surtout coat. Amongst these
are many pure Indians, short sturdy men, who make the
steadiest workmen, patient and industrious, but with
little appreciation of the value of money, and spending
the whole of their wages at the end of the month, before
they resume work. At these times the commandant
comes in from the town of Libertad, about nine miles
distant, with half-a-dozen bare-footed soldiers carrying
old muskets on their shoulders, and levies black mail
upon the poor patient "Mosas," as they are called, in
the shape of a fine for drunkenness. But the "aguardiente," a native-made rum, is nevertheless always kept
on hand, being a government monopoly, and ever ready,
so that the Mosas may have no excuse to be sober and
escape being fined.

Even in their drink the poor Indians are not very
violent, and get intoxicated with surprising stolidity
and quietness. Amongst the half-breeds, especially
where the Negro element exists, there are often quarrel-
lings and rows, when they slash away at each other with
their long knives or "machetes," and get ugly cuts,
which, however, heal again quickly.

Both the Negroes and Indians are decidedly inferior
to the whites in intellect ; but they do not differ so much
from the Europeans as they do from each other. The
Negro will work hard for a short while, on rare occasions,
or when compelled by another, but is innately lazy. The
Indian is industrious by nature, and works steadily and
well for himself; but if compelled to work for another,
loses all heart, and pines away and dies. The Negro
is talkative, vivacious, vain, and sensual ; the Indian

taciturn, stolid, dignified, and moderate. As freemen, regularly though poorly paid and kindly treated, the Indians work well and laboriously in the mines; but the Negro seldom engages either in that or any other settled employment, unless compelled as a slave, in which condition he is happy and thoughtless. I do not defend slavery, but I believe it to be a greater curse to the masters than to the slaves, more deteriorating to the former than to the latter. The Spaniards at first enslaved the Indians, but they died away so rapidly that in a very short time the indigenes of the whole of the once-populous islands of the West Indies were exterminated, and large numbers of Indians were carried off from the mainland to supply their places, but died with equal rapidity; so that the Spaniards found it more profitable to bring negroes from Africa, who thrived and multiplied in captivity as readily as the enslaved Indians pined away and died. In Central America there never were many black slaves; since the States threw off the yoke of Spain there have been none; and this comparative scarcity of the Negro element makes these countries much more pleasant and safer to dwell in than the West Indies, where it is much larger. The Indian seldom or never molests the whites, excepting in retaliation for some great injury; whilst amongst the free Negroes, robbery, violence, and murder need no other incentives than their own evil passions and lust.

The women at Santo Domingo are much the same as those found at all the small provincial towns of Central America. Morality is at a low ebb, and most of them live as mistresses, not as wives, for which they do not seem to suffer in the estimation of their neighbours. This

is greatly due in Nicaragua, as it is throughout Central
and South America, to the profligate lives led by the
priests, who, with few rare exceptions, live in concubin-
age more or less open. The women have children at
an early age, and make kind and indulgent mothers.

The village is bounded to the eastward by the mines
and hacienda of the Chontales Mining Company, whose
houses, workshops, and machinery are on rising ground
on each side of the valley, with the brook running down
between. About fifty acres of the forest have been cut
down, and a great deal of this is fenced in and covered
with grass. Going up the valley from the village, on
the right-hand side, about fifty yards from the road, on
a grass-covered slope, stand the houses of the commissioner and cashier, in the latter of which the medical
officer also lives. The former, a large, white-washed,
square, two-storied, wooden house, with verandahs round
three sides of it, and communicating by a covered passage
with a detached kitchen behind, had been built by one
of my predecessors, Captain Hill, R.N., who did not
live to inhabit it. It was a roomy, comfortable house,
commanding a view of the machinery, workshops, and
part of the mines on the other side of the valley, and
formed my residence for upwards of four years.

The slope in front of the house, down to the river, was
covered with weedy bushes when I arrived; but I had
these cleared away, and a fine greensward of grass took
their place. On this I planted young orange, lime, and
citron trees; and I had the pleasure, before I left, to see
them beginning to bear their fine fruit. To the west of
the house was a dell, covered with fallen logs and rubbish
thrown from the hill, in which was a perennial spring

E

of limpid water. I had the logs and rubbish gathered together and burnt, put a light fence round it, and formed a small vegetable, fruit, and flower garden. The mango and avocado trees had not come into bearing before I left; but pineapples, figs, grenadillas, bananas, pumpkins, plantains, papaws, and chioties fruited abun-

COMMISSIONER'S HOUSE AT SANTO DOMINGO.

dantly. The last named is a native of Mexico; it is a climbing plant with succulent stems and vine-like leaves, and grows with great rapidity. The fruit, of which it bears a great abundance, is about the size and shape of a pear, covered with soft prickles. It is boiled and eaten as a vegetable, and resembles vegetable marrow.

At Santo Domingo, it continues to bear a succession of fruits during eight months of the year.

Next to maize, plantains and bananas form the principal sustenance of the natives. The banana tree shoots up its succulent stem, and unfolds its immense entire leaves with great rapidity; and a group of them waving their silky leaves in the sun, or shining ghostly white in the moonlight, forms one of those beautiful sights that can only be seen to perfection in the tropics. There are a great many varieties of them, and they are cooked in many ways—boiled, baked, made into pastry, or eaten as a fruit. The varieties differ not only in their fruits, but in the colour of their leaves and stems; the natives can distinguish them without seeing the fruit, and have names for each, by which they are known throughout all Central America, Mexico, and Peru. These names are of Spanish origin; and this fact, together with the absence of any native, Mexican, or Peruvian name for the fruit, inclines me to adopt the opinion of Clavigero, who contends, in opposition to other writers, that the plantain and banana were not known in these countries before the Spanish conquest, but were first brought from the Canaries to Hayti in 1516, and from thence taken to the mainland.

Neither the sugar-cane * nor the plantain is given in the list of the indigenous productions of Mexico by the careful and accurate Hernandez. The natives made sugar from the green stems of the maize. Humboldt thinks that some species of plantain were indigenous to

---

* The sugar-cane is said never to bear seed in the West Indies, Malaga, India, Cochin China, or the Malay Archipelago.—Darwin's " Animals and Plants under Domestication," vol. ii. p. 169.

America ; but it seems incredible that such an important fruit could have been overlooked by the early historians. In the old world the cultivation of the banana dates from the earliest times of which tradition makes mention. One of the Sanscrit names was *bhanu*—fruit, from which probably the name " banana " was derived.*

Both the plantain and the banana are always propagated from shoots or suckers that spring from the base of the plants ; and it is to be remarked that the pineapple and the bread-fruit, that are also universally grown from cuttings or shoots, and have been cultivated from remote antiquity, have in a great measure lost the faculty of producing mature seed. Such varieties could not arise in a state of nature, but are due to selection by early races of mankind, who would naturally propagate the best varieties ; and, to do this, seed was not required. As the finest kinds of bananas, pineapples, and bread-fruit are almost seedless, it is probable that the nutriment that would have been required for the formation of the seeds has been expended in producing larger and more succulent fruits. We find some varieties of oranges, which also have been cultivated from very early ages, producing fruits without seeds ; but as these trees are propagated from seeds, these varieties could not become so sterile as those just mentioned. There can be no doubt that the seedless varieties of bananas, bread-fruits, and pineapples have been propagated for hundreds of years ; and this fact ought to modify the opinions generally entertained by horticulturists that the life of plants and trees propagated from shoots or cuttings cannot be indefinitely prolonged in that way. Perhaps this may be

* Humboldt's "Aspects of Nature," vol. ii. p. 141.

the case in trees, such as apples, that have come under their notice ; and the reason that the varieties die out after a certain time, if not reproduced from seed, may be that the vigour of the trees is at last used up by the production of mature seed, but that in the seedless bananas, pineapples, and bread-fruits this does not happen.

Figs grow well in Nicaragua, and by many their luscious fruit is preferred to all others. My trees suffered greatly from the attacks of a large and fine longicorn beetle (*Tæniotes scalaris*, Fab.) which laid its eggs in the green bark, and produced white grubs that mined into the stem. I had to dig down to them with a knife to extricate them and prevent them destroying the young trees. We were surrounded at a short distance by the forest, in which grow many species of wild fig-trees ; and this probably was the reason that my trees suffered so much, for at Granada the fig-gowers were not troubled with this insect.

The grenadilla is the fruit of one of the passion-flowers (*Passiflora quadrangularis*), and is shaped like a large oblong apple, which it also resembles in perfume. It makes fine tarts and puddings, being somewhat like the gooseberry in taste. I had much difficulty in preserving it from being eaten by small forest rats that came out of the woods, where they had already been accustomed to eat the wild fruit of this climber.

The moist, warm climate seemed to suit the papaw tree, as it grew with great vigour, and produced very large and fine melon-like fruits. The green fruits are excellent for making pastry, if flavoured with a little lime-juice.

In vegetables, I grew three species of sweet potatoes—
yellow, purple, and white skinned, and which differ also
in their leaves and flowers; cabbages, kidney-beans,
pumpkins, yuccas (*Jatropha manihot*), quequisque (a
species of arum, *Colocasia esculenta*), lettuces, tomatoes,
capsicums, endives, parsley, and carrots.

The climate was too damp to grow onions; neither
could I succeed with peas, potatoes, or turnips. Scarlet
runners (*Phaseolus multiflorus*) grew well, and flowered
abundantly, but never produced a single pod. Darwin
has shown that this flower is dependent, like many
others, for its fertilisation upon the operations of the
busy humble-bee, and that it is provided with a wonderful mechanism, by means of which its pollen is rubbed
into the head of the bee, and received on the stigma of
the next plant visited.* There are many humble-bees,
of different species from ours, in tropical America;
but none of them frequented the flowers of the scarlet
runner, and to that circumstance we may safely ascribe
its sterility. An analogous case has been long known.
The vanilla plant (*Vanilla planifolia*) has been introduced from tropical America into India, but though it
grows well, and flowers, it never fruits without artificial
aid. It is the same in the hothouses of Europe. Dr.
Morren, of Liége, has shown that, if artificially fertilised,
every flower will produce fruit; and ascribes its sterility
to the absence, in Europe and India, of some insect that
in America carries the pollen from one flower to another.†
When those interested in the acclimature of the natural

* "Gardener's Chronicle," Oct. 24, 1857, and Nov. 14, 1858; also
T. H. Farrer, in "Annals of Natural History," Oct. 1868.

† Taylor's "Annals of Natural History," vol. iii. p. 1.

productions of one country on the soil of some distant one, study the mutual relations of plants and animals, they will find that in the case of many plants it is important that the insects specially adapted for the fertilisation of their flowers should be introduced with them. Thus, if the insect or bird that assists in the fertilisation of the vanilla could be introduced into and would live in India, the growers of that plant would be relieved of much trouble, and it might be thoroughly naturalised. Judging from my experience, it would be useless to attempt the acclimature of the scarlet-runner bean in Chontales unless the humble-bee were also introduced.

Caterpillars, plant-lice, bugs, and insect pests of all kinds were numerous, and did much harm to my garden; but the greatest plague of all were the leaf-cutting ants, and I had to wage a continual warfare against them. During this contest I gained much information regarding their habits, and was successful in checking their ravages, and I shall occupy the remainder of this chapter with an account of them.

LEAF-CUTTING ANTS.—Nearly all travellers in tropical America have described the ravages of the leaf-cutting ants (*Œcodoma*); their crowded, well-worn paths through the forests, their ceaseless pertinacity in the spoliation of the trees—more particularly of introduced species— which are stripped bare and ragged, with the midribs and a few jagged points of the leaves only left. Many a young plantation of orange, mango, and lemon trees has been destroyed by them. Again and again have I been told in Nicaragua, when inquiring why no fruit-trees were grown at particular places, " It is no use planting

them ; the ants eat them up." The first acquaintance a
stranger generally makes with them is on encountering
their paths on the outskirts of the forest crowded with
the ants ; one lot carrying off the pieces of leaves, each
piece about the size of a sixpence, and held up vertically
between the jaws of the ant; another lot hurrying along
in an opposite direction empty-handed, but eager to get
loaded with their leafy burdens. If he follows this last
division, it will lead him to some young trees or shrubs,
up which the ants mount; and then each one, stationing
itself on the edge of a leaf, commences to make a circular
cut, with its scissor-like jaws, from the edge, its hinder
feet being the centre on which it turns. When the piece
is nearly cut off, it is still stationed upon it, and it looks
as though it would fall to the ground with it ; but, on
being finally detached, the ant is generally found to have
hold of the leaf with one foot, and soon righting itself,
and arranging its burden to its satisfaction, it sets off at
once on its return. Following it again, it is seen to
join a throng of others, each laden like itself, and, without a moment's delay, it hurries along the well-worn
path. As it proceeds, other paths, each thronged with
busy workers, come in from the sides, until the main
road often gets to be seven or eight inches broad, and
more thronged than the streets of the city of London.

After travelling for some hundreds of yards, often for
more than half a mile, the formicarium is reached. It
consists of low, wide mounds of brown, clayey-looking
earth, above and immediately around which the bushes
have been killed by their buds and leaves having been
persistently bitten off as they attempted to grow after
their first defoliation. Under high trees in the thick

forest the ants do not make their nests, because, I believe, the ventilation of their underground galleries, about which they are very particular, would be interfered with, and perhaps to avoid the drip from the trees. It is on the outskirts of the forest, or around clearings, or near wide roads that let in the sun, that these formicariums are generally found. Numerous round tunnels, varying from half an inch to seven or eight inches in diameter, lead down through the mounds of earth; and many more, from some distance around, also lead underneath them. At some of the holes on the mounds ants will be seen busily at work, bringing up little pellets of earth from below, and casting them down on the ever-increasing mound, so that its surface is nearly always fresh and new-looking.

Standing near the mounds, one sees from every point of the compass ant-paths leading to them, all thronged with the busy workers carrying their leafy burdens. As far as the eye can distinguish their tiny forms, troops upon troops of leaves are moving up towards the central point, and disappearing down the numerous tunnelled passages. The outgoing, empty-handed hosts are partly concealed amongst the bulky burdens of the incomers, and can only be distinguished by looking closely amongst them. The ceaseless, toiling hosts impress one with their power, and one asks—What forests can stand before such invaders? How is it that vegetation is not eaten off the face of the earth? Surely nowhere but in the tropics, where the recuperative powers of nature are immense and ever active, could such devastation be withstood.

Further acquaintance with the subject will teach the

inquirer that, just as many insects are preserved by
being distasteful to insectivorous birds, so very many
of the forest trees are protected from the ravages of the
ants by their leaves either being distasteful to them, or
unfitted for the purpose for which they are required,
whilst some have special means of defence against their
attacks. None of the indigenous trees appear so suitable for them as the introduced ones. Through long
ages the trees and the ants of tropical America have been
modified together. Varieties of plants that arose unsuitable for the ants have had an immense advantage over
others that were more suitable ; and thus through time
every indigenous tree that has survived in the great
struggle has done so because it has had originally, or has
acquired, some protection against the great destroyer.
The leaf-cutting ants are confined to tropical America ;
and we can easily understand that trees and vegetables
introduced from foreign lands where these ants are unknown could not have acquired, excepting accidentally,
and without any reference to the ants, any protection
against their attacks, and now they are most eagerly
sought by them. Amongst introduced trees, some
species of even the same genus are more acceptable than
others. Thus, in the orange tribe, the lime (*Citrus
lemonum*) is less liked than the other species ; it is
the only one that I ever found growing really wild in
Central America : and I have sometimes thought that
even in the short time since the lime was first introduced, about three hundred years ago, a wild variety
may have arisen, less subject to the attacks of the ants
than the cultivated variety ; for in many parts I saw
them growing wild, and apparently not touched. The

orange (*Citrus aurantium*) and the citron (*Citrus medi-cus*), on the other hand, are only found where they have been planted and protected by man ; and, were he to give up their cultivation, the only species that would ultimately withstand the attacks of the ants, and obtain a permanent footing in Central America, would be the lime.   The reason why the lime is not so subject to the attacks of the ants is unknown ; and the fact that it is so is another instance of how little we know why one species of a particular genus should prevail over another nearly similar form.   A little more or less acridity, or a slight chemical difference in the composition of the tissues of a leaf, so small that it is inappreciable to our senses, may be sufficient to ensure the preservation or the destruction of a species throughout an entire continent.

The ravages of this ant are so great that it may not be without interest for me to enter upon some details respecting the means I took to protect my own garden against their attacks, especially as the continual warfare I waged against them for more than four years made me acquainted with much of their wonderful economy.

In June 1869, very soon after the formation of my garden, the leaf-cutting ants came down upon it, and at once commenced denuding the young bananas, orange and mango trees of their leaves.   I followed up the paths of the invading hosts to their nest, which was about one hundred yards distant, close to the edge of the forest. The nest was not a very large one, the low mound of earth covering it being about four yards in diameter. At first I tried to stop the holes up, but fresh ones were immediately opened out : I then dug down below the mound, and laid bare the chambers beneath, filled with ant-food and young ants in every stage of growth; but I soon found that the underground ramifications extended so far, and to so great a depth, while the ants were continually at work making fresh excavations, that it would be an immense task to eradicate them by such means; and notwithstanding all the digging I had done the first day, I found them the next as busily at work as ever at my garden, which they were rapidly defoliating. At this stage, our medical officer, Dr. J. H. Simpson,* came to my assistance, and suggested pouring carbolic acid, mixed with water, down their burrows. The suggestion proved a most valuable one. We had a quantity of common brown carbolic acid, about a pint of which I mixed with four buckets of water, and, after stirring it well about, poured it down the burrows; I could hear it rumbling down to the lowest depths of the formicarium four or five feet from the surface. The effect was all that I could have wished : the marauding parties were at once drawn off from my garden to meet the new danger at home. The whole formicarium was disorganised. Big fellows came stalking up from the cavernous regions below, only to descend again in the utmost perplexity.

Next day I found them busily employed bringing up the ant-food from the old burrows, and carrying it to a new one a few yards distant ; and here I first noticed a wonderful instance of their reasoning powers. Between the old burrows and the new one was a steep slope.

* This gentleman, beloved by all who knew him, of rare talent, and with every prospect of a prosperous career before him, died at Jamaica from hydrophobia, between two and three months after being bitten by a small dog that had not itself shown any symptoms of that disease.

Instead of descending this with their burdens, they cast them down on the top of the slope, whence they rolled down to the bottom, where another relay of labourers picked them up and carried them to the new burrow. It was amusing to watch the ants hurrying out with bundles of food, dropping them over the slope, and rushing back immediately for more. They also brought out great numbers of dead ants that the fumes of the carbolic acid had killed. A few days afterwards, when I visited the locality again, I found both the old burrows and the new one entirely deserted, and I thought they had died off; but subsequent events convinced me that the survivors had only moved away to a greater distance.

It was fully twelve months before my garden was again invaded. I had then a number of rose-trees and also cabbages growing, which the ants seemed to prefer to everything else. The rose-trees were soon defoliated, and great havoc was made amongst the cabbages. I followed them to their nest, and found it about two hundred yards from the one of the year before. I poured down the burrows, as before, several buckets of water with carbolic acid. The water is required to carry the acid down to the lowest chambers. The ants, as before, were at once withdrawn from my garden; and two days afterwards, on visiting the place, I found all the survivors at work on one track that led directly to the old nest of the year before, where they were busily employed making fresh excavations. Many were bringing along pieces of the ant-food from the old to the new nests; others carried the undeveloped white pupæ and larvæ. It was a wholesale and entire migration; and the next day the formicarium down which I had last

poured the carbolic acid was entirely deserted. I afterwards found that when much disturbed, and many of
the ants destroyed, the survivors migrate to a new
locality. I do not doubt that some of the leading
minds in this formicarium recollected the nest of the
year before, and directed the migration to it.

Don Francisco Velasquez informed me, in 1870, that
he had a powder which made the ants mad, so that they
bit and destroyed each other. He gave me a little of it,
and it proved to be corrosive sublimate. I made several
trials of it, and found it most efficacious in turning a
large column of the ants. A little of it sprinkled across
one of their paths in dry weather has a most surprising
effect. As soon as one of the ants touches the white
powder, it commences to run about wildly, and to attack
any other ant it comes across. In a couple of hours,
round balls of the ants will be found all biting each other;
and numerous individuals will be seen bitten completely
in two, whilst others have lost some of their legs or
antennæ. News of the commotion is carried to the formicarium, and huge fellows, measuring three-quarters of an
inch in length, that only come out of the nest during a
migration or an attack on the nest or one of the working
columns, are seen stalking down with a determined air,
as if they would soon right matters. As soon, however,
as they have touched the sublimate, all their stateliness
leaves them: they rush about; their legs are seized
hold of by some of the smaller ants already affected by
the poison; and they themselves begin to bite, and in a
short time become the centres of fresh balls of rabid ants.
The sublimate can only be used effectively in dry
weather. At Colon I found the Americans using coal

tar, which they spread across their paths when any of them led to their gardens. I was also told that the Indians prevent them from ascending young trees by tying thick wisps of grass, with the sharp points downwards, round the stems. The ants cannot pass through the wisp, and do not find out how to surmount it, getting confused amongst the numberless blades, all leading downwards. I mention these different plans of meeting and frustrating the attacks of the ants at some length, as they are one of the greatest scourges of tropical America, and it has been too readily supposed that their attacks cannot be warded off. I myself was enabled, by using some of the means mentioned above, to cultivate successfully trees and vegetables of which the ants were extremely fond.

Notwithstanding that these ants are so common throughout tropical America, and have excited the attention of nearly every traveller, there still remains much doubt as to the use to which the leaves are put. Some naturalists have supposed that they use them directly as food ; others, that they roof their underground nests with them. I believe the real use they make of them is as a manure, on which grows a minute species of fungus, on which they feed ;—that they are, in reality, mushroom growers and eaters. This explanation is so extraordinary and unexpected, that I may be permitted to enter somewhat at length on the facts that led me to adopt it. When I first began my warfare against the ants that attacked my garden, I dug down deeply into some of their nests. In our mining operations we also, on two occasions, carried our excavations from below up through very large formicariums, so that

all their underground workings were exposed to observation. I found their nests below to consist of numerous
rounded chambers, about as large as a man's head,
connected together by tunnelled passages leading from
one chamber to another. Notwithstanding that many
columns of the ants were continually carrying in the cut
leaves, I could never find any quantity of these in the
burrows, and it was evident that they were used up
in some way immediately they were brought in. The
chambers were always about three parts filled with a

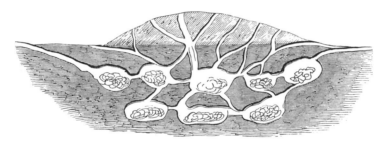

NEST OF LEAF-CUTTING ANT.

speckled, brown, flocculent, spongy-looking mass of a
light and loosely connected substance. Throughout these
masses were numerous ants belonging to the smallest
division of the workers, which do not engage in leaf-
carrying. Along with them were pupæ and larvæ, not
gathered together, but dispersed, apparently irregularly,
throughout the flocculent mass. This mass, which I
have called the ant-food, proved, on examination, to
be composed of minutely subdivided pieces of leaves,
withered to a brown colour, and overgrown and lightly
connected together by a minute white fungus that rami-

fied in every direction throughout it. I not only found
this fungus in every chamber I opened, but also in the
chambers of the nest of a distinct species that generally
comes out only in the night-time, often entering houses
and carrying off various farinaceous substances, and
which does not make mounds above its nests, but long,
winding passages, terminating in chambers similar to
the common species, and always, like them, three parts
filled with flocculent masses of fungus-covered vegetable
matter, amongst which are the ant-nurses and immature ants. When a nest is disturbed, and the masses of
ant-food spread about, the ants are in great concern to
carry every morsel of it under shelter again ; and sometimes, when I had dug into a nest, I found the next
day all the earth thrown out filled with little pits that
the ants had dug into it to get out the covered up food.
When they migrate from one part to another, they also
carry with them all the ant-food from their old habitations. That they do not eat the leaves themselves I convinced myself; for I found near the tenanted chambers,
deserted ones filled with the refuse particles of leaves
that had been exhausted as manure for the fungus, and
were now left, and served as food for larvæ of *Staphy-
linidæ* and other beetles.*

These ants do not confine themselves to leaves, but
also carry off any vegetable substance that they find
suitable for growing the fungus on. They are very
partial to the inside white rind of oranges, and I have

* This theory that the leaf-cutting ants feed on a fungus which they
cultivate has been confirmed by Mr. Fritz Müllar, who had arrived at
it independently in Brazil. His observations on this and various other
habits of insects are contained in a letter to Mr. Charles Darwin, published in *Nature* of June 11, 1874.

also seen them cutting up and carrying off the flowers
of certain shrubs, the leaves of which they neglected.
They are particular about the ventilation of their underground chambers, and have numerous holes leading up
to the surface from them.   These they open out or close
up, apparently to keep up a regular degree of temperature below.   The great care they take that the pieces of
leaves they carry into the nest should be neither too dry
nor too damp, is also consistent with the idea that the
object is the growth of a fungus that requires particular
conditions of temperature and moisture to ensure its
vigorous growth.   If a sudden shower should come on,
the ants do not carry the wet pieces into the burrows,
but throw them down near the entrances.   Should the
weather clear up again, these pieces are picked up when
nearly dried, and taken inside ; should the rain, however,
continue, they get sodden down into the ground, and are
left there.   On the contrary, in dry and hot weather,
when the leaves would get dried up before they could be
conveyed to the nest, the ants, when in exposed situations, do not go out at all during the hot hours, but
bring in their leafy burdens in the cool of the day and
during the night.   As soon as the pieces of leaves are
carried in they must be cut up by the small class of
workers into little pieces.   I have never seen the smallest
class of ants carrying in leaves ; their duties appear to
be inside, cutting them up into smaller fragments, and
nursing the immature ants.   I have, however, seen them
running out along the paths with the others ; but instead
of helping to carry in the burdens, they climb on the top
of the pieces which are being carried along by the middle-
sized workers, and so get a ride home again.   It is very

probable that they take a run out merely for air and exercise. The largest class of what are called workers are, I believe, the directors and protectors of the others. They are never seen out of the nest, excepting on particular occasions, such as the migrations of the ants, and when one of the working columns or nests is attacked; they then come stalking up, and attack the enemy with their strong jaws. Sometimes, when digging into the burrows, one of these giants has unperceived climbed up my dress, and the first intimation of his presence has been the burying of his jaws in my neck, from which he would not fail to draw the blood. The stately observant way in which they stalk about, and their great size, compared with the others, always impressed me with the idea that in their bulky heads lay the brains that directed the community in its various duties. Many of their actions, such as that I have mentioned of two relays of workmen carrying out the ant-food, can scarcely be blind instinct. Some of the ants make mistakes, and carry in unsuitable leaves. Thus grass is nearly always rejected by them, yet I have seen some ants, perhaps young ones, carrying in leaves of grass. After a while these pieces were invariably brought out again and thrown away. I can imagine a young ant getting a severe earwigging from one of the major-domos for its stupidity.

I shall conclude this long account of the leaf-cutting ants with an instance of their reasoning powers. A nest was made near one of our tramways, and to get to the trees the ants had to cross the rails, over which the waggons were continually passing and repassing. Every time they came along a number of ants were crushed to death. They persevered in crossing for several days, but at last set to work and tunnelled underneath each rail. One day, when the waggons were not running, I stopped up the tunnels with stones; but although great numbers carrying leaves were thus cut off from the nest, they would not cross the rails, but set to work making fresh tunnels underneath them. Apparently an order had gone forth, or a general understanding been come to, that the rails were not to be crossed.

These ants do not appear to have many enemies, though I sometimes found holes burrowed into their nests, probably by the small armadillo. I once saw a minute parasitic fly hovering over a column of ants, near a nest, and every now and then darting down and attaching an egg to one entering. Large, horned beetles (*Cœlosis biloba*) and a species of Staphylinus are found in the nests, but probably their larvæ live on the rotten leaves, after the ants have done with them.

CHAPTER VI.

THERE is scarcely any level land around Santo Domingo,
but in every direction a succession of hills and valleys.
The hills are not isolated ; they run in irregular ranges,
having mostly an east and west direction, but with
many modifications in their trend. From the main
valleys numerous auxiliary ones cut deeply into the
ranges, and bifurcate again and again, like the branches
of a tree, forming channels for carrying off the great
quantity of water that falls in these rainy forests. The
branching valleys, all leading into main ones, and these
into the rivers, have been excavated by sub-aërial agency,
and almost entirely by the action of running water. It
is the system that best effects the drainage of the
country, and has been caused by that drainage.

The wearing out of valleys near Santo Domingo proceeds more rapidly than in regions where less rain falls,
and where the rocks are not so soft and decomposed.
Even during the few years I was in Nicaragua there
were some modifications of the surface effected ; I saw

the commencement of new valleys, and the widening and lengthening of others, caused not only by the gradual denudation of the surface, but by landslips, some of which occur every wet season.

The rocks of the district are dolerytes, with bands and protrusions of hard greenstones. The decomposition of the dolerytes is very great, and extends from the tops of the hills to a depth (as proved in the mines), of at least two hundred feet. Next the surface they are often as soft as alluvial clay, and may be cut with a spade. This decomposition of the rocks near the surface prevails in many parts of tropical America, and is principally, if not always, confined to the forest regions. It has been ascribed, and probably with reason, to the percolation through the rocks of rain-water charged with a little acid from the decomposing vegetation. If this be so, the great depth to which it has reached tells of the immense antiquity of the forests.

Gold-mining at Santo Domingo is confined almost entirely to auriferous quartz lodes, no alluvial deposits having been found that will pay for working. The lodes run east and west, and are nearly perpendicular, sometimes dipping a little to the north, sometimes a little to the south, and near the surface, generally turning over towards the face of the hill through which they cut. The trend of the main ranges, also nearly east and west, is probably due to the direction of the outcrops of the lodes which have resisted the action of the elements better than the soft dolerytes. The quartz veins now form the crests of many of the ranges, but are everywhere cut through by the lateral valleys. The beds of doleryte lie at low angles, through which the quartz veins cut

nearly vertically.   Excepting that they are very irregular
in thickness, and often branch and send thin offshoots
into the enclosing rocks, they resemble coal seams that
have been turned up on edge, so as to be vertical instead
of horizontal.   They run for a great distance.   Near
Santo Domingo they had been traced for two miles in
length, and probably they extend much further.   They
are what are called fissure-veins, owing their origin to
cracks or fractures in the rocks that have been filled
up with mineral substances through chemical, thermal,
aqueous, or plutonic agencies.   In depth, the bottom of
fissure-veins has never been reached, and taking into
consideration the deep-seated forces required to produce
fissures of such great length and regularity, we may
safely assume that they run for miles deep into the earth
—that their extension vertically is as great as it is horizontally.   The probability that they extend to immense
depths is increased when we reflect that mineral veins
occur in parallel groups that run with great regularity
for hundreds of miles ; and further by the fact that, in
all the changes of the earth's surface, by which deep-
seated rocks have been brought up and exposed by
denudation, no instance is known of the bottom of a
fissure-vein having been brought by such movements
within the reach of man.

The gold-mines of Santo Domingo are in veins or lodes
of auriferous quartz that run parallel to each other, and
are so numerous that across a band more than a mile in
width one may be found every fifty yards.   All that have
been worked vary greatly in thickness ; sometimes within
a hundred yards a lode will thicken out from one to
seventeen feet.   Their auriferous contents vary still more

than their width. The richest ore, worth from one to four
ounces per ton, occurs in irregular patches and bands
very small in comparison with the bulk of the ore stuff,
which varies in value from two to seven pennyweights
per ton. The average value of all the ore treated by the
Chontales Mining Company, up to the end of 1871, has

MACHINERY OF CHONTALES GOLD-MINING COMPANY.

been about seven pennyweights per ton, and during that
time small patches have been met with worth one hundred ounces of gold per ton. The gold does not occur
pure, but is a natural alloy of gold and silver, containing
about three parts of the former to one of the latter.
Besides this metallic alloy (to which, for brevity, I shall,
in the remarks I have to make, give its common designa-

tion of gold), the quartz lodes contain sulphide of silver, peroxide of manganese, peroxide of iron, sulphides of iron and copper, and occasionally ores of lead.

The quartz is generally very friable, full of drusy cavities, and broken up into innumerable small pieces that are often coloured black by the peroxide of manganese. The gold is in minute grains, and generally distributed loosely amongst the quartz. Pieces as large as a pin's head are rare, and specimens of quartz showing the gold in it are seldom met with, even in the richest portions of a lode. The fine gold-dust can, however, easily be detected by washing portions of the lode-stuff in a horn. The quartz and clay is washed away, and the gold-dust sinks to the bottom, and is retained in the horn. This is the usual way in which a lode is tested by the mining agents, and long practice has made them very expert in valuing the ore by the wash in the " spoon." Although most of the gold occurs loose, amongst the soft portions of the lode, the hard quartz also contains it disseminated in minute grains throughout. These can be obtained in the horn by pounding the quartz to powder and then washing it.

One feature in the distribution of gold in the quartz lodes of Santo Domingo led to a most exaggerated opinion of their value when they were first mined by English companies. On the hills, near the outcrops of the lodes, the ore was in some places exceedingly rich. One thousand ounces of gold were obtained from a small patch of ore near the surface of the Consuelo lode, and at Santo Domingo, San Benito, San Antonio, and Javali lodes, very rich ore was also discovered within a few fathoms of the surface. When, however, these deposits were followed downwards, they invariably got poorer, and at one hundred feet from the surface, no very rich ore had been met with. Below that, when the works are prosecuted still deeper, there does not appear to be any further progressive deterioration in the value of the ore, and it varies in yield from two to seven penny-weights of gold per ton, upon which yield further depth does not seem to have any effect. The cause of these rich deposits near the surface does not appear to me to be that the lodes originally, before they were exposed by denudation, contained more gold in their upper portions than below, but to be the effect of the decomposition and wearing down of the higher parts, and the concentration of the gold they contained in the lode below that worn away. We have seen that in the decomposed parts of the lode, the gold exists in loose fine grains. During the wet season water percolates freely from the surface down through the lodes, and the gold set free by the decomposition of the ore at the surface must be carried down into it, so that in the course of ages, during the gradual degradation and wearing away of the surface, there has, I believe, been an accumulation of the loose gold in the upper parts of the lodes from parts that originally stood much higher, and have now been worn away by the action of the elements.

This accumulation of loose gold near the surface of auriferous veins, set at liberty from its matrix by the decomposition of the ore, and concentrated by degradation, is probably the reason of the great richness of many of what are called the *caps* of quartz veins; that is, the parts next the existing surface, and has, also, perhaps, originated the belief that auriferous lodes de-

teriorate in value in depth. I at one time, after having
studied the auriferous quartz veins of Australia, advocated this theory, which was first insisted upon by Sir
R. I. Murchison, but further experience in North Wales,
Nova Scotia, Brazil, and Central America, has led me
to doubt its correctness, excepting in cases such as
we have been considering, where there has been an
accumulation of gold in the superficial portions of lodes,
since their original formation. Gold is distributed in
quartz veins in bands, and in patches of richer stone of
more or less extent. These richer portions of the lodes,
if sunk upon perpendicularly, will be passed through,
but so also they would be if followed horizontally, their
extent in one direction being as great as it is in the
other. The chances of meeting with further patches of
rich ore in depth, after one has been passed through,
are about the same as they are in driving horizontally,
and the frequency therefore with which the auriferous
ores are met with along the surface will, as a rule, be
an index of their occurrence in depth, if we be careful
in distinguishing deposits belonging to the original condition of the lodes, and those due to subsequent concentration. To do this we must get below the immediate
surface, and take as our guide the gold occurring in
the solid undecomposed quartz, and not the loose grains
contained in the fissures and cavities.

The lodes of Santo Domingo are worked by means of
levels driven from near the bottoms of the valleys that
intersect them. When these levels have entered sufficiently far into the hills, shafts are driven upwards from
them to the surface, and other levels driven sixty feet
higher than the first. This process is continued until

the lode lying above the lowest level has been divided
off into horizontal bands, each about sixty feet in depth.
The quartz is then excavated above the topmost level,
and thrown down the shafts to the lowest, where it is
received into waggons and conveyed to the reduction
works.   As both the ore and the enclosing rocks are
greatly decomposed and very soft, the whole of the
ground has to be securely timbered as the work proceeds.   The levels are timbered with " nispera," a wood
of great durability and strength, but the excavated

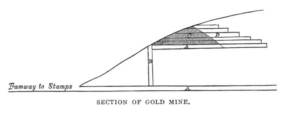

SECTION OF GOLD MINE.

Diagram showing method of excavating ore at Santo Domingo Mines.

A, Levels; B, Rise, down which the ore is thrown; D, Stopes; C, Stopes refilled
with clay and barren rock.

portions between them are only temporarily secured
with common soft wood, and at the end of every fortnight filled up with clay and barren rock.   The mining
is entirely executed by native workmen, principally
Mestizos from the border lands of Honduras and Nicaragua, where they have been engaged in silver-mining.
They are paid according to the amount of ground excavated, and are very industrious when poor; but
when they accumulate a little money, they take fits
of idleness and dissipation until it is spent.

The ore is taken down to the reduction works in

waggons that run down by gravitation, and are drawn up by mules. It is then stamped to powder by iron beaters, each of which is lifted by cams, and let fall seventy times per minute. The stamped ore, in the form of fine sand, is carried by a stream of water over inclined copper plates covered with mercury, with which is mixed a little metallic sodium. Nearly the whole of the free gold is caught by the mercury, for which it has a great affinity, and accumulates as amalgam on the copper plates, from which it is cleaned off every twelve hours. The sand and water then pass over inclined tables covered with blankets, the fibres of which intercept particles of gold and mercury that have escaped from the first process, and afterwards into a concentrating box, where the coarsest grains of sand and the sulphurets of iron, copper, and silver, are caught, and with the sand from the blankets retreated in arrastres. These arrastres are round troughs, twelve feet in diameter, paved with stones. Four large stones of quartz are dragged round and round in this trough, and grind the coarse sand to fine powder. The gold liberated sinks into the crevices in the stone pavement, a little mercury being put into the trough to form it into amalgam. The arrastres and all the amalgamating apparatus is cleaned up once a month. The amalgam obtained is squeezed through thin dressed skins, and is then of the consistence of stiff putty, and of a silver colour. These balls of amalgam are placed in iron retorts, and the mercury driven off by heat and condensed again in water. The balls of gold so obtained are then melted into bars weighing about one hundred ounces each, and in that state sent to England. At

Santo Domingo about two thousand tons of ore are treated monthly, and the whole cost of treatment, including all charges for mining, carriage, reduction, amalgamation, and management, is only about eight shillings per ton. The loss of mercury is about twenty pounds for every thousand tons of ore treated; the smallness of

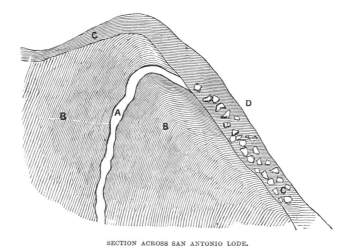

SECTION ACROSS SAN ANTONIO LODE.

A, Lode; B, Decomposed doleryte; C, Surface soil;
D, Quartz rocks in surface soil.

the loss in comparison with that of many other goldextracting establishments being greatly due to the employment of sodium in the amalgamating processes. The loss of mercury usually occurring in amalgamation work is principally caused by its mineralisation, and sodium has such an intense affinity for oxygen and sulphur, that it reduces the mercury to its metallic

form again, and prevents its being carried off in light
mineralised flakes and powder.

The band of auriferous quartz veins worked at Santo
Domingo continues westward for eight miles, as far as
the savannahs near Libertad, and has been largely
mined in the neighbourhood of that town, and between
that point and Santo Domingo. Besides the working
of the mines proper, some surface deposits, called by
the Spaniards " Mantos," are also worked for gold,
especially in the neighbourhood of Libertad. The
" Mantos " consist of broken quartz, covering the
faces of the hills in the neighbourhood of some of the
lodes. In some places they form a broken but regular
stratum over the whole side of a hill, and I was much
puzzled at first to account for their origin.

I have already mentioned that the lodes near their
summit incline over towards the face of the hill through
which they cut. In some cases, as in the San Antonio
mine, the lode is in parts bent completely round, as
shown in the annexed section. This bending over of
the lodes is always towards the face of the hill, and is,
I think, produced by successive small landslips. It is
evident that if carried still further than in the case
shown in the diagram, the lode would be brought down
over the face of the hill, and the result has, I think,
been achieved in some places, and a regular " *Manto* "
produced. I have already stated that small landslips
are of frequent occurrence on the sides of the hills. We
had several times the entrance to our mines temporarily
closed by them in the wet season.

Mr. David Forbes,* in his account of the geology of

* Quart. Journ. Geol. Soc., vol. xvii.

Peru and Bolivia, has advanced the opinion that auriferous quartz veins belong to two different systems, one
occurring in connection with Granitic, the other with
Diorytic intrusive rocks.   In later papers he has shown
that this occurrence of gold is not confined to South
America, but appears to prevail in all parts of the
world.*   One of the latest writers on the subject, Mr.
R. Daintree, in his "Notes on the Geology of Queens-
land," has shown that the auriferous veinstones in that
colony occur in connection with, or in the near vicinity
of certain intrusive trap-rocks, and that even some of
the trappean dykes themselves are auriferous.†   Several
years ago, I endeavoured to show that mineral veins in
granitic districts occurred in regular sequences, with
certain intrusive rocks, as follows :—1st, Intrusion of
main mass of granite ; 2nd, Granitic veins ; 3rd, Elvan
dykes ; and, lastly, Mineral veins, cutting through all
the other intrusive rocks.‡   Later observations have
led me to conclude that a similar sequence of events
characterised the occurrence of auriferous quartz veins
in connection with the intrusive rocks, commonly desig-
nated Greenstones, in some districts consisting of diabase, as in North Wales, near Dolgelly ; in others of
dioryte, as in Santo Domingo ; and in many parts of
South America and Australia.   In North Wales we
have, firstly, an intrusion of diabase, occurring in great
mountain masses ; 2ndly, Irregular tortuous dykes of
diabase ; 3rdly, Elvan dykes ; and, lastly, auriferous
quartz veins.   In every region of intrusive plutonic

* Geological Magazine, September 1866.
† Quart. Journ. Geol. Soc., vol. xxviii. p. 308.
‡ See "Geol. Survey of Canada," pp. 141 and 173.

rocks that has been thoroughly explored, a similar
succession of events, culminating in the production of
mineral veins, has been proved to have taken place,*
and it appears that the origin of such veins is the
natural result of the plutonic intrusion.   There is, also,
sometimes a complete gradation from veins of perfectly
crystallised granite, through others abounding in quartz
at the expense of the other constituents, up to veins
filled with pure quartz, as at Porth Just, near Cape
Cornwall; and, again, the same vein will in some parts
be filled with felspar; in others, contain irregular masses
of quartz, apparently the excess of silica beyond what
has been absorbed in the trisilicate compound of felspar.†
Granitic, porphyritic, and trappean dykes ‡'also sometimes contain gold and other metals; and I think the
probability is great that quartz veins have been filled
in the same manner,—that if dykes and veins of granite
have been an igneous injection, so have those of quartz.
By an igneous injection, I do not mean that the fused
rock owed its fluidity to dry heat.   The celebrated
researches of Sorby on the microscopical fluid cavities
in the quartz of granite and quartz veins, have shown
beyond a doubt that the vapour of water was present
in comparatively large quantities when the quartz was
solidifying.   All strata below the surface contain water,
and if melted up would still hold it as superheated
steam; and M. Angelot has suggested that fused rock
under great pressure may dissolve large quantities of

* "Mineral Veins," p. 16.

† Mr. John Phillips in "Memoirs, Geological Survey of Great
Britain," vol. ii. p. 45.

‡ Sir R. I. Murchison, "Siluria," pp. 479, 481, 488, and 500; and
R. Daintree, Quart. Jour. Geol. Soc., vol. xxviii. pp. 308, 310.

the vapour of water, just as liquids dissolve gases. The presence of the vapour of water would cause the lique-faction of quartz at a much lower temperature than would be possible by heat alone, unaided by water.*   I know that this opinion is contrary to that usually held by geologists, the theory generally accepted being that mineral veins have been produced by deposits from hot springs; but during twenty years I have been engaged in auriferous quartz-mining in various parts of the world, and nowhere have I met with lodes, the pheno-mena of which could be explained on this hypothesis. The veinstone is pure quartz containing water in micro-scopical cavities, as in the quartz crystals of granite, but not combined as in the hydrous siliceous sinter deposited from hot springs.   The lodes are not ribboned, but consist of quartz, jointed across from side to side, exactly like trappean dykes.   There is often a banded arrangement produced by the repeated re-opening and filling of the same fissure; but never, in quartz veins, a regular filling up from the sides towards the centre, as in veins produced by deposits from springs.   Quartz veins extend sometimes for miles, and it is necessary to suppose on the hydro-thermal theory that the fissures remained open sufficiently long for the gradual deposition of the veinstones, without the soft and shattered rocks at their sides falling in, nor yet fragments from above; although there are many lodes, fully twenty feet in width, filled entirely with quartz and mineral ores, without any included fragments of fallen rocks, and nowhere showing any trace of regular deposition on the sides.   The gold also found in auri-

* H. C. Sorby, Jour. Geol. Soc., vol. xiv.

ferous lodes is never pure, but forms various alloys of
gold, silver, copper, lead, iron, and bismuth; and no
way is known of producing these alloys except by fusion.

It is true that mineral veins contain many minerals
that could not exist together undecomposed with even a
moderate degree of heat; but it is only here contended
that the original filling of the lodes was an igneous injection, not that the present arrangement and composition
of all the minerals is due to the same action. Since
the lodes were first filled they have been subjected to
every variety of hydro-thermal and aqueous influence;
for the cooling of the heated rocks must have been a
slow process, and undoubtedly the veins have often been
the channels both for the passage of hot water and steam
from the interior, and of cold water charged with carbonic
acid and carbonate of lime from the surface, and many
changes must have taken place. Auriferous quartz veins
have resisted these influences better than others, because
neither the veinstone nor the metal is easily altered, and
such veins therefore form better guides for the study of
the origin of mineral lodes than fissures filled with calc
spar and ores of the baser metals, all readily dissolved
and reformed by hydro-thermal agencies. Our miner-
alogical museums are filled with beautiful specimens of
crystals of quartz, fluor spar, and various ores deposited
one on the other; and the student who confines his
attention to these is naturally led to believe that he
sees before him the process by which mineral veins
have been filled. But the miner, working far underground, knows that such crystals are only found in
cavities and fissures, and that the normal arrangement
of the minerals is very different. The deposition of

various spars one on the other in cavities is a secondary
operation even now going on, and has nothing neces-
sarily to do with the original filling of the lodes; indeed,
their arrangement is so different that it helps to prove
they have been differently formed.

It would take a volume to discuss this question in all
its bearings, and as I have already entered more fully
into it in another place,* I shall only now give a brief
résumé of the conclusions I have arrived at respecting
the origin of mineral veins.

1. Sedimentary strata have been carried down, by
movements of the earth's crust, far below the surface,
covered by other deposits, and subjected to great heat,
which, aided by the water contained in the rocks and
various chemical reactions, has effected a re-arrange-
ment of the mineral contents of the strata, so that
by molecular movements, the metamorphic crystalline
rocks, including interstratified granites and greenstones, have been formed.

2. Carried to greater depths and subjected to more
intense heat, the strata have been completely fused,
and the liquid or pasty mass, invading the contorted
strata above it, has formed perfectly crystalline intrusive granites and greenstones.

3. As the heated rocks cooled from their highest
parts downwards, cracks or fissures have been formed
in them by contraction, and these have been filled from
the still-fluid mass below.   At the beginning these
injections have been the same as the first massive
intrusive rocks, either granite or greenstone ; but as
the rocks gradually cooled, the fissures reached greater

* "Mineral Veins," by Thomas Belt.   John Weale, 1861.

and greater depths; and the lighter constituents having been drawn off and exhausted, only the heavier molten silica, mingled with metallic and aqueous vapours, has been left, and with these the last-formed and deepest fissures have been filled. These injections never reached to the surface, — probably never beyond the area of heated rocks; so that there have been no overflows from them, and they have only been exposed by subsequent great upheaval and denudation.

4. Probably the molten matter was injected into the fissures of rocks already greatly heated, and the cooling of these rocks has been prolonged over thousands of years, during which the lodes have been exposed to every degree of heat, from that of fusion to their present normal temperature. During the slow upheaval and denudation of the lodes, they have been subjected to various chemical, hydro-thermal, and aqueous agencies, by which many of their contents have been re-arranged and re-formed, new minerals have been brought in by percolation of water from the surrounding rocks, and possibly some of the original contents have been carried out by mineral springs rising through the lines of fissures which are not completely sealed by the igneous injection, as the contraction of the molten matter in cooling has left cracks and crevices through which water readily passes.

5. Some of the fissures may have been re-opened since they were raised beyond the reach of molten matter, and the new rent may have been filled by hydro-thermal or aqueous agencies, and may contain, along with veinstones of calcite derived from neighbouring beds of limestone, some minerals due to a previous

igneous injection.   Crevices and cavities, called *vughs* by the miners, have been filled more or less completely with crystals of fluor spar, quartz, and various ores of metals from true aqueous solutions, or by the action of super-heated steam.

6. By these means the signs of the original filling of many mineral lodes, especially those of the baser metals, have been obscured or obliterated ; but in auriferous quartz lodes both the metal and the veinstone have generally resisted all these secondary agencies, and are presented to us much the same as they were first deposited, excepting that the associated minerals have been altered, and in some cases new ones introduced, by the passage of hot springs from below or percolation of water from the surface.

CHAPTER VII.

THE climate of Santo Domingo and of the whole north-
eastern side of Nicaragua is a very damp one. The
rains set in in May, and continue with occasional intermission until the following January, when the dry
season of a little more than three months begins. Even
during the short-lived summer there are occasional rains,
so that although the roads dry up, vegetation never
does, the ground in the woods is ever moist, and the
brooks perennial. In the shady forest, mosquitoes and
sand-flies are rather troublesome ; but the large cleared
space about the houses of the mining company is almost
free from them, and in the beautiful light evenings one
can sit under the verandahs undisturbed, watching the
play of the moonbeams on the silky leaves of the
bananas, the twinkling north star just peeping over the
range in front, with " Charlie's Wain " in the upper half
of its endless circlings, whilst in the opposite direction
the eye rests on the beautiful constellations of the
southern hemisphere. On the darkest nights innumerable fire-flies flash their intermittent lights as they pass

amongst the low bushes or herbage, making another twinkling firmament on earth. On other evenings, sitting inside with lighted candles and wide opened doors, great bats flap inside, make a round of the apartment, and pass out again, whilst iris-winged moths, attracted by the light, flit about the ceiling, or long-horned beetles flop down on the table. In this way I made my first acquaintance with many entomological rarities.*

The heaviest rains fall in July and August, and at these times the brooks are greatly swollen. The one in front of my house sometimes carried away the little wooden bridge that crossed it, and for an hour or two became impassable, but subsided again almost as soon as the heavy rain ceased falling, for the watershed above does not extend far. Every year our operations were impeded by runs in the mines, or by small landslips stopping up our tramways and levels, or floods carrying away our dam or breaking our watercourses ; but after August we considered our troubles on this score at an end for the season. Occasionally the rains lasted three or four days without intermission, but generally they would come on in the afternoon, and there would be a downpour, such as is only seen in the tropics, for an hour or two, then some clear weather, until another great bank of clouds rolled up from the north-east and sent down another deluge. In September, October, and November there are breaks of fine weather, sometimes lasting for a fortnight ; but December is generally a very wet month, the rains ex-

* In moths, numerous fine Sphingidæ and Bombycidæ ; and in beetles, amongst many others, the rare *Xestia nitida* (Bates) and *Hexoplon albipenne* (Bates) were first described from these evening captures.

tending far into January, so that it is not until February
that the roads begin to dry up.

I had much riding about.   The mines worked by us,
when I first went out, extended from Consuelo, a mile
higher up the valley, to Pavon, a mile below Santo Domingo ; and even after I had concentrated our operations to those nearer to our reduction works, there were
many occasions for me to ride into the woods.   I had
to look after our woodcutters and charcoal-burners, to
see that they did not encroach upon the lands of our
neighbours, as they were inclined to do, and involve us
in squabbles and lawsuits ; paths had to be opened out,
to bring in nispera and cedar timber, our property surveyed, and new mines, found in the woods, visited and
explored.   Besides this, I spent most of my spare time
in the forest, which surrounded us on every side.   Longer
excursions were frequent.   The Nicaraguans, like all
Spanish Americans, are very litigious, and every now
and then I would be summoned, as the representative
of the company, to appear at Libertad, Juigalpa, or
Acoyapo, to answer some frivolous complaint, generally
made with the expectation of extorting money, but entertained and probably remanded from time to time by
unscrupulous judges, who are so badly paid by the
government that they have to depend upon the fees of
suitors for their support, and are much open to corruption.   These rides and strolls into the woods were very
fruitful in natural-history acquisitions and observations.
I shall give an account of some of those made in the
immediate vicinity of Santo Domingo, and I wish I
could transfer to my readers some of the pleasure that
they afforded me.   They gave the relief that enabled

me to carry on for years an incessant struggle, under
great difficulties, to bring the mines into a paying state,
continually hampered for want of sufficient capital, with
most inadequate machinery, and all the annoyances,
delays, and disappointments inevitable in carrying on
such a precarious enterprise as gold-mining far in the
interior of a half-civilised country.

The brook that ran at the foot of the bank below my
house, and there called the "Quebrada de Santo Domingo," is dignified half a mile lower down, after passing the mines of the Javali Company and receiving the
waters of another brook coming down from the westward,
by the name of the Javali river. The Indians, however,
both at the Indian village of Carca, seven miles back in
the mountains, and those lower down the river itself, call
it "Artígua." The preservation of these old Indian names
is important, as they might sometime or other throw
considerable light on the early inhabitants of the country.
In all parts of the world the names of mountains, valleys,
lakes, and rivers are among the most certain memorials
of the ancient inhabitants. The reason the names of the
natural features of a country remain unchanged under
the sway of successive nations, speaking totally different
languages, appears to be this. The successful invaders of
a country, even in the most cruel times, never exterminated the people they conquered ; at the least, the young
women were spared. The conquerors established their
own language, and to everything they had known in their
own land they gave their own names ; but to things quite
new to them, which nearly always included the mountains, valleys, lakes, and rivers, and often the towns and
many of the natural productions, they accepted the exist-

ing names from the survivors of the conquered people.
Often the names were corrupted, the new inhabitants
altering them just a little, to render their pronuncia-
tion easier, or to make them significant in their own
language.   Thus the fruit of the *Persea gratissima*
was called "ahuacatl" by the ancient Mexicans; the
Spaniards corrupted it to "avocado," which means an
advocate; and our sailors still further, to "alligator
pears."   The town of Comelapa, in Chontales, the
name of which means, in Spanish, "Eat a macaw," is
undoubtedly a corruption of some old Indian name
of similar form to that of the neighbouring village of
Comoapa, although the Spaniards give an absurd explanation of it, evidently invented, according to which
it was so called because a sick man was cured of a
deadly disease by eating the bird indicated.

The Artígua—I shall call it so, to do what I can to
save the name from oblivion—is woefully polluted by
the gold-mining on its banks, and flows, a dark muddy
stream, through the village of Santo Domingo, and just
below it precipitates itself one hundred and twenty feet
over a rocky fall.   One of the forest roads leads down its
banks for several miles to some small clearings, where a
few scattered, Spanish-speaking Indians and half-breeds
cultivate maize and plantains.   After leaving Santo
Domingo, it at first follows the left bank of the stream,
through low bushes and small trees of second growth,
then crosses a beautiful clear brook coming down from
the east, and finally winding round a slope covered with
great trees and dense undergrowth, reaches the site
chosen for the machinery at Pavon, where a large space
has been cleared, much of which is covered with grass.

After descending a steep hill, the Artígua, with its muddy water, is crossed. Here, in the dry season, in the hot afternoons, the wet sandy banks were the favourite resorts of multitudes of butterflies, that gathered in great masses on particular moist spots in such numbers that with one swoop of my net I have enclosed more than thirty in its gauzy folds. These butterflies were principally different species of *Callidryas*, yellow and white, mixed with brown and red species of *Timetes*, which, when disturbed, rose in a body and circled about; on the ground, looking like a bouquet; when rising, like a fountain of flowers. In groups, by themselves, would be five or six specimens of yellow and black *Papilios*, greedily sucking up the moisture, and vibrating their wings, now and then taking short flights and settling again to drink. Hesperidæ, too, abounded; and in a favourable afternoon more than twenty different species of butterflies might be taken at these spots, the finest being a lovely white, green, and black swallow-tailed *Papilio*, the first capture of which filled me with delight. Near the river were some fallen-down wooden sheds, partly overgrown with a red-flowered vine. Here a large spider (*Nephila*) built strong yellow silken webs, joined one on to the other, so as to make a complete curtain of web, in which were entangled many large butterflies, generally forest species, caught when flying across the clearing. I was at first surprised to find that the kinds that frequent open places were not caught, although they abounded on low white-flowered shrubs close to the webs; but, on getting behind them, and trying to frighten them within the silken curtain, their instinct taught them to avoid it, for, although startled,

they threaded their way through open spaces and between
the webs with the greatest ease. It was one instance
of many I have noticed of the strong instinct implanted
in insects to avoid their natural enemies. I shall mention two others. The *Heliconidæ*, a tribe of butterflies
peculiar to tropical America, with long, narrow, weak
wings, are distasteful to most animals: I have seen even
spiders drop them out of their webs again; and small
monkeys, which are extremely fond of insects, will not
eat them, as I have proved over and over again. Probably, in consequence of this special protection, they
have not needed stronger wings, and hence their weak
flight. They are also very bold, allowing one to walk
close up to flowers on which they alight. There is one
genus with transparent wings that frequents the white-
flowered shrubs in the clearings, and I have sometimes
advanced my hand within six inches of them without
frightening them. There is, however, a yellow and
black banded wasp that catches them to store his nest
with; and whenever one of these came about, they
would rise fluttering in the air, where they were safe,
as I never saw the wasp attack them on the wing. It
would hawk round the groups of shrubs, trying to
pounce on one unawares; but their natural dread of
this foe made it rather difficult to do so. When it did
catch one, it would quietly bite off its wings, roll it up
into a ball, and fly off with it. Again, the cockroaches
that infest the houses of the tropics are very wary, as
they have numerous enemies—birds, rats, scorpions, and
spiders: their long, trembling antennæ are ever stretched
out, as if feeling the very texture of the air around them;
and their long legs quickly take them out of danger.

Sometimes I tried to chase one of them up to a corner where on the wall a large cockroach-eating spider stood motionless, looking out for his prey ; the cockroach would rush away from me in great fear; but as soon as it came within a foot of its mortal foe nothing would force it onwards, but back it would double, facing all the danger from me rather than advance nearer to its natural enemy.

To return to the spiders. Besides the large owner and manufacturer of each web who was stationed near its centre, there were on the outskirts several very small ones, belonging, I think, to two different species.   I sometimes threw a fly into one of the webs.   The large spider would seize it and commence sucking its blood. The small ones, attracted by the sight of the prey, would advance cautiously from the circumference, but generally stop short about half-way up the web, evidently afraid to come within reach of the owner ; thus having to content themselves with looking at the provisions, like hungry urchins nosing the windows of an eating-house.   Sometimes a more audacious one would advance closer, but the owner would, when it came within reach, quickly lift up one of its feet and strike at it, like a feeding horse kicking at another that came near its provender, and the intruder would have to retire discomfited. These little spiders probably feed on minute insects entangled in the web, too small for the consideration of the huge owner, to whom they may be of assistance in clearing it.

Soon after crossing the muddy Artígua below Pavon, a beautifully clear and sparkling brook is reached, coming down to join its pure waters with the soiled river below. In the evening this was a favourite resort of many birds that came to drink at the pellucid stream, or catch insects playing above the water. Amongst the last was the beautiful blue, green, and white humming-bird (*Florisuga mellivora*, Linn.); the head and neck deep metallic-blue, bordered on the back by a pure white

HUMMING-BIRDS.

collar over the shoulders, followed by deep metallic-green; on the underside the blue neck is succeeded by green, the green from the centre of the breast to the end of the tail by pure white; the tail can be expanded to a half circle, and each feather widening towards the end makes the semicircle complete around the edge. When catching the ephemeridæ that play above the water, the tail is not expanded: it is reserved for times of courtship. I have seen the female sitting quietly on a branch, and two males displaying their charms in front of her. One would shoot up like a rocket, then suddenly expanding the snow-white tail like an inverted parachute, slowly descend in front of her, turning round gradually to show off both back and front. The effect was heightened by the wings being invisible from a distance of a few yards, both from their great velocity of movement and from not having the metallic lustre of the rest of the body. The expanded white tail covered more space than all the rest of the bird, and was evidently the grand feature in the performance. Whilst one was descending, the other would shoot up and come slowly down, expanded. The entertainment ended in a fight between the two performers; but whether the more beautiful or the more pugnacious were the accepted suitor, I know not. Another fine humming-bird seen about this brook was the long-billed, fire-throated *Heliomaster pallidiceps*, (Gould), generally engaged in probing long narrow-throated red flowers, forming, with their attractive nectar, complete traps for the small insects on which the humming-birds principally feed, the bird returning the favour by carrying the pollen of one flower to another. A third species, also seen at this brook, *Petasophora delphinæ*, Less., is of a dull brown colour, with brilliant purple ear-feathers and metallic-green throat. Both it and *Florisuga mellivora* are short billed, generally catching flying insects, and do not frequent flowers so much as other humming-birds. I have seen the *Petasophora* fly into the centre of a dancing column of midges and

rapidly darting first at one and then at another secure
half-a-dozen of the tiny flies before the column was
broken up; then retire to a branch and wait until it
was re-formed, when it made another sudden descent on
them. A fourth species (*Heliothrix barroti*, Bourc.),
brilliant green above, white below, with a shining
purple crest, has also a short bill, and I never saw it
about flowers, but always hovering underneath leaves
and searching for the small soft-bodied spiders that
are found there. Two of them that I examined had
these spiders in their crops. I have no doubt many
humming-birds suck the honey from flowers, as I have
seen it exude from their bills when shot, but others do
not frequent them. The principal food of all is small
insects. I have examined scores of them, and never
without finding insects in their crops. Their generally long bills have been spoken of by some naturalists
as tubes into which they suck the honey by a piston-
like movement of the tongue; but suction in the usual
way would be just as effective; and I am satisfied
that this is not the primary use of the tongue, nor of
the mechanism which enables it to be exserted to a
great length beyond the end of the bill. The tongue,
for one-half of its length, is semi-horny and cleft in two,

Tongue of Humming-bird, with the blades a little opened.

the two halves are laid flat against each other when at
rest, but can be separated at the will of the bird and
form a delicate pliable pair of forceps, most admirably
adapted for picking out minute insects from amongst the

stamens of the flowers. The woodpecker, which has a similar extensile mechanism for exserting its tongue to a great length, also uses it to procure its food—in its case soft grubs from holes in rotten trees—and to enable it to pull these out, the end of the tongue is sharp and horny, and barbed with short stiff recurved bristles.

Tongue of large red-crested Woodpecker.

Continuing down the river, the road again crosses it, and enters on the primeval forest almost untouched by the hand of man, excepting in spots where the trees that furnish the best charcoal have been cut down by the charcoal-burners, or a gigantic isolated cedar (*Cedrela odorata*) has been felled for shingles, bringing down in its fall a number of the neighbouring trees entangled in the great bush ropes. Such open spots, letting in the sunshine into the thick forests, were favourite stopping-places; for numerous butterflies frequent them, all beautiful and most varied in their colours and marking. The fallen trees, too, are the breeding-places of multitudes of beetles, whose larvæ riddle them with holes. Some beetles frequent different varieties of timber, others are peculiar to a single tree. The most noticeable of these beetles are the numerous longicorns, to the collection of which I paid a great deal of attention, and brought home more than three hundred species. More than one-half of these were new to science, and have been described by Mr. Bates. To show how prolific the locality was in insect life, I need only state that about two hundred and ninety of the species were taken within a radius of four miles, having on one side the savannahs near Pital, on the other the ranges around Santo Domingo.   Some run and fly only in the daytime, others towards evening and in the short twilight ; but the great majority issue from their hiding-places only in the night-time, and during the day lie concealed in withered leaves, beneath fallen logs, under bark, and in crevices amongst the moss growing on the trunks of trees, or even against the bare trunk, protected from observation by their mottled brown, grey, and greenish tints—assimilating in colour and appearance to the bark of the tree.   Up and down the fallen timber would stalk gigantic black ants, one inch in length, provided with most formidable stings, and disdaining to run away from danger.   They are slow and stately in their movements, seeming to prey solely on the slow-moving wood-borers, which they take at a great disadvantage when half buried in their burrows, and bear off in their great jaws.   They appear to use their sting only as a defensive weapon ; but other smaller species that hunt singly, and are very agile, use their stings to paralyse their prey.   I once saw one of these on the banks of the Artígua chasing a wood-louse (*Oniscus*), very like our common English species, on a nearly perpendicular slope.   The wood-louse, when the ant got near it, made convulsive springs, throwing itself down the slope, whilst the ant followed, coursing from side to side, and examining the ground with its vibrating antennæ.   The actions of the wood-louse resembled that of the hunted hare trying to throw the dog off its scent, and the ant was like the dog in its movements to recover the trail.   At last the wood-louse reached the bottom of the slope, and concealed itself amongst some leaves; but the ant soon discovered it, paralysed it with a sting, and was running away with it, turned back downwards, beneath itself, when I secured the hunter for my collection. All these ants that hunt singly, have the eyes well developed, and thus differ greatly from the *Ecitons*, or army ants.

The road, continuing down the Artígua, crosses it again, winds away from it, then comes to it again, at a beautiful rocky spot overhung by trees; the banks covered with plants and shrubs, and the rocks with a great variety of ferns, whilst a babbling, clear brook comes down from the ranges to the right. Some damp spots near the river are covered with a carpet of a beautiful variegated, velvety-leaved plant (*Cyrtodeira chontalensis*) with a flower like an achimenes, whilst the dryer slopes bear melastomæ and a great variety of dwarf palms, amongst which the Sweetie (*Geonoma sp.*), used for thatching houses, is the most abundant. About here grows a species of cacao (*Herrania purpurea*) differing from the cultivated species (*Theobroma cacao*). Amongst the larger trees is the " côrtess," having a wood as hard as ebony, and at the end of March entirely covered with brilliant yellow flowers, unrelieved by any green, the tree casting its leaves before flowering. The great yellow domes may be distinguished amongst the dark green forest at the distance of five or six miles. Near at hand they are absolutely dazzling when the sun is shining on them; and when they shed their flowers, the ground below is carpeted as with gold. Another valuable timber tree, the " nispera " (*Achras sapota*), is also common, growing on the dryer ridges. It attains to a great size, and its timber is almost in-

destructible, so that we used it in the construction of
all our permanent works.   White ants do not eat it,
nor, excepting when first cut, and before it is barked,
do any of the wood-boring beetles.   It bears a round
fruit about the size of an apple, hard and heavy when
green, and at this time is much frequented by the large
yellowish-brown spider-monkeys (*Ateles*), which roam
over the tops of the trees in bands of from ten to twenty.
Sometimes they lay quiet until I was passing underneath, and then shaking a branch of the nispera tree,
they would send down a shower of the hard round fruit.
Fortunately I was never struck by them.   As soon as I
looked up, they would commence yelping and barking,
and putting on the most threatening gestures, breaking
off pieces of branches and letting them fall, and shaking
off more fruit, but never throwing anything, simply
letting it fall.   Often, when on lower trees, they would
hang from the branches two or three together, holding on
to each other and to the branch with their fore feet and
long tail, whilst their hind feet hung down, all the time
making threatening gestures and cries.   Occasionally a
female would be seen carrying a young one on its back,
to which it clung with legs and tail, the mother making
its way along the branches, and leaping from tree to tree,
apparently but little encumbered with its baby.   A large
black and white eagle is said to prey upon them, but I
never witnessed this, although I was constantly falling
in with troops of the monkeys.   Don Francisco Velasquez,
one of our officers, told me that one day he heard a
monkey crying out in the forest for more than two hours,
and at last, going to see what was the matter, he saw one
on a branch and an eagle beside it trying to frighten it

to turn its back, when it would have seized it. The monkey, however, kept its face to its foe, and the eagle did not care to engage with it in this position, but probably would have tired it out. Velasquez fired at the eagle, and frightened it away. I think it likely from what I have seen of the habits of the spider-monkeys that they defend themselves from this peril by keeping two or three together, thus assisting each other, and that it is only when the eagle finds one separated from its companions that it dares to attack it.

Sometimes, but more rarely, we would fall in with a troop of the white-faced cebus monkey, rapidly running away, throwing themselves from tree to tree. This monkey feeds also partly on fruit, but is incessantly on the look-out for insects, examining the crevices in trees and withered leaves, seizing the largest beetles and munching them up with great relish. It is also very fond of eggs and young birds, and must play havoc amongst the nestlings. Probably owing to its carnivorous habits, its flesh is not considered so good by monkey - eaters as that of the fruit-feeding spider-monkey, but I never myself tried either. It is a very intelligent and mischievous animal. I kept one for a long time as a pet, and was much amused with its antics. At first, I had it fastened with a light chain; but it managed to open the links and escape several times, and then made straight for the fowls' nests, breaking every egg it could get hold of. Generally, after being a day or two loose, it would allow itself to be caught again. I tried tying it up with a cord, and afterwards with a raw-hide thong, but had to nail the end, as it could loosen any knot in a few minutes. It would sometimes entangle itself round a pole to which it was fastened, and then unwind the coils again with great discernment. Its chain allowed it to swing down below the verandah, but it could not reach to the ground. Sometimes, when there were broods of young ducks about, it would hold out a piece of bread in one hand, and, when it had tempted a duckling within reach, seize it by the other, and kill it with a bite in the breast. There was such an uproar amongst the fowls on these occasions, that we soon knew what was the matter, and would rush out and punish Mickey (as we called him) with a switch which ultimately cured him of his poultry-killing propensities. Once, when whipping him, I held up the dead duckling in front of him, and at each blow of the light switch told him to take hold of it, and at last, much to my surprise, he did so, taking it and holding it tremblingly in one hand. He would draw things towards him with a stick, and even use a swing for the same purpose. It had been put up for the children, and could be reached by Mickey, who now and then indulged himself with a swing on it. One day, I had put down some bird-skins on a chair to dry, far beyond, as I thought, Mickey's reach; but, fertile in expedients, he took the swing and launched it towards the chair, and actually managed to knock the skins off in the return of the swing, so as to bring them within his reach. He also procured some jelly that was set out to cool in the same way. Mickey's actions were very human-like. When any one came near to fondle him, he never neglected the opportunity of pocket-picking. He would pull out letters, and quickly take them from their envelopes. Anything eatable disappeared into his mouth immediately.   Once he abstracted a small bottle of turpentine from the pocket of our medical officer.   He drew the cork, held it first to one nostril then to the other, made a wry face, recorked it, and returned it to the doctor.   Another time, when he got loose, he was detected carrying off the cream-jug from the table, holding it upright with both hands, and trying to move off on his hind limbs.   He gave the jug up without spilling a drop, all the time making an apologetic grunting chuckle he often used when found out in any mischief, and which meant, " I know I have done wrong, but don't punish me ; in fact, I did not mean to do it,—it was accidental."   Whenever, however, he saw he was going to be punished, he would change his tone to a shrill, threatening note, showing his teeth, and trying to intimidate.   He had quite an extensive vocabulary of sounds, varying from a gruff bark to a shrill whistle ; and we could tell by them, without seeing him, when it was he was hungry, eating, frightened, or menacing ; doubtless, one of his own species would have understood various minor shades of intonation and expression that we, not entering so fully into his feelings and wants, passed over as unintelligible. There is a third species of monkey (*Mycetes palliatus*), called by the natives the congo, which occasionally is heard howling in the forest ; but they are not often seen, as they generally remain quiet amongst the upper branches of particular trees.

One day, when riding down this path, I came upon a pack of pisotes (*Nasua fusca*, Desm.), a raccoon-like animal, that ascends all the small trees, searching for birds' nests and fruits.   There were not less than fifty

in the pack I saw, and nothing seemed likely to escape
their search in the track they were travelling. Sometimes solitary specimens of the pisoti are met with,
hunting alone in the forest. I once saw one near
Juigalpa, ascending tree after tree, and climbing every
branch, apparently in search of birds' nests. They are
very fond of eggs ; and the tame ones, which are often
kept as pets, play havoc amongst the poultry when they
got loose. They are about the size of a hare, with a
taper snout, strong tusks, a thick hairy coat, and bushy
tail. When passing down this road, I at times saw the
fine curl-crested curassow (*Crax globicera*), as large as a
turkey, jet black, excepting underneath. This kind
would always take to the trees, and was easy to shoot,
and as good eating as it was noble in appearance. The
female is a very different-looking bird from the male,
being of a fine brown colour. Dr. Sclater, in a paper
read before the Zoological Society of London, June 17th,
1873, stated that in the South and Central American
species of *Crax* there is a complete gradation from a
species in which the sexes scarcely differ, through
others in which they differ more and more, until in
Crax globicera they are quite distinctly coloured, and
have been described as different species. The natives
call them " pavónes," and often keep them tame ; but I
never heard of them breeding in confinement. Another
fine game bird is a species of *Penelope*, called by the
natives " pávos." It feeds on the fruits of trees, and I
never saw it on the ground. A similar, but much
smaller, bird, called " chachalakes," is often met with
in the low scrub.

Mountain hens (species of *Tinamus*) were not uncommon, about the size of a plump fowl, and tasting like a pheasant. There were also two species of grouse and a ground pigeon, all good eating.

Amongst the smaller birds were trogons, mot-mots, toucans, and wood-peckers. The trogons are general feeders. I have taken from their crops the remains of fruits, grasshoppers, beetles, termites, and even small crabs and land shells. Three species are not uncommon in the forest around Santo Domingo. In all of them the females are dull brown or slaty black on the back and neck, these parts being beautiful bronze green in the males. The largest species (*Trogon massena,* Gould) is one foot in length, dark bronze green above, with the smaller wing feathers speckled white and black, and the belly of a beautiful carmine. Sometimes it sits on a branch above where the army ants are foraging below ; and when a grasshopper or other large insect flies up and alights on a leaf, it darts after it, picks it up, and returns to its perch. I found them breaking into the nests of the termites with their strong bills, and eating the large soft-bodied workers; and it was from the crop of this species that I took the remains of a small crab and a land shell (*Helicina*). Of the two smaller species, one (*Trogon atricollis,* Viell.) is bronze green above, with speckled black and white wings, belly yellow, and under feathers of the tail white, barred with black. The other (*Trogon caligatus,* Gould) is rather smaller, of similar colours, excepting the head, which is black, and a dark blue collar round the neck. Both species take short, quick, jerky flights, and are often met with along with flocks of other birds—fly-catchers, tanagers, creepers, woodpeckers, &c., that hunt together, traversing the forests in flocks of hundreds together, belonging to more than a score different species; so that whilst they are passing over, the trees seem alive with them.   Mr. Bates has mentioned similar gregarious flocks met with by him in Brazil; and I never went any distance into the woods around Santo Domingo without seeing them.   The reason of their association together may be partly for protection, as no rapacious bird or mammal could approach the flock without being discovered by one or other of them, but the principal reason appears to be that they play into each other's hands in their search for food.   The creepers and wood-peckers and others drive the insects out of their hiding-places under bark, amongst moss, and in withered leaves. The fly-catchers and trogons sit on branches, and fly after the larger insects, the fly-catchers taking them on the wing, the trogons from off the leaves on which they have settled.   In the breeding season, the trogons are continually calling out to each other, and are thus easily discovered.   They are called "viduas," that is, "widows," by the Spaniards.

Woodpeckers are often seen along with the hunting flocks of birds, especially a small one (*Centrurus puche-rani*, Mahl), with red and yellow head and speckled back. This species feeds on fruits, as well as on grubs taken out of dead trees.   A large red-crested species is common near recently-made clearings, and I successively met with one of an elegant chocolate-brown colour, and another brown with black spots on the back and breast, with a lighter-coloured crested head (*Celeus castaneus*, Wagl.).

Of the mot-mots, I met with four species in the forest, all more or less olive green in colour (*Momotus martii* and *lessoni*, and *Prionyrhynchus carinatus* and *platyrhyn-chus*), having two of the tail-feathers very long, with the shafts denuded about an inch from the end. The mot-mots have all hoarse croak-like cries, heard at a great distance in the forest, and feed on large beetles and other insects.

The toucans are very curious-looking birds, with their enormous bills. They hop with great agility amongst the branches. The largest species at Santo Domingo was the *Rhamphastus tocard*, Vieill., twenty-three inches in length, of which one-fourth was taken up by the long bill and another fourth by the tail; above, all black, excepting the tail-coverts, which are white; below, throat and breast clear lemon yellow, bordered with red, the rest black, excepting the under tail-coverts, red. When alive, the bill is beautifully painted with red, brown, and yellow. I kept a young one for some time as a pet until it was killed by my monkey. It became very tame, and was expert in catching cockroaches, swallowing them with a jerk of its bill.

After passing through some low scrubby forest, very thick with tangled second growth, the clearings of the mestizoes were reached, about five miles below Santo Domingo. Maize, plantains, and a few native vege-tables were grown here, and the owners now and then came up to the village to sell their produce. Their houses were open-sided low huts, thatched with palm-leaves; their furniture, rude bedsteads made out of a few rough poles, tied together with bark, supported on crutches stuck in the ground, with raw-hides stretched across them; their cooking utensils a tortilla-stone and a few coarse earthenware jars and pans ; their clothing dirty cotton rags. This was the limit of my journeys in this direction, although the path continued on to the savannahs towards San Thomas. The soil at this place is good, and I think that it has been long cultivated, as much of the forest appears of second growth, in which small palms and prickly shrubs abound.

CHAPTER VIII.

ON the northern side of the Santo Domingo valley, opposite to my house, a branch valley came down from the
north, which we called the San Antonio Valley. It intersected all the lodes we were working, and I constructed a
tramway up it as far as the most northern mine, called San
Benito, by which we brought down the ore to the stamps
and the firewood for the steam-engine, and in a short time
we had cleared all the timber from the lower part of the
valley ; and a dense scrub or second growth sprang up,
through which numerous paths were made by the woodcutters. I was almost daily up this valley, visiting the
mines, or in the evening after the workmen had left, and
on Saturdays afternoons, when they discontinued work at
two o'clock. On Sundays, too, it was our favourite walk,
for the tramway was dry to walk on ; there were tunnels,
mines, and sheds at various parts to get into if one of the
sudden heavy showers of rain came on ; and there were
always flowers or insects, or birds to claim one's attention. I planned the whole of the tramway; the upper

half I surveyed and levelled myself; and my almost
daily walks up it familiarised me with every bush and
fallen log by its side, and with every turn of the clear
cool brook that came prattling down over the stones,
soon at the machinery to lose its early purity, and be
soiled in the ceaseless search for gold.

The sides of the valley rose steeply, and a fair view
was obtained from the tramway in the centre over the
shrubs and small trees on each side, so that the walk was
not so hemmed in with foliage as is usual in the forest
roads. Insects were plentiful by this path. In some parts
brown tiger beetles ran or flew with great swiftness; in
others, leaf-cutting ants in endless trains carried aloft
their burdens of foliage, looking, as they marched along
with the segments of leaves, held up vertically, like green
butterflies, or a mimic representation of a moving Birnam
wood. Sometimes the chirping of the ant-thrushes drew
attention to where a great body of army-ants were
foraging amongst the fallen branches, sending the spiders,
cockroaches, and grasshoppers fleeing for their lives, only
to fall victims to the surrounding birds. On the fallen
branches and logs I obtained many longicorn beetles;
the woodcutters brought me many more, and from this
valley were obtained some of the rarest and finest species
in my collection. On the myrtle-like flowers of some of
the shrubs, large green cockchafers were to be found
during the dry season, and a bright green rosechafer was
also common. I was surprised to find on two occasions
a green and brown bug (*Pentatoma punicea*) sucking the
juices from dead specimens of this species. The bug has
weak limbs, and the beetle is more than twice its size
and weight, and is very active, quickly taking wing; so

that the only way in which it could be overcome that
I can think of, is by the bug creeping up when it is
sleeping, quietly introducing the point of its sharp
proboscis between the rings of its body, and injecting
some stupefying poison.   In both instances that I witnessed, the bug was on a leaf up a shrub, with the bulky
beetle hanging over suspended on its proboscis.   Other
species of bugs certainly inject poisonous fluids.   One
black and red species in the forest, if taken in the hand,
would thrust its sharp proboscis into the skin, and produce a pain worse than the sting of a wasp.   Amongst
the bushes were always to be found the beautiful scarlet
and black tanager (*Rhamphocœlus passerinii*, Bp.), and
more rarely another species (*R. sanguinolentus*, Less.).
Along with these, a brownish-coloured bird, reddish on
the breast and top of the head (*Phœnicothraupis fusi-
cauda*, Cab.), flew sociably ; whilst generally somewhere
in the vicinity, as evening drew on, a brown hawk
might be seen up some of the low trees, watching the
thoughtless chirping birds, and ready to pounce down
when opportunity offered.   Higher up the valley more
trees were left standing, and amongst these small
flocks of other birds might often be found, one green
with red head (*Calliste laviniæ*, Cass.) ; another, shining green, with black head (*Chlorophanes guatema-
lensis*) ; and a third, beautiful black, blue, and yellow,
with yellow head (*Calliste larvata*, Du Bus.).   These and
many others were certain to be found where the climbing *Marcgravia nepenthoides* expanded its curious flowers.
The flowers of this lofty climber are disposed in a circle,
hanging downwards, like an inverted candelabrum.   From
the centre of the circle of flowers is suspended a number

of pitcher-like vessels, which, when the flowers expand, in February and March, are filled with a sweetish liquid. This liquid attracts insects, and the insects numerous insectivorous birds, including the species I have mentioned and many kinds of humming-birds. The flowers are so disposed, with the stamens hanging downwards, that the birds, to get at the pitchers, must brush against them, and thus convey the pollen from one plant to

FLOWER OF MARCGRAVIA NEPENTHOIDES.

another. A second species of Marcgravia that I found in the woods around Santo Domingo has the pitchers placed close to the pedicels of the flowers, so that the birds must approach them from above; and in this species the flowers are turned upwards, and the pollen is brushed off by the breasts of the birds. In temperate latitudes we find many flowers fertilised by insects, attracted by honey-bearing nectaries; and in tropical

I

America not only bees, moths, and other large insects carry the pollen from one flower to another, but many flowers, like the Marcgravia, are specially adapted to secure the aid of small birds, particularly humming-birds, for this purpose. Amongst these, the " palosabre," a species of *Erythrina*, a small tree, bearing red flowers,

FLOWER OF PALOSABRE.

that grew in this valley, near the brook, often drew my attention. The tree blooms in February, and is at the time leafless, so that the large red flowers are seen from a great distance. Each flower consists of a single long, rather fleshy petal, doubled over, flattened, and closed, excepting a small opening on one edge, where the stamens protrude. Only minute insects can find access to the flower, which secretes at the base a honey-like fluid. Two long-billed humming-birds frequent it; one (*Heliomaster pallidiceps*, Gould), which I have already mentioned, is rather rare; the other (*Phæthornis longirostris*, De Latt.) might be seen at any time when the tree was in bloom, by watching near it for a few minutes. It is mottled brown above, pale below, and the two middle tail feathers are much longer than the others. The bill is very long and curved, enabling the bird easily to probe the long flower, and with its extensile cleft tongue pick up the minute insects from the bottom of the tube, where they are caught as if in a trap, their only way of exit being closed by the bill of the bird.

Whilst the bird is probing the flower, the pollen of the stamens is rubbed in to the lower part of its head, and thus carried from one flower to fecundate another. The bottom of the flower is covered externally with a thick, fleshy calyx—an effectual guard against the attempts of bees or wasps to break through to get at the honey. Humming-birds feed on minute insects, and the honey would only be wasted if larger ones could gain access to it, but in the flower of the palosabre this contingency is simply and completely guarded against.

Many flowers have contrivances for preventing useless insects from obtaining access to the nectaries. Amongst our English flowers there are scores of interesting examples, and I shall describe the fertilisation of one, the common foxglove, on account of the exceeding simplicity with which this object is effected, and to draw the attention of all lovers of nature to this other branch of a subject on which the labours of Darwin and other naturalists have of late years thrown a flood of light. The pollen of the foxglove (*Digitalis purpurea*) is carried from one flower to another by the humble-bee, who, far more than the hive bee, that " improves each shining hour," deserves to be considered the type of steady, persevering industry. It improves not only the hours of sunshine, but those of cloud, and even rain ; and, long before the honey-bee has ventured from its door, is at work bustling from flower to flower, its steady hum changing to an importunate squeak as it rifles the blossoms of their sweets. The racemes of purple bells held up by the foxglove are methodically visited by it, commencing at the bottom flower, and ascending step by step to the highest. The four stamens and the pistil of the foxglove are laid closely against the upper side of the flower. First a stamen on one side opens its anthers and exposes its pollen. The humble-bee, as it bustles in and out, brushes this off. Then another stamen exposes its pollen on the other side, then another and another; but not till all the pollen has been brushed off does the cleft-end of the pistil open, and expose its viscid stigma. The humble-bee brushes off the pollen unto its hairy coat from the upper flowers of one raceme and carries it direct to the lowest flowers of another, where the viscid stigmas are open and ready to receive it. If the humble-bee went first to the upper flowers of the spike and proceeded downwards, the whole economy of this plant to procure cross fertilisation would be upset.* The open flower of the foxglove hangs downwards. The lower part, or dilated opening of the tube, is turned outwards, and has scattered stiff hairs distributed over its inner surface ; above these the inside of the flower hangs almost perpendicularly, and is smooth and pearly. The large humble-bee bustles in with the greatest ease, and uses these hairs as footholds whilst he is sucking the honey ; but the smaller honey-bees are impeded by them, and when, having at last struggled through them, they reach the pearly, slippery precipice above, they are completely baffled. I passed the autumn of 1857 in North Wales, where the foxglove was very abundant, and watched the flowers throughout the season, but only once saw

* Darwin mentions having seen humble-bees visiting the flowering spikes of the *Spiranthes autumnalis* (ladies' tresses), and notices that they always commenced with the bottom flowers, and crawling spirally up sucked one flower after the other, and shows how this proceeding ensures the cross fertilisation of different plants.—" Fertilisation of Orchids," p. 127.

a small bee reach the nectary, though many were seen trying in vain to do so.

Great attention has of late years been paid by naturalists to the wonderful contrivances amongst flowers to secure cross fertilisation; but the structure of many cannot, I believe, be understood, unless we take into consideration not only the beautiful adaptations for securing the services of the proper insect or bird, but also the contrivances for preventing insects that would not be useful, from obtaining access to the nectar. Thus the immense length of the nectary of the *Angræcum sesquipedale* of Madagascar might, perhaps, have been completely explained by Mr. Wallace, if this important purpose had been taken into account.*

The tramway in some parts was on raised ground, in others excavated in the bank side. In the cuttings the nearly perpendicular clay slopes were frequented by many kinds of wasps that excavated round holes of the diameter of their own bodies, and stored them with sting-paralysed spiders, grasshoppers, or horse-flies. Amongst these they lay their eggs, and the white grubs that issue therefrom feed on the poor prisoners. I one day saw a small black and yellow banded wasp (*Pompilus polistoides*) hunting for spiders; it approached a web where a spider was stationed in the centre, made a dart towards it—apparently a feint to frighten the spider clear of its web; at any rate it had that effect, for it fell to the ground, and was immediately seized by the wasp, who stung it, then ran quickly backwards, dragging the spider after it, up a branch reaching to the

* "Natural Selection," by A. R. Wallace, p. 272.

ground, until it got high enough, when it flew heavily
off with it.   It was so small, and the spider so heavy,
that it probably could not have raised it from the ground
by flight.   All over the world there are wasps that store
their nests with the bodies of spiders for their young to
feed on.   In Australia, I often witnessed a wasp combat-
ing with a large flat spider that is found on the bark of
trees.   It would fall to the ground, and lie on its back,
so as to be able to grapple with its opponent ; but the
wasp was always the victor in the encounters I saw,
although it was not always allowed to carry its prey off
in peace.   One day, sitting on the sand-banks on the
coast of Hobson's Bay, I saw one dragging along a
large spider.   Three or four inches above it hovered
two minute flies, keeping a little behind, and advancing
with it.   The wasp seemed much disturbed by the
presence of the tiny flies, and twice left its prey to fly
up towards them, but they darted away immediately.
As soon as the wasp returned to the spider, there they
were hovering over and following it again.   At last,
unable to drive away its small tormentors, the wasp
reached its burrow and took down the spider, and the
two flies stationed themselves one on each side the
entrance, and would, doubtless, when the wasp went
away to seek another victim, descend and lay their own
eggs in the nest.

The variety of wasps, as of all other insects, was very
great around Santo Domingo.   Many made papery
nests, hanging from the undersides of large leaves.
Others hung their open cells underneath verandahs and
eaves of houses.   One large black one was particularly
abundant about houses, and many people got stung by

them.   They also build their pendent nests in the
orange and lime trees, and it is not always safe to
gather the fruit.   Fortunately they are heavy flyers,
and can often be struck down or evaded in their attacks.
They do good where there are gardens, as they feed
their young on caterpillars, and are continually hunting for them.   Another species, banded brown and
yellow (*Polistes carnifex*), has similar habits, but is not
so common.   Bates, in his account of the habits of the
sand-wasps at Santarem, on the Amazon, gives an interesting account of the way in which they took a few turns
in the air around the hole they had made in the sand,
before leaving to seek for flies in the forest, apparently
to mark well the position of the burrow, so that on their
return they might find it without difficulty.   He remarks
that this precaution would be said to be instinctive, but
that the instinct is no mysterious and unintelligible
agent, but a mental process in each individual differing
from the same in man only by its unerring certainty.*
I had an opportunity of confirming his account of the
proceedings of wasps when quitting a locality to which
they wished to return, in all but their unerring certainty.
I could not help noting how similar they were to the
way in which a man would act who wished to return to
some spot not easily found out, and with which he was
not previously acquainted.   A specimen of the *Polistes
carnifex* was hunting about for caterpillars in my garden.
I found one about an inch long, and held it out towards
the wasp on the point of a stick.   The wasp seized the
caterpillar immediately, and commenced biting it from
head to tail, soon reducing the soft body to a mass of pulp.

* "Naturalist on the Amazon," p. 222.

Then rolling up about one-half of the pulp into a ball, it carried it off. Being at the time amidst a thick mass of a fine-leaved climbing plant, it proceeded, before flying away, to take note of the place where the other half was left. To do this, it hovered in front for a few seconds, then took small circles in front, then larger ones round the whole plant. I thought it had gone, but it returned again, and had another look at the opening in the dense foliage down which the other half of the caterpillar lay. It then flew away, but must have left its burden for distribution with its comrades at the nest, for it returned in less than two minutes, and making one circle around the bush, descended to the opening, alighted on a leaf, and ran inside. The green remnant of the caterpillar was lying on another leaf inside, but not connected with the one on which the wasp alighted, so that in running in it missed the object and soon got hopelessly lost in the thick foliage. Coming out, it took another circle, and pounced down on the same spot again, as soon as it came opposite to it. Three small seed-pods, which here grew close together, formed the marks that I had myself taken to note the place, and these the wasp seemed also to have taken as its guide, for it flew directly down to them, and ran inside; but the small leaf on which the fragment of caterpillar lay, not being directly connected with any on the outside, it again missed it, and again got far away from the object of its search. It then flew out again, and the same process was repeated again and again. Always when in circling round it came in sight of the seed-pods down it pounced, alighted near them, and recommenced its quest on foot. I was surprised at

its perseverance, and thought it would have given up
the search ; not so, however, for it returned at least
half-a-dozen times, and seemed to get angry, hurrying
about with buzzing wings.   At last it stumbled across
its prey, seized it eagerly, and as there was nothing
more to come back for, flew straight off to its nest,.
without taking any further note of the locality.   Such
an action is not the result of blind instinct, but of a
thinking mind ; and it is wonderful to see an insect so
differently constructed using a mental process similar
to that of man.   It is suggestive of the probability of
many of the actions of insects that we ascribe to instinct
being the result of the possession of reasoning powers.

Where the tramway terminated at San Benito mine,
the valley had greatly contracted in width, and the
stream, excepting in time of flood, had dwindled to a
little rill.   A small rough path, made by the miners to
bring in their timber, continued up the brook, crossing
and recrossing it.   The sides of the valley were very
steep, and covered with trees and undergrowth.   The
foliage arched over the water, forming beautiful little
dells, with small, clear pools of water.   One of these was
a favourite resort of humming-birds, who came there to
bathe, for these gem-like birds are very frequent in their
ablutions, and I spent many a half-hour in the evenings
leaning against a trunk of a tree that had fallen across
the stream four or five yards below the pool, and watching
them.   At all times of the day they occasionally came
down, but during the short twilight there was a crowd of
bathers, and often there were two or three at one time
hovering over the pool, which was only three feet across,
and dipping into it.   Some would delay their evening

toilet until the shades of night were thickening, and it became almost too dark to distinguish them from my stand. Three species regularly frequented the pool, and three others occasionally visited it. The commonest was the *Thalurania venusta* (Gould), the male of which is a most beautiful bird,—the front of the head and shoulders glistening purple, the throat brilliant light green, shining in particular lights like polished metal, the breast blue, and the back dark green. It was a beautiful sight to see this bird hovering over the pool, turning from side to side by quick jerks of its tail, now showing its throat a gleaming emerald, now its shoulders a glistening amethyst, then darting beneath the water, and rising instantly, throw off a shower of spray from its quivering wings, and fly up to an overhanging bough and commence to preen its feathers. All humming-birds bathe on the wing, and generally take three or four dips, hovering, between times, about three inches above the surface.

Sometimes when the last-mentioned species was suspended over the water, its rapidly vibrating wings showing, like a mere film, a speck shot down the valley, swift as an arrow, as white as a snowflake, and stopping suddenly over the pool, startled the emerald-throat, and frightened it up amongst the overhanging branches. The intruder was the white-cap (*Microchera parvirostris*, Lawr.), the smallest of thirteen different kinds of humming-birds that I noticed around Santo Domingo; being only a little more than two and a half inches in length, including the bill; but it was very pugnacious, and I have often seen it drive some of the larger birds away from a flowering tree. Its body is purplish-red,

with green reflections, the front of its head flat, and
pearly white, and, when flying towards one, its white
head is the only part seen. Sometimes the green-throat
would hold its ground, and then it was comical to see
them hovering over the water, jerking round from side
to side, eyeing each other suspiciously, the one wishing
to dip, but apparently afraid to do so, for fear the other
would take a mean advantage, and do it some mischief
whilst under water ; though what harm was possible
I could not see, as there were no clothes to steal.   I
have seen human bathers acting just like the birds,
though from a different cause, bobbing down towards the
water, but afraid to dip their heads, and the idea of comi-
cality arose, as it does in most of the ludicrous actions
of animals, from their resemblance to those of mankind.
The dispute would generally end by the green-throat
giving way, and leaving the pugnacious little white-cap
in possession of the pool.

Besides the humming-birds I have mentioned, there
were four or five other small ones that we used to call
squeakers, as it is their habit for a great part of the day
to sit motionless on branches and every now and then to
chirp out one or two shrill notes.   At first I thought
these sounds proceeded from insects, as they resemble
those of crickets ; but they are not so continuous.
After a while I got to know them, and could distinguish
the notes of the different species.   It was not until then
that I found out how full the woods are of humming-birds,
for they are most difficult to see when perched amongst
the branches, and when flying they frequent the tops of
trees in flower, where they are indistinguishable.   I
have sometimes heard the different chirps of more than

a dozen individuals, although unable to get a glimpse
of one of them, as they are mere brown specks on the
branches, their metallic colours not showing from below,
and the sound of their chirpings—or rather squeakings
—being most deceptive as to their direction and distance
from the hearer. My conclusion, after I got to know
their voices in the woods, was that the humming-birds
around Santo Domingo equalled in number all the rest
of the birds together, if they did not greatly exceed them.
Yet one may sometimes ride for hours without seeing
one. They build their nests on low shrubs—often on
branches overhanging paths, or on the underside of the
large leaves of the shrubby palm-trees. They are all
bold birds, suffering you to approach nearer than any
other kinds, and often flying up and hovering within
two or three yards from you. This fearlessness is
probably owing to the great security from foes that
their swiftness of flight ensures to them. I have
noticed amongst butterflies that the swiftest and
strongest flyers, such as the *Hesperidæ*, also allow you
to approach near to them, feeling confident that they
can dart away from any threatened danger,—a mis-
placed confidence, however, so far as the net of the
collector is concerned.

At the head of the tramway, near the entrance to the
San Benito mine, we planted about three acres of the
banks of the valley with grass. In clearing away the
fallen logs and brushwoods, many beetles, scorpions, and
centipedes were brought to light. Amongst the last was
a curious species belonging to the sucking division of the
Myriapods (*Sugantia*, of Brandt), which had a singular
method of securing its prey. It is about three inches

long, and sluggish in its movements; but from its tubular
mouth it is able to discharge a viscid fluid to the distance
of about three inches, which stiffens on exposure to the
air to the consistency of a spider's web, but stronger.
With this it can envelop and capture its prey, just as a
fowler throws his net over a bird. The order of *Myriapoda*
is placed by systematists at the bottom of the class of
insects; the sucking Myriapods are amongst the lowest
forms of the order, and it is singular to find one of these
lowly organised species furnished with an apparatus of
such utility, and the numberless higher forms without
any trace of it.   Some of the other centipedes have two
phosphorescent spots in the head, which shine brightly
at night, casting a greenish light for a little distance in
front of them.   I do not know the use of these lights,
but think that they may serve to dazzle or allure the
insects on which they prey.   We planted two kinds of
grasses, both of which have been introduced into Nicaragua within the last twenty years.   They are called
Pará and Guinea grasses, I believe, after the places from
which they were first brought.   The former is a strong
succulent grass, rooting at the joints; the latter grows in
tufts, rising to a height of four to five feet.   Both are
greatly liked by cattle and mules; large bundles were
cut every day for the latter whilst they were at work
on the tramway, and they kept in good condition on it
without other food.   The natural, indigenous grass that
springs up in clearings in the neighbouring forest is
a creeping species, and is rather abundant about Santo
Domingo.   It has a bitter taste, and cattle do not thrive
on it, but rapidly fall away in condition if confined to it.
They do better when allowed to roam about the outskirts

of the forest amongst the brushwood, as they browse on the leaves of many of the bushes. This grass is not found far outside the forest, but is replaced on the savannahs by a great variety of tufted grasses, which seem gradually to overcome the creeper in the clearings on the edge of the forest; but at Santo Domingo the latter was predominant, and although I sowed the seeds of other grasses amongst it, they did not succeed, on account of the cattle picking them out and eating them in preference to the other.

There were many other paths leading in different directions into the forest, and I shall describe one of them, as it differed from those already mentioned, leading to the top of a bare rock, rising fully 1000 feet above Santo.Domingo.

This rock, on the southern and most perpendicular side, weathers to a whitish colour, and is called Peña Blanca, meaning the white peak. It is visible from some points on the savannahs. During the summer months it is, on the northern side, covered with the flowers of a caulescent orchid (*Ornithorhynchos*) that has not been found anywhere else in the neighbourhood; and the natives, who are very fond of flowers, inheriting the taste from their Indian ancestors, at this time, often on Sundays ascend the peak and bring down large quantities of the blossoms. Its colour, when it first opens, is scarlet and yellow. With it grows a crimson *Mackleania*. Once when I made an ascent, in March, these flowers were in perfection, and in great abundance, and the northern face of the rock was completely covered with them. When I emerged from the gloomy forest, the sun was shining brightly on it, and the combination

of scarlet, crimson, and yellow made a perfect blaze of
colour, approaching more nearly to the appearance of
flames of fire than anything I have elsewhere seen in
the floral world.

The last ascent I made to the summit of Peña Blanca
was in the middle of June 1872, after we had had
about two weeks of continuously wet weather.   On the
17th, the rain clouds cleared away, the sun shone out,
and only a few fleecy cumuli sailed across the blue sky,
driven by the north-east trade wind.   I had on previous
visits to the peak noticed the elytra of many beetles
lying on the bare top.   They were the remnants of
insects caught by frogs; great bulky fellows that excited one's curiosity to know how ever they got there.
Amongst the elytra were those of beetles that I had
never taken, and as they were night-roaming species,
I determined to go up some evening and wait until
dark, with a lanthorn, to see if I could take any of
them.   We had one heavy shower of rain in the afternoon, so that the forest was very wet, and the hills
slippery and difficult for the mule.   The path ascends
the valley of Santo Domingo, then crosses a range
behind a mine called the " Consuelo," enters the forest,
descending at first a steep slope to a clear brook; after
crossing this, the ascent of the hill of Peña Blanca
begins, and is continuous for about a mile to the top
of the rock.   The ground was damp, and the forest
gloomy, but here and there glimpses of sunshine glanced
through the trees, and enlivened the scene a little.   I
startled a mountain hen (*Tinamus sp.*) which whirred
off amongst the bushes.   The dry slopes of hills are
their favourite feeding-places, and around Peña Blanca

they are rather plentiful; and so, also, in their season, are the curassows and penelopes. In the lower ground, the footmarks of the tapir are very frequent, especially along the small paths, where I have sometimes traced them for more than a mile. They are harmless beasts. One of our men came across one near Peña Blanca, and attacked and killed it with his knife. He brought in the head to me. It was as large as that of a bullock. I often tried to track them, but never succeeded in seeing one. One day in my eagerness to get near what I believed to be one, I rushed into rather unpleasant proximity with a jaguar, the "tigre" of the natives. I had just received a fresh supply of cartridge cases for my breech-loader, and wishing to get some specimens of the small birds that attend the armies of the foraging ants, I made up three or four small charges of No. 8 shot, putting in only a quarter of an ounce of shot into each charge, so as not to destroy their plumage. I went back into the forest along a path where I had often seen the great footmarks of the tapir. After riding about a couple of miles, I heard the notes of some birds, and, dismounting, tied up my mule, and pushed through the bushes. The birds were shy, and in following them I had got about fifty yards from the path, to a part where the big trees were more clear of brushwood, when I heard a loud hough in a thicket towards the left. It was something between a cough and a growl, but very loud, and could only have been produced by a very large animal. Never having seen or heard a jaguar before in the woods, and having often seen the footprints of the tapir, I thought it was the latter, and thinking I would have to get very close up

ADVENTURE WITH A JAGUAR.

to it to do it any damage with my little charge of small
shot, I ran along towards the sound, which was continued at intervals of a few seconds.　Seeing a large
animal moving amongst the thick bushes, only a few
yards from me, I stopped, when, to my amazement, out
stalked a great jaguar (like the housekeeper's rat, the
largest I had ever seen), in whose jaws I should have
been nearly as helpless as a mouse in those of a cat.
He was lashing his tail, at every roar showing his great
teeth, and was evidently in a bad humour.　Notwithstanding I was so near to him, I scarcely think he saw
me at first, as he was crossing the open glade about
twenty yards in front of me.　I had not even a knife
with me to show fight with if he attacked me, and my
small charge of shot would not have penetrated beyond
his skin, unless I managed to hit him when he was very
near to me.　To steady my aim, if he approached me, I
knelt down on one knee, supporting my left elbow on
the other.　He was just opposite to me at the time, the
movement caught his eye, he turned half round, and put
down his neck and head towards the ground as if he
was going to spring, and I believe he could have cleared
the ground between us at a single bound, but the next
moment he turned away from me, and was lost sight
of amongst the bushes.　I half regretted I had not fired
and taken my chance ; and when he disappeared, I followed a few yards, greatly chagrined that in the only
chance I had ever had of bagging a jaguar, I was not
prepared for the encounter, and had to let " I dare not,"
wait upon " I would."　I returned the next morning
with a supply of ball cartridges, but in the night it had
rained heavily, so that I could not even find the jaguar's

K

tracks, and although afterwards I was always prepared, I never met with another. From the accounts of the natives, I believe that in Central America he never attacks man unless first interfered with, but when wounded is very savage and dangerous. Velasquez told me that his father had mortally wounded one, which, however, sprang after him, and had got hold of him by the leg, when it fortunately fell down dead.

The path up Peña Blanca hill gets steeper and steeper, until about fifty yards from the rock it is too precipitous and rugged to ride with safety, so that the rest of the ascent must be made on foot. Tying my mule to a sapling, I scrambled up the path, and soon emerging from the dark forest, stood under the grey face of the rock towering up above me. It has two peaks, of which the highest is accessible, footholds having been cut into the face of it, and the most difficult part being surmounted by a rude ladder made by cutting notches in a pole. Above it the rock is shelving, and the top is easily reached. I found a strong north-east wind blowing, which made it rather uncomfortable on the top, but the view was very fine and varied. To the south-east and east the eye roams over range beyond range all covered with dark forest, that partly hides the inequalities of the ground, the trees in the hollows growing higher than those on the hills. On this side the rock is a sheer precipice, going down perpendicularly for more than three hundred feet; the face of the cliff all weathered white. The tops of the trees are far below, and as one looking down upon them hears the various cries and whistles of the birds come up, and marks the vultures wheeling round in aërial circles over the trees far below one's feet, then it is that you realise that at last the forest, with its world of foliage, has been surmounted. Looking down on the trees, every shade of green meets the eye, here light as grass, there dark as holly, whilst the fleecy clouds above cast lines of dark shadows over hill and dale.

Directly south-east is a high rock, about three miles distant, and beyond it the Carca and the Artígua rivers must meet, judging from the fall of the country. The course of the Carca is marked by some patches of light green, that look like grass, and are probably clearings made by the Indians.

To the south the eye first passes over about six miles of forest, then savannahs and grassy ranges stretching to the lake, which is only dimly seen, with the peaks of Madera and Ometépec more distinct, the latter bearing south-west by west. Alone on the summit of a high peak, with surging green billows of foliage all around, dim misty mountains in the distance, and above the blue heavens, checkered with fleecy clouds, that have travelled up hundreds of miles from the north-east, thoughts arise that can be only felt in their full intensity amid solitude and nature's grandest phases. Then man's intellect strives to grapple with the great mysteries of his existence, and like a fluttering bird that beats itself against the bars of its cage, falls back baffled and bruised.

Another shower of rain came on, quickly followed by sunshine again. Great banks of vapour began to rise from the forest, and fill the valleys, and now looking down over the precipice, instead of foliage there was a glistening white cloud spread out below, up through

which came the cries of birds. The hills stood up
through the cloud of mist like islands. To the south-
west, over the savannahs, the air was clear, and the peak
of Ometépec was a fine object in the distance. A white
cloud enveloping its top looked like a snow-cap, and
this, as the night came on, descended lower and lower,

PEÑA BLANCA.

mantling closely around it, and conforming to its out-
line. That the savannahs should not give off the same
vapour as the forest has been ascribed, and, I believe,
with reason, to the fact that their evaporating surfaces
are much smaller than those of the latter, with their
numberless leaves heated by the previous sunshine.

As night came on, a wetting mist drove over the top of the peak, and the wind increased in strength, making it very cold and bleak, for there was no shelter of any kind on the summit.   Such a night was not a favourable one for insects, but I got a few beetles that were new to me on the very top of the rock, where only rushes are growing.   They appeared to be travelling with the north-east trade wind, and were sifted out by the rushes as they passed over.   On a finer night I have no doubt many species might be obtained.   I suppose that the wind was moving at the rate of not less than thirty miles an hour, so that the beetles, when they got up to it from the forest below, where it was comparatively calm, might easily be carried hundreds of miles without much labour to themselves.   I added two fine new Carabidæ to my collection; and about eleven o'clock started back again, having many a fall on the slippery steep before I reached the place where I had left my mule.   It was a very dark night, and the oil of my small bull's-eye lanthorn was exhausted, but the mule knew every step of the way, and, though slipping often, never fell, and carried me safely home.

CHAPTER IX.

TOWARDS the end of June, in 1872, I had to go to Juigalpa, one of the principal towns of the province of Chontales, on business connected with a lawsuit brought against the mining company by a litigious native. I started early in the morning, taking with me my native boy, Rito, who carried on his mule behind him my blankets and a change of clothes. I carried in my hand a light fowling-piece. The roads through the forest were excessively muddy, and it took us four hours to get over the seven miles to Pital ; the poor mules struggling all the way through mud nearly three feet deep. Shortly after leaving Pital, we passed the river Mico ; and two miles further on, across some grassy hills, reached the small town of Libertad. It is the principal mining centre of Chontales. There are a great number of gold mines in its vicinity, several of which are worked by intelligent Frenchmen. The gold and silver mines of Libertad are richer than those of Santo

Domingo, and many of the owners of them have ex-
tracted great quantities of the precious metals.

The town is situated near to the edge of the forest,
being separated by the Rio Mico, across which it is
proposed to build a wooden bridge, as during floods the
river is impassable. Whether the bridge will ever be
built or not I cannot tell. Several times rates have
been levied, and money collected to build it, but the
funds have always melted away in the hands of the
officials. There is an alcalde and a judge at Libertad.
Every one worth two hundred dollars is liable to be
elected to the latter office. Only unimportant cases are
tried by him, and his decisions depend generally on the
private influence that is brought to bear upon him. He
is often a tool in the hands of some unprincipled lawyer.
The church at Libertad is a great barn-like edifice, with
tiled roof. At one side is a detached small bell-tower,
in which hang two bells, one sound and whole, the other
cracked and patched. The latter was a present from
one of the mining companies, and had excited a great
scandal. The mining company had a fine large bell,
with which they called together their workmen. The
priest of Libertad, thinking it might be much better
employed in the service of the church, made an applica-
tion for it. The superintendent of the mine could not
part with it, but having an old broken bell, he had it
patched up, and sent it out with a letter, explaining
that he could not let them have the other, but that if
this one was of any use, they were welcome to it. The
priest heard that the bell was on the road, and thinking
it was the one he had coveted, got up a procession to
go and meet it, to take it to its place with befitting

ceremony. But when he saw the old battered and broken article that had been sent, his satisfaction was changed to rage, instead of blessing he cursed it, threw it to the ground, and even kicked and spat upon it. His rage for a time knew no bounds, as he thought that he had been mocked by the heretical foreigners, and his indignation was at first shared by some of the principal inhabitants of the town, but when the explanatory letter had been interpreted to them, their feelings changed, and the poor bell was put up to do what duty it could. There are some good stores in Libertad, the best being branches of Granada houses that buy the produce of the country—hides, india-rubber, and gold—for export, and import European manufactured goods.

Captain Velasquez joined me at Libertad, and, after getting breakfast, we started. The road passes over grassy hills, on which cattle and mules were feeding. The edge of the forest is not far distant to the right, and all the way along it, there have been clearings made and maize planted. As we rode along, great numbers of a brown, tailed butterfly (*Timetes chiron*) were flying over to the south-east. They occurred, as it were, in columns. The air would be comparatively clear of them for a few hundred yards, then we would pass through a band perhaps fifty yards in width, where hundreds were always in sight, and all travelling one way. I took the direction several times with a pocket compass, and it was always south-east. Amongst them were a few yellow butterflies, but these were not so numerous as in former years. In some seasons these migratory swarms of butterflies continue passing over to the south-east for three to five weeks, and must consist of millions upon

millions of individuals, comprising many different species
and genera. The beautiful tailed green and gilded day-
flying moth (*Urania leilus*) also joins in this annual
movement. When in Brazil, I observed similar flights
of butterflies at Pernambuco and Maranham, all travelling south-east. Mr. R. Spruce describes a migration
which he witnessed on the Amazon, in November 1849,
of the common white and yellow butterflies. They were
all passing to the south-south-east.* Darwin mentions
that several times when off the shores of Northern
Patagonia, and at other times when some miles off the
mouth of the Plata, the ship was surrounded by butterflies; so numerous were they on one occasion, that it
was not possible to see a space free from them, and the
seamen cried out that it was " snowing butterflies." †
These butterflies must also come from the westward.
I know of no satisfactory explanation of these immense
migrations. They occurred every year whilst I was in
Chontales, and always in the same direction. I thought
that some of the earlier flights in April might be caused
by the vegetation of the Pacific side of the continent
being still parched up, whilst on the Atlantic slope the
forests were green and moist. But in June there had
been abundant rains on the Pacific side, and vegetation
was everywhere growing luxuriantly. Neither would
their direction from the north-west bring them from the
Pacific, but from the interior of Honduras and Guatemala. The difficulty is that there are no return swarms.
If they travelled in one direction at one season of the
year, and in an opposite at another, we might suppose

* " Journal of the Linnæan Society," vol. ix.
† " Naturalist's Voyage," p. 158.

that the vegetation on which the caterpillars feed was at one time more abundant in the north-west, at another in the south-east; but during the five years I was in Central America, I was always on the look-out for them, and never saw any return swarms of butterflies. Their migration every year in one definite direction is quite unintelligible to me.

We gradually ascended the range that separates the water-shed of the Lake of Nicaragua from that of the Blewfields river, passing over grassy savannahs. About two leagues from Libertad there are many old Indian graves, covered with mounds of earth and stones. A well-educated Englishman, Mr. Fairbairn, has taken up his abode at this place, and is growing maize and rearing cattle. There are many evidences of a large Indian population having lived at this spot, and their pottery and fragments of their stones for bruising maize have been found in some graves that have been opened. Mr. Fairbairn got me several of these curiosities, amongst them are imitations of the heads of armadillos, and other animals. Some of these had formed the feet of urns, others were rattles, containing small balls of baked clay. The old Indians used these rattles in their solemn religious dances, and the custom is probably not yet quite obsolete, for as late as 1823 Mr. W. Bullock saw, in Mexico, Indian women dancing in a masque representing the court of Montezuma, and holding rattles in their right hands, to the noise of which they accompanied their motions. Several stone axes have been found, which are called "thunderbolts" by the natives, who have no idea that they are artificial, although it is less than four hundred years ago since their forefathers used them. Like

most of the sites of the ancient Indian towns, the place
is a very picturesque one. At a short distance to the
west, rise the precipitous rocks of the Amerrique range,
with great perpendicular cliffs, and huge isolated rocks
and pinnacles. The name of this range gives us a clue
to the race of the ancient inhabitants. In the highlands
of Honduras, as has been noted by Squiers, the termination of *tique* or *rique* is of frequent occurrence in the
names of places, as *Chaparristique*, *Lepaterique*, *Llotique*,
Ajuterique, and others. The race that inhabited this
region were the Lenca Indians, often mentioned in the
accounts given by the missionaries of their early expeditions into Honduras. I think that the Lenca Indians
were the ancient inhabitants of Chontales, that they
were the "Chontals" of the Nahuatls or Aztecs of the
Pacific side of the country, and that they were partly
conquered, and their territories encroached upon by the
latter before the arrival of the Spaniards, as some of the
Aztec names of places in Nicaragua do not appear to be
such as could be given originally by the first inhabitants;
thus Juigalpa, pronounced Hueygalpa, is southern Aztec
for "Big Town." No town could be called the big town
at first by those who saw it grow up gradually from
small beginnings, but it is a likely enough name to be
given by a conquering invader. Again Ometépec is nearly
pure Aztec for Two Peaks, but the island itself only
contains one, and the name was probably given by an
invader who saw the two peaks of Ometépec and Madera
from the shore of the lake, and thought they belonged
to one island. The Lenca Indians nowhere appear to
have built stone buildings, like the Quiches, and La-
candones of Guatemala, and the Mayas of Yucatan,

who were probably much more nearly affiliated to the
Nahuatls of Mexico than the Lencas.

We reached the top of the dividing range, and now
left the main road, taking a path to the left, that is
very rocky and narrow.   We began rapidly to descend,
and found an entire change of climate on this side of the
range.   It had been raining for weeks at Libertad, and
everywhere the ground was wet and swampy, but two
miles on the other side of the range the ground was quite
dry, and so it continued to Juigalpa.   Dry gravelly hills,
covered with low scrubby bushes and trees, succeeded
the damp grassy slopes we had been for hours travelling
over.   Prickly acacias, nancitos, guayavas, jicaras, were
the principal trees, with here and there the one whose
thick coriaceous leaves are used by the natives instead
of sandpaper.   The beds of the rivers were dry, or at
the most contained only stagnant pools of water, until we
reached the Juigalpa river, which rises far to the eastward ; the north-east trade wind in crossing the great
forest that clothes the Atlantic slope of the continent,
gives up most of its moisture ; and this range, rising
about three thousand feet above the sea, intercepts nearly
all that remains, so that only occasional showers reach
Juigalpa.

On one of the low gravelly hills that we passed, not
far from the path, we saw a troop of the white-faced
monkey (*Cebus albifrons*) on the ground, amongst low
scattered trees.   Their attitudes, some standing up on
their hind legs to get a better look at us, others with
their backs arched like cats, were amusing.   Though
quite ready to run away, they stood all quite still,
watching us, and looked as if they had been grouped for

a photograph. A few steps towards them sent them scampering off, barking as they went.

Soon after this, I got severely stung by a number of small wasps, whose nest I had disturbed in passing under some bushes. About thirty were upon me, but I got off with about half-a-dozen stings, as I managed to kill the rest as they made their way through the hair of my head and beard, for these wasps, having generally to do with animals covered with hair, do not fly at the open face, but at the hair of the head, and push down through it to the skin before they sting. On this and on another occasion on which I was attacked by them, I had not a single sting on the exposed portions of my face, although my hands were stung in killing them in my hair. It is curious to note that the large black wasp that makes its nest under the verandahs of houses and eaves of huts, and has had to deal with man as his principal foe, flies directly at the face when molested.

Without further adventure we reached Juigalpa at dusk, and took up our quarters not far from the plaza, in a house where one large room was set apart for the accommodation of travellers. We found we should have to stay for a couple of days before our business was concluded; and whilst waiting for some law papers to be made out, I determined to try to see some of the Indian antiquities in the neighbourhood. We had hard leather stretchers to sleep on, the use of mattresses being almost unknown.

Next morning I was up at daylight, and, after getting a cup of coffee and milk, started off on horseback on the lower road towards Acoyapo. This led over undulating savannahs, with grass and jicara trees, and

small clumps of low trees and shrubs on stony hillocks.
Wild pigeons were very numerous, and their cooings
were incessant. On the rocky spots grew spiny cactuses,
with flattened pear-shaped joints and scarlet fruit. I
reached the Juigalpa river about two miles below the
town. Near the crossing it ran between shelving rocky
banks, with here and there still reaches and pebbly shores.
Shady trees overhung the clear water; and behind were
myrtle-leaved shrubs and grassy openings. The morning was yet young, and the banks were vocal with
the noises of birds, that chattered, whistled, chirruped,
croaked, cooed, warbled, or made discordant cries. I
doubt if any other part of the earth's surface could show
a greater variety of the feathered tribe. A large brown
bittern stood motionless amongst the stones of a rapid
portion of the stream, crouching down with his neck and
head drawn back close to his body, so that he looked
like a brown rock himself. Kingfishers flitted up and
down, or dashed into the water with a splashing thud.
At a sedgy spot were some jacanas stalking about.
When disturbed, these birds rise chattering their dis-
pleasure, and showing the lemon yellow of the underside
of their wings, which contrasts with the deep chocolate
brown of the rest of their plumage. Parrots flew past
in screaming flocks, or alighted on the trees and nestled
together in loving couples, changing their screaming to
tender chirrupings. Numerous brown and yellow fly-
catchers sat on small dead branches, and darted off
every now and then after passing insects. A couple of
beautiful mot-mots (*Eumomota superciliaris*) made short
flights after the larger insects, or sat on the low branches
by the river-bank, jerking their curious tails from side

to side. Swallows skimmed past in their circling flights,
whilst in the bushes were warbling orange-and-black
Sisitotis and many another bird of beautiful feather.
One class of birds, and that the most characteristic
of tropical America, was decidedly scarce. I did not
see a single humming-bird by the river-side. On the
savannahs they are much less frequent than in the forest
region. Insects were not so numerous as they had been
in preceding years. Over sandy spots two speckled
species of tiger-beetles ran and flew with great swiftness. I saw one rise from the ground and take an
insect on the wing that was flying slowly over. On
one myrtle-like bush, with small white flowers, there
were dozens of a small Longicorn new to me, which,
when flying, looked like black wasps.

It was very pleasant to sit in the cool shade, and listen
to, and watch, the birds. There was here no fear of
dangerous animals, the only annoyance being stinging
ants or biting sand-flies, neither of which were at this
place very numerous. Snakes also were scarce. I saw
but one, a harmless green one, that glided away with
wavy folds amongst the brushwood. The natives say
that alligators are plentiful in the river, but that they
are harmless. I saw one small one, about five feet long,
floating with his eyes, nostrils, and the serratures of his
back only above water. Every one bathes in the river
without fear, which would not be the case if there had
been any one seized by them during the last fifty years ;
for no traditions are more persistent than tales of the
attacks of wild beasts. Anxious parents pass on from
generation to generation the stories they themselves
were told when children.

As I sat upon the rocks in the cool shade, enjoying the scene, there came hobbling along, with painful steps, on the other side of the river, a poor cripple, afflicted with that horrible disease, elephantiasis. He crossed the river with great difficulty, as his feet were swollen to six times their natural size, with great horny callosities. One of his hands was also disabled; and altogether he was a most pitiable object. Such a sight seemed a blot upon the fair face of nature; but it is our sympathy for our kind that makes us think so. If the trees were sympathetic beings, not a poor crippled specimen of humanity would have their pity, but the gnarled and half-rotten giants of the forest, threatening to topple down with every breeze; whilst to our eyes the dying tree, covered with moss and ferns, and, maybe, clasped by climbing vines, is a picturesque and pleasing sight. So, the fishes would pity their comrades caught by the kingfisher, the birds those in the claws of the hawk— every creature considering the fate that overtook its fellows, and which might befall itself—the great blot in nature's plan.

The poor cripple told me he was going into Juigalpa. He had, doubtless, heard that a stranger had arrived in the town; for every time I had been there he had turned up. His best friends are the foreigners, who look with greater pity on his misfortune than his neighbours, who have grown accustomed to it.

The blind, the lame, and the sick are the only beggars I ever saw in Nicaragua. The necessaries of life are easily procured. Very little clothing is required. Any one may plant maize or bananas; and there is plenty of work for all who are willing or obliged to labour; so

the healthy and strong amongst the poorer classes lead
an easy and pleasant life, but the sick and incapacitated
amongst them are really badly off.   There is a great
indifference amongst the natives to the wants of their
comrades struck down by sickness or accident, and
hospitals and asylums are unknown.

I was told that the cripple, lame as he was, often
took long journeys, and had even gone as far as Granada.
He had been a soldier in one of the revolutions, when
John Chamorro was President, and ascribed the commencement of the disease to getting a chill by bathing
when he was heated.

After he had hobbled off, I bathed in the cool river,
and then rambled about on the other side, where I found
some large mango trees, full of delicious ripe fruit.   It
was getting on towards noon : the sun was high and
hot, and the birds had mostly retired into the deepest
shades for their mid-day sleep.   I could have lingered
all day, but it was time for me to return, as I had
arranged with Velasquez to accompany him in search
of some Indian graves he had heard of about three miles
away.

As I left the river, I heard the whistle of the beautiful
" toledo," so called because its note resembles these
syllables, clearly and slowly whistled, with the emphasis
on the last two.   Following the sound, it led me to a
deep, thickly-timbered gully, at the bottom of which
was the bed of a brook, consisting now only of detached
pools, over one of which, on the limb of a tree, sat a
large dark - coloured hawk, with white - banded tail
watching for fresh-water and land crabs, on which it'
feeds.   I had a long chase after the toledo.   As soon as

L

I got within sight of it, sometimes before, it would dart away through the brushwood, generally across the brook, and in a few minutes I would hear its deep-toned whistle again as if in mockery of my pursuit. I had to climb and reclimb the steep banks of the gully : but at last, creeping cautiously, and just getting my head above the bank, I got a shot. There were two of them sitting close together. I brought both down, and they proved to be in fine plumage. The toledo (*Chirosciphia lineata*) is about the size of a linnet, of a general velvety black colour. The crown of the head is covered with a flat scarlet crest, and the back with what looks like a shawl of sky-blue. From the tail spring two long ribbon-like feathers. Its curious note is often heard on the savannahs, in the thick timber that skirts the small brooks; but it is not often seen, as it is a shy bird, and frequents the deepest shades.

There were several of the yellow-breasted trogon (*T. melanocephalus*) sitting amongst the branches, and now and then darting off after insects. This species often breaks into the nests of the termites, and feeds on the soft-bodied workers. Another trogon about here, with red breast (*T. elegans*), has a peculiarly harsh, croaking voice, very different from the other species, and more resembling the cry of a mot-mot.

As I rode back over the savannahs to Juigalpa, the nearly vertical rays of the sun were reflected from the dry, hot, sandy soil. Not a sound was now heard from the numerous birds. The shrill cicada still piped its never-ending treble. No wind was stirring, and the air over the parched soil quivered with heat.

I was glad to get back to my "hotel," and have

breakfast, with chocolate served up in jicaras. After
an hour's rest, I started with Velasquez in search of the
Indian antiquities. We rode up the right side of the
river, high up above the stream, as the banks are rocky
and precipitous ; then down a shelving road to a lower
level, and across undulating savannahs thinly timbered.
After about three miles, we came out on a small flat
plain, probably alluvial, about twenty acres in extent,
mostly covered with grass, with a few scattered jicara
trees. On the further end of this plain was a mud-
walled, thatched hut, called " El Salto," from a fall of
the river close by. A man was lounging about, and a
woman bruising maize for tortillas. The man told us
that the " worked stones," as he called them, were on
the side of the plain we had crossed. Before going to
look at them, we went down to the river to see the
waterfall. Just opposite the house the Juigalpa river,
which comes flowing down over a flat bed of trachyte,
leaps down a deep narrow chasm that it has cut in the
hard rock. This chasm is about fifty feet deep, and
only twenty wide. The river was low, and poured all
its water in at the end of the deep notch ; but when
flooded, it must rush in over the sides also, and make a
magnificent turmoil of waters. Even when I saw it,
the water, as it rushed along at the bottom of the
narrow chasm, boiling and surging amongst great
masses of fallen rock with a steady roar, looked as if
it would carry all before it. Deep pot-holes, some of
them ten feet deep, were worn into the trachyte rock,
and sections of several were shown in the sides of the
chasm, which could only have been formed when the
falls were many yards lower down. The trachyte is

very hard and tough.   The sections of the pot-holes are
as fresh as if they had been made but yesterday.

In reply to my assertion that the falls had produced,
and were now working back the chasm, our guide, the
lounging man from the house, said the rocks had always
been as they were : he had lived there ten years, and
there had been no change in them.   Perhaps, if the
buried Indians could rise from their graves where they
were laid to rest more than three hundred years ago,
they, too, would testify that there had been no change,
that the rocks and the leaping river were as they had
been and would be for ever.   The untrained mind
cannot grasp the idea of the effect of slowly-acting
influences extending over vast periods of time.

We asked the guide if there were any cairns near, and
he said there was one on the top of a neighbouring hill.
Up this we climbed.   It was the rounded spur of a range
behind, jutting out into the small plain before mentioned,
and might be partly artificial.   On the summit, which
commanded a fine view of the country around, with the
white cliffs and dark woods of the Amerrique range in
front, was an Indian cairn, elliptical in shape, about
thirty feet long and twenty broad.   Several small trees
had sprung up amongst the stones.   Near the centre two
holes had been dug down about four feet deep.   Our
guide told us that he and his brother had made them, to
hide themselves in from the soldiers during the last
revolutionary outbreak.   Not a very likely story, that
they should have chosen the top of a bare hill for a
hiding-place, when all around in the valleys there were
thickets of brushwood.   He said they had found nothing
in the holes.   We, however, soon found fragments of two

INDIAN STATUES. Page 165.

broken cinerary urns, one of fine clay, painted with red and black, the other much coarser and stronger, without ornament. The custom of the Chontales Indians appears to have been to burn their dead, and place the ashes in a thin painted urn, inclosed within a stronger one. This was buried, along with the stone for grinding maize, and a cairn of stones built over the grave, in the centre of which was sometimes set up the statue of the deceased.

It was evident that the tomb had been ransacked in search of treasure ; but our guide was very reticent about it.   He admitted, however, on further questioning, that he had found a broken "metlate," or maize-grinder, in the grave. Velasquez got down into the deepest hole, and unearthed some more fragments of pottery, but nothing more.

We then descended the steep face of the hill again, and crossed the plain to where the "worked stones" were lying. We found them to be broken fragments of statues, one larger, better worked, and in much fairer preservation than the others.   They had all been much battered and broken.   The greater size and solidity of this one had made it more difficult to deface.   It was in two parts, the head being severed from the body. The total length of the two fragments was about five feet.   The face had been much shattered.   The nose was gone, and the mouth defaced, but enough was left to show that the latter had been protruding.   The eyes were in good preservation, prominent, and with the eyeballs projecting.   Around the head was an ornamented circlet, like a crown.   The arms were laid over the breast, and were continued upwards over the shoulder, and partly down the back, as if it had been intended to indicate the shoulder-blades. The legs were doubled up, and continued round to the back, in the same way as the arms.

The back of the figure was elaborately carved, the most noticeable features being a wide ornamented belt around the waist, and two well-carved crosses, one on each shoulder.

The other stones lying about were broken portions of other smaller figures and of pedestals. All were made out of very hard, tough trachyte ; and the labour required to make the principal one out of such difficult material without tools of iron must have been immense.

The fragments were all lying out on the bare plain. I thought they must have been brought from some burial-place of the ancient Indians. Our guide, on being asked, said he had seen other cairns of stones besides these on the hill-top, but could not recollect where. He was very uneasy when questioned ; and at last said he had business to attend to, and left us abruptly. In his absence we examined all around for traces of graves. Between the plain and the river was a thicket of low trees and undergrowth. Peering into this, we saw some heaps of stones ; and, pushing in amongst the bushes found it was full of old Indian graves, marked by heaps of stones, in the centres of some of which still stood the pedestals on which the statues had been placed. Most of the heaps were about twenty feet in diameter, and composed of stones of the average size of a man's head : but one, from the centre of which grew an immense cotton-wood tree, was made of about a dozen very large stones, some about five feet long, three broad, and one thick. Here we got a clue to the behaviour of our guide.   When he told us that he knew not where there were any more cairns, he was standing within thirty feet of one hidden by the thicket, which bore evident marks of having been recently disturbed.   It was the cairn of big stones.   One of these had been overturned, and some fresh-cut poles, that had been used as levers, were lying alongside, with the green bark broken and bruised.   A hole had been dug underneath it, and filled up with stones again.   Our lounging friend had been doing a little exploring on his own account.   Many of the natives believe that treasure is buried under these heaps of stones ; and the interest that foreigners take in them they ascribe to their wish to obtain these treasures.   Our guide, wishing to get these himself, had taken us to the single grave on the top of the hill, which he had already ransacked, and professed ignorance of the others.   I only hope that he did not compound with his conscience for the lies he had told us by coming back after we left, and trying to break off the nose of another idol, as the natives call the images. They think they show their zeal for Christianity by defacing them.   This is why scarcely any of the noses of the images are left.   They form the most salient points for attack.   And that the images have not been utterly destroyed by the ill-usage they have had for three hundred years is due to the hard, tough rock of which they are made.   It is probable that the statues at El Salto were brought out from the cairns into the plain, and publicly thrown down, defaced, and broken, when the Spaniards first took possession of the Juigalpa district, and forced Christianity upon the Indians ; for the conquerors everywhere overthrew and mutilated the " idols " of the Indians, set up the cross and their own images, and forced the people to be baptized. The change was not a great one. Already the cross was an emblem amongst them, and baptism a rite; and the images they were called upon to adore did not differ so greatly from those they had worshipped before. They easily conformed to the new faith. D'Avila is said to have overthrown the idols at Rivas, and to have baptized nine thousand Indians. Then the Spaniards, having Christianised the Indians, made slaves of them, and ground them to the dust with merciless cruelties and overwork, which quickly depopulated whole towns and districts.

The presence of the cross in Central America greatly astonished the Spanish discoverers. In Yucatan and throughout the Aztec Empire it was the emblem of the " god of rain." There has been much speculation by various authors respecting its origin, as a religious emblem, in Mexico and Central America. It has even been supposed that some of the early Icelandic Christians of the ninth century may have reached the coast of Mexico, and introduced some knowledge of the Christian religion. But the cross was a religious emblem of the greatest antiquity, both in Syria and Egypt, and baptism was a pre-Christian rite. This and other observances, such as auricular confession and monastic institutions, were so mixed up with the worship of a great number of gods, at the head of which was the worship of the sun, and were associated with such horrid human sacrifices and pagan ceremonials, that it is more likely that they acquired the cross, with other pagan traditions handed down to them from a remote antiquity, from the common stock from whence both the inhabitants of the Eastern and Western hemispheres were descended. There is good evidence for supposing that young children were offered up in sacrifice to Thaloc, the god of rain, the very god whose emblem was the cross—a contrast too great to the " Suffer little children to come unto me " of the loving Saviour, not to make the mind revolt against the idea that the cross of the god of rain was derived from the cross of the Christian.

I see no reason for supposing that the images of El Salto were idols, as supposed by the early Spaniards, and still by the degenerate half-breeds. They are more likely portrait-statues of famous chieftains who led the tribe to many a victory. When they died, a loving people, with wailings and lamentations, celebrated their obsequies. The funeral pyre was built, the body burnt, and the ashes carefully gathered together, and placed in the finely-wrought urn and painted cinerary, and this in one larger and coarser. These were buried with the stone maize-grinder, and sometimes weapons and earthen dishes and food. Over the grave a pile of stones was raised, and skilful artificers were set to work on the hardest and toughest stone they could find to make a statue of the chief whose memory they reverenced. It must have taken months, if not years, to have fashioned the statue I have figured, out of the trachyte, without tools of iron, and it strikes one with wonder to think of the patience and perseverance with which the details were worked out. No eye-servers were these Indians ; before and behind they bestowed equal pains and labour on their work, undeterred by the hardness of the materials or the rudeness of their tools.

When we turn from these works and remains of a

great and united tribe to the miserable huts of the
present natives, we feel how great a curse the Spanish
invasion has in some respects been to Central America.
The half-breed, wrapped up in himself, lives from year
to year in his thatched hut, looking after a few cows,
and making cheese from their milk.   He perhaps plants
a small patch of maize once a year, and grows a few
plantains, content to live on the plainest fare, and in
the rudest style, so that he may indulge in indolence
and sloth.   So he vegetates and drops into his grave,
and in a year or two no mark or sign tells where he
was laid.   The graves of the old Indians are still to
be found, but no mounds mark the spots where the
inhabitants of the valley since the conquest have been
laid to rest.   They have passed away, as they lived,
without a record or memorial.

The builders of these cairns and the fashioners of these
statues were a different and a better race.   They stood
by each other, and reverenced and obeyed their chiefs.
They tilled the ground and lived on the fruits of it.
From the accounts of all the historians of the Spanish
conquest, the Pacific side of Nicaragua was so densely
populated when the Spaniards first arrived, that the
greater part of it must have been cultivated like a
garden; and it is probable that the population was
ten times greater than it is now.   Another point that
strikes the observer is, that not only the descendants
of the Spaniards and the Mestizos are sunk far below
the level of the old Indians, but that the nearly pure
Indians, of whom there are many large communities,
have so degenerated that it is hard to believe that they
are the very same people that, four hundred years ago,

had advanced so far in their peculiar civilisation. They
are not so sunk in sloth as the half-breeds. They still
till the ground, grow maize, cacao, and many fruits;
they still make the earthenware dishes of the country,
though far inferior to those of their ancestors; but they
have lost their tribal instincts, they do not support
each other; they acknowledge no chiefs; each one is
absorbed in his own affairs, and they are only a little
less slothful than the half-breeds. Will these Indians
ever again attain to that pitch of civilisation at which
they had arrived before the conquest?—I fear not. The
whip that kept them to the mark in the old days was the
continual warfare between the different tribes, and this
has ceased for ever. War is not always a curse. "There
is some soul of goodness in things evil." Before the
Spanish conquest no small isolated communities could
exist. Those in which the tribal instinct was strongest,
who stood shoulder to shoulder with their fellows, reverenced and obeyed their chiefs, and excelled in feats of
strength and agility, would annihilate or subjugate the
weaker and less warlike races. It was this constant
struggle between the different tribes that weeded out
the weak and indolent, and preserved the strong and
enterprising; just as amongst many of the lower animals
the stronger kill off the weaker, and the result is the
improvement of the race, or at any rate the maintenance
of the point of excellence at which it had arrived in
former times.

Since the Spanish conquest there has been no such process of selection in operation amongst the Indians. The
most indolent can obtain enough food, whilst the climate
makes clothing almost a superfluity. The idle and

improvident live their natural terms of years, and increase their kind even faster than the provident and industrious. The tribal feeling is destroyed; the selfish and sensual instincts are developed, and year by year the Indian degenerates.

Mr. Bates, at the end of his admirable work on the natural history of the Amazon, speculates on the future of the human race, and thinks that under the equator alone will it attain the highest form of perfection. I have had similar thoughts when riding over hundreds of miles of fertile savannahs in Central America, where an everlasting summer and fertile land yield a harvest of fruits and grain all the year round—where it is not even necessary "to tickle the ground with a hoe to make it laugh with a harvest." But thinking over the cause of the degeneracy of the Spaniards and Indians, I am led to believe that in climes where man has to battle with nature for his food, not to receive it from her hands as a gift; where he is a worker, and not an idler; where hard winters kill off the weak and brace up the strong; there only is that selection at work that keeps the human race advancing, and prevents it retrograding, now that Mars has been dethroned and Vulcan set on high.

In destroying the ancient monarchies of Mexico and Central America, the Spaniards inflicted an irreparable injury on the Indian race; for whether or not a republic is the highest ideal form of government (and doubtless it would be if man were perfect), it is not adapted for savage or half-civilised communities, and I cordially agree with the truth enunciated by Darwin when, writing of the natives of Terra del Fuego, he says, " Perfect equality among the individuals composing the

Fuegian tribes must for a long time retard their civilisation. As we see those animals whose instinct compels them to live in society, and obey a chief, are most capable of improvement, so is it with the races of mankind. Whether we look at it as a cause or a consequence, the most civilised always have the most artificial governments. For instance, the inhabitants of Otaheite, who, when first discovered, were governed by hereditary kings, had arrived at a far higher grade than another branch of the same people, the New Zealanders, who, although benefited by being compelled to turn their attention to agriculture, were republicans in the most absolute sense." *

Dusk was coming on before we left the small plain, with its broken statues, and the steep hill overlooking it, on which probably religious rites had been celebrated and human sacrifices offered up. This people have entirely passed away, and the sparse inhabitants of the once thickly-populated province have not even a tradition about them. In Europe and North America more is known about them, and more interest taken in gleaning what little vestiges of their history can be recovered from the dim past, than among their own degenerate descendants.

Half way to Juigalpa was an Indian hut and a small clearing made for growing maize. The fallen trunks of trees were a likely place for beetles, and as I had brought a lantern with me, I stayed to examine them whilst Velasquez rode on to get some food ready. At night many species of beetles, especially longicorns, are to be found running over the trunks, that lie closely hidden in

* "Naturalist's Voyage," p. 229.

the day-time. The night-world is very different from that
of the day. Things that blink and hide from the light
are all awake and astir when the sun goes down. Great
spiders and scorpions prowl about, or take up advan-
tageous positions where they expect their prey to pass.
Cockroaches of all sizes, from that of one's finger to that
of one's finger-nail, stand with long quivering antennæ,
pictures of alert outlook, watching for their numerous
foes, or scurry away as fast as their long legs can
carry them; but if they come within reach of the great
spider they are pounced upon in an instant, and with
one convulsive kick give up the hopeless struggle.
Centipedes, wood-lice, and all kinds of creeping things
come out of cracks and crevices; even the pools are
alive with water-beetles that have been hiding in the
ooze all day, excepting when they come up with a dash
to the surface for a bubble of fresh air. Owls and
night-jars make strange unearthly cries. The timid
deer comes out of its close covert to feed in the grassy
clearings. Jaguars, ocelots, and opossums slink about in
the gloom. The skunk goes leisurely along, holding up
his white tail as a danger-flag for none to come within
range of his nauseous artillery. Bats and large moths
flitter around, whilst all the day-world is at rest and
asleep. The night speeds on; the stars that rose in the
east are sinking behind the western hills; a faint tinge
of dawn lights the eastern sky; loud and shrill rings
out the awakening shout of chanticleer; the grey dawn
comes on apace; a hundred birds salute the cheerful
morn, and the night-world hurries to its gloomy dens
and hiding-places, like the sprites and fairy elves of
our nursery days.

It was very dark when I started to return, excepting that flashes of lightning now and then illumined the path, but I left my mule to herself, and she carried me safely into Juigalpa, where I found dinner awaiting me.   It took me until midnight to skin the birds I had shot during the day; and as I had been up since six in the morning, I was quite ready for, and took kindly to, my hard leathern couch.

CHAPTER X.

THE site of Juigalpa is beautifully chosen, as is usual
with the old Indian towns. It is on a level dry piece
of land, about three hundred feet above the river. A
rocky brook behind the town supplies the water for
drinking and cooking purposes. The large square or
plaza has the church at one end; on the other three
sides are red-tiled adobe houses and stores, with floors of
clay or red bricks. Streets branch off at right angles
from the square, and are crossed by others. The best
houses are those nearest the square. Those on the outskirts are mere thatched hovels, with open sides of
bamboo poles. The house I stayed at was at the corner
of one of the square blocks, and from the angle the view
extended in four directions along the level roads. Each
way the prospect was bounded by hills in the distance.
North-east were the white cliffs of the Amerrique range,
mantled with dark woods. The intervening country
could not be seen, and only a small portion of the
range itself; framed in, as it were, by the sides of the
street. It looked close at hand, like a piece of arti-

ficial rockery, or the grey walls of a castle covered with ivy. The range to the south-west is several miles distant; and is called San Miguelito by the Spaniards, but I could not learn its Indian name.

Our host was a musician, and his wife attended to the guests. As usual, a number of relations lived with them, including the mother of our hostess and two of her brothers. It was a very fair sample of a family amongst what may be called the middle class in Nicaragua. The master of the house plays occasionally in a band at dances and festas, and holds a respectable position at Juigalpa, where the highest families keep stores and shops.

The only work is done by the females—the men keep up their dignity by lounging about all day, or lolling in a hammock, all wearied with their slothfulness, and looking discontented and unhappy. One brother told me he was a carpenter, the other a shoemaker, but that there was nothing to do in Juigalpa. I suggested that they should go to Libertad, where there was plenty of work. They said there was too much rain there. As long as their brother-in-law will allow them, they will remain lounging about his house; and that will probably be as long as he has one, for I noticed that the wealthier Nicaraguans are rather proud of having a lot of relations hanging about and dependent on them. Now and then they do little spells of work—get in the cows or doctor one that is sick—but I doubt if any of them average more than half an hour's work per day. Even this may be an equivalent for their board, which does not cost much, being only a few tortillas and beans.

To this have the descendants of the Spanish con-

M

querors come, throughout the length and breadth of the
land. With perennial summer and a fertile soil they
might drink the waters of abundance, but the bands
of indolence have wound round them generation after
generation, and now they are so bound up in the
drowsy folds of slothfulness that they cannot break
their silken fetters. Not a green vegetable, not a fruit,
can you buy at Juigalpa. Beef, or a fowl—brown beans,
rice, and tortillas—form the only fare. When Mexico
becomes one of the United States, all Central America
will soon follow. Railways will be pushed from the
north into the tropics, and a constant stream of immigration will change the face of the country, and fill it with
farms and gardens, orange groves, and coffee, sugar,
cacao, and indigo plantations. No progress need be
expected from the present inhabitants.

Having finished our business in Juigalpa, we arranged
to start on our return early the next morning, Velasquez going round by Acoyapo whilst Rito accompanied
me to the mines. I had a fowl cooked overnight to
take with us, and set off at six o'clock. I shall make
some remarks on the road on points not touched on in
my account of the journey out. After leaving Juigalpa,
we descended to the river by a rocky and steep path,
crossed it, and then passed over alluvial-like plains,
intersected by a few nearly dry river beds, to the foot
of the south-western side of the Amerrique hills, then
gradually ascended the range that separates the Juigalpa
district from that of Libertad. The ground was gravelly
and dry, with stony hillocks covered with low trees and
bushes. After ascending about a thousand feet, the
ground became much moister, and we reached an Indian

hut on the side of the range, where a few bananas and
a little maize was grown. Indian women, naked to the
waist, were, as usual, bruising maize, this being their
employment from morning to night, whilst the men were
sitting about idle. Some mangy-looking dogs set up a
loud barking as we approached. To one of them clung
a young spider-monkey. A number of parrots also gave
evidence of the great fondness the Indians have for
animal pets. There is scarcely a house where some bird
or beast is not kept; and the Indian women are very
clever in taming birds, probably by their constant kindness and gentleness to them, and by feeding them out
of their mouths and fondling them. From near here
we had a fine view, and saw that we had come up the
side of a wide valley, bounded on the right by the
Amerrique range, on the left by high rounded grassy
hills, on one of which we could make out the cattle
hacienda of La Puerta. Lines of trees and bamboo
thickets marked the course of numerous brooks that
joined lower down and formed the small rivers we had
crossed. Looking down the valley it opened out into
a wide plain, with here and there sharp-topped conical
hills, such as abound in Central America, where they
appear to have been taken as landmarks by the Indians,
as many of the old roads lead past them. Beyond the
plain in the grey distance were the waters of the lake
and the peaks of Ometépec and Madera.

We had now to ascend the side of a ravine, the road,
or rather path, being through a bamboo thicket for about
a mile, the bamboos touching our knees on either side
and arching close overhead, so that we had to lie on the
mules' necks a great part of the way. Some portions of

the road were dangerously steep and rocky ; but as fully
a league in distance is saved by taking this by-path,
instead of the main road by way of La Puerta, I generally preferred travelling by it, especially as I often took
rare and new beetles on the bushes. I usually, when
travelling, carried a net fixed to a short stick, and caught
the insects as I passed along, off the leaves, without
stopping ; so abundant were they, that it was very rare
for me to take the shortest journey without finding
some new species to add to my collection. On this
journey I did not, however, take many insects, as the
latter half of the year 1872, for some reason or other,
was a very unfavourable season for them. The scarcity
of beetles was very remarkable. The wet season set in
a little earlier than usual, but I do not think that this
caused the dearth of insects, as at Juigalpa, where there
had been scarcely any rain, there were very few compared with the two former years. The year before,
when the season was nearly as wet, beetles, especially
longicorns, had been very abundant ; and the first half
of 1872 had not been characterised by any scarcity of
them. Some of the fine longicorns that appear in April
were numerous. No less than five specimens of a large
and beautiful one (*Deliathis nivea*, Bates), white, with
black spots, that we considered one of our greatest
rarities, were taken in that month. It was not until the
end of May that the great scarcity of beetles, compared
with their abundance in former years, became apparent.
I think all classes of beetles had suffered. Many fine
lamellicorns, that were generally numerous, were not seen
at all ; neither were many species of longicorns, usually
common. A fig-tree that I had growing in my garden

had been much injured by a longicorn (*Tæniotes scalaris*) in 1870 and 1871, but was not touched in 1872.

Butterflies were also scarce, but it was the second season that they had been so. Some ants were affected ; in others, such as the leaf-cutter, I noted no perceptible diminution in number. A little ant (*Pheidole sp.*) that used to swarm on a passion flower which grew over the house, attending on the honey glands, and scale insects, disappeared altogether ; and another species (*Hypoclinea sp.*) that it used to drive away, took its place. A small stinging black ant (*Solenopsis sp.*), that was a great plague in the houses, was also fortunately scarce. In the beginning of June nearly all the white ants or termites (" Comiens " of the Nicaraguans) died. In some parts of my house they lay in little heaps, just as they dropped from the nests above in the roof, and most of the nests were entirely depopulated. I examined some of the dead termites with a magnifier, but could detect no difference in them, excepting that they seemed a little swollen.

That some epidemic prevailed amongst the insects there can be no doubt ; and it is curious that it should have attacked so many different species and classes. I am not sure that it was confined to the insects, for there was also a great mortality amongst the fowls, many dying from inflammation of the crop, and two large parrots fell victims to the same disease. This disease amongst the birds may not, however, have been connected in any way with that amongst the insects. I recollect that in 1865 there was a somewhat similar mortality amongst the wasps in North Wales. In the autumn of the preceding year they had been exceedingly abundant, and very destructive to the fruit. In the next spring, numerous females that had hybernated commenced making their paper nests, and I anticipated a still greater plague of wasps in the autumn than we had had the year before ; but some epidemic carried off nearly all the females before they finished building their nests, and in the autumn scarcely a wasp was to be seen. I saw also in the Natural History magazines notices of their scarcity in all parts of England.

The great mortality amongst the insects of Chontales in 1872 has some bearing on the origin of species, for in times of such great epidemics we may suspect that the gradations that connect extreme forms of the same species may become extinct. Darwin has shown how very slight differences in the colour of the skin and hair are sometimes correlated with great immunity from certain diseases, and from the action of some vegetable poisons, and the attacks of certain parasites.*   Any varieties of species of insects that could withstand better than others these great and probably periodical epidemics, would certainly obtain a great advantage over those not so protected ; and thus the survival of one form, and the extinction of another, might be brought about.   We see two species of the same genus, as in many insects, differing but little from each other, yet quite distinct, and we ask why, if these have descended from one parent form, do not the innumerable gradations that must have connected them exist also ?   There is but one answer ; we are ignorant what characters are

* "Descent of Man," vol. i. p. 242 ; and "Animals and Plants under Cultivation," vol. ii. pp. 227–230. I have taken the examples given from the same author.

of essential value to each species ; we do not know why white terriers are more subject than darker-coloured ones to the attacks of the fatal distemper ; why yellow-fleshed peaches in America suffer more from diseases . than the white-fleshed varieties ; why white chickens are most liable to the *gapes ;* or why the caterpillars of silkworms, which produce white cocoons, are not attacked by fungus so much as those that produce yellow cocoons ?   Yet in all these cases, and many others, it has been shown that immunity from disease is correlated with some slight difference in colour or structure, but as to the cause of that immunity we are entirely ignorant.

At last we reached the summit of the range, which is probably not less than three thousand feet above the sea, and entered on the district of Libertad.   Rounded boggy hills covered with grass, sedgy plants and stunted trees, replaced the dry gravelly soil of the Juigalpa district.   The low trees bore innumerable epiphytal plants on their trunks and boughs.   Many of these are species of *Tillandsia,* which sit perched up on the small branches like birds.   They have sheathing leaves that hold at their base a supply of water that must be very useful to them in the dry season.   Insects get drowned in this water, and the plants·may derive some nourishment from their decomposing bodies, but I believe the principal object is to obtain a supply of moisture, as the roots of the plants do not hang down to the ground, like those of many other epiphytes in the tropics, nor are they provided with bulbs like the orchids.   Some plants that hold liquids in cup-shaped leaves are simply insect traps, many of them growing in bogs, where the supply of moisture is perennial and constant. Such is the Indian-cup (*Sarracenia*) that grows in the bogs of Canada, and the Californian pitcher-plant (*Darlingtonia californica*), which also grows in bogs, and is such an excellent fly-trap, that there is generally a layer of from two to five inches of decomposing insects lying at the bottom of the cup.* The different species of *Drosera*, or sun-dews, possess quite a different apparatus for catching insects, and they also live in bogs, which supports the inference that plants growing in such situations have some especial need to obtain nutriment, which they cannot draw from the decaying vegetation on which they live. Possibly they obtain the salts of potash in this way. I did not notice any provision in the leaves of the Bromeliaceous epiphytes of Chontales to ensure the capture of insects, but often saw their dead bodies in the water held at the base of the leaves, and any that came to drink would be very liable to slip into the water from off the nearly perpendicular side of the leaf and be drowned. It is not impossible that the small supply of mineral salts required for the organisation of these plants that do not draw any nutriment from the earth may be obtained from dead insects, but, as I have already stated, I believe that the principal object is to lay up a store of water to carry them safely through the dry season. Incidentally, the further advantage has been gained that insects fall into the receptacles of water and are drowned, affording in their decomposition nourishment to the plants.

Our road now lay over the damp grassy hills of the Libertad district. It edged away from the Amerrique

* See "Nature," vol. iii. pp. 159 and 167.

range on our right.   To our left, about three miles
distant, rose the dark sinuous line of the great forest
of the Atlantic slope.   Only a fringe of dark-foliaged
trees in the foreground was visible, the higher ground
behind was shrouded in a sombre pall of thick clouds
that never lifted, but seemed to cover a gloomy and
mysterious country beyond.   Though I had dived into
the recesses of these mountains again and again, and
knew that they were covered with beautiful vegetation
and full of animal life, yet the sight of that leaden-
coloured barrier of cloud resting on the forest tops,
whilst the savannahs were bathed in sunshine, ever
raised in my mind vague sensations of the unknown
and the unfathomable.   Our course was nearly parallel
to this gloomy forest, but we gradually approached it.
The line that separates it from the grassy savannahs is
sinuous and irregular.   In some places a dark promontory
of trees juts out into the savannahs, in others a green
grassy hill is seen almost surrounded by forest.   When
I first came to the country, I was much puzzled to understand why the forest should end just where it did.   It
is not because of any change in the nature of the soil or
bed-rock.   It cannot be for lack of moisture, for around
Libertad it rains for at least six months out of the
twelve.   The surface of the ground is not level on the
savannahs, but consists of hill and dale, just as in the
forest.   Altogether the conditions seemed to be exactly
the same, and it appeared a difficult matter to account
for the fact that the forest should end at an irregular but
definite line, and that at that boundary grassy savannahs
should commence.   After seeing the changes that were
wrought during the four and a half years that I was in

the country, I have been led to the conclusion that
the forest formerly extended much further towards the
Pacific, and has been beaten back principally by the
agency of man.   The ancient Indians of Nicaragua
were an agricultural race, their principal food then, as
now, being maize ; and in all the ancient graves, the
stone for grinding corn is found placed there, as the one
thing that was considered indispensable.   They cut
down patches of the forest and burnt it to plant their
corn, as all along the edge of it they do still.   The first
time the forest is cut down, and the ground planted,
the soil contains seeds of the forest trees, which, after
the corn is gathered, spring up and regain possession
of the ground, so that in twenty years, if such a spot
is left alone, it will scarcely differ from the surrounding
untouched forest.   But it does not remain unmolested.
After two or three years it is cut down again and a
great change takes place.   The soil does not now contain seeds of forest trees, and in their stead a great
variety of weedy-looking shrubs, only found where the
land has been cultivated, spring up.   Grass, too, begins
to get a hold on the ground ; if it prevails, the Indian,
or Mestizo, does not attempt to grow corn there again,
as he knows the grass will spoil it, and he is too indolent to weed it out.   Often, however, the brushwood
has been cut down and burnt, and fresh crops of corn
grown several times before the grass has gained such
an advantage that the cultivator gives up the attempt
to plant maize.   There is then a struggle between the
weedy shrubs and the grass.   The leaf-cutting ants
come to the aid of the latter.   Grass they will not
touch, excepting to clear it away from their paths.

The thick forest they do not like, possibly because beneath its shade the ground is kept too damp for their fungus beds.   But along the edge of the forest, by the sides of roads through it, that let in the air and sunshine, and in clearings, they abound.   They are especially fond of the leaves of young trees, many of which are destroyed by them.   Should the brushwood ultimately prevail, and cover the ground, the Indian, or Mestizo, comes again after a few years, cuts it down, and replants it with maize.   But as most of his old clearings get covered with grass, he is continually encroaching on the edge of the forest, beating it back gradually, but surely, towards the north-east.   As this process has probably been going on for thousands of years, I believe that the edge of the forest is several miles nearer the Atlantic than it was originally.

In this way many acres in the neighbourhood of Pital were taken from the forest, and added to the grass-lands, whilst I was in the country.   The brush-wood-land does not yield such good crops as the virgin forest, but it is nearer to the huts of the cultivators, who live out on the savannahs, so that whenever the weedy shrubs gain possession of a spot sufficiently large for a clearing, and choke off the grass, these places are again cut down and burnt, and thus the forest is never allowed to establish outposts, or advanced stations, in the disputed ground.   What would be the result if man were withdrawn from the scene, I do not know, but I believe that the forest would slowly, but surely, regain the ground that it has lost through long centuries.   The thickets and dense brushwood that always spring up along the edge of the forest, and consist of many shrubs that the leaf-cutting ants do not touch, would gradually spread, and beat back the grass. In their shade and shelter, seeds from the forest would vegetate and grow, and thus, I think, very slowly, inch by inch, the forest would regain its long-lost territory, and gradually extend its limits towards the south-west, until it reached its old boundaries, where a change in the physical character of the land, or in the amount of moisture precipitated, would stay its further progress. It is far more likely, however, that man will drive back the forest to the very Atlantic than that he will quit the scene.

After passing the Indian graves, about a league from Libertad, we turned off to the right, by a path that led directly to the Mico, without going through the town. After crossing several rounded grassy hills, we reached the river, and found it swollen with recent rains, but fordable. Sometimes travellers are detained several days, unable to cross, and I was always glad when, returning to the mines, I had put it behind me. Now and then a traveller is drowned when attempting to cross the swollen river, but these accidents are rare, as it is well known, by certain rocks being covered, when it is unfordable. If carried away, a traveller has little chance to save his life, as just below the crossing, the river is rapid and the banks precipitous. I heard of one man who had had a very narrow escape. He was trying to cross on muleback, but his beast lost its footing, rolled over, and was rapidly washed away. The poor man was carried into the roaring rapids, and would soon have been drowned, but a herdsman on the bank, who was looking for cattle, threw his lasso cleverly over the drowning traveller, and

dragged him on shore.   Some of the " vacqueros," as the
herdsmen are called, are wonderfully adroit in throwing
the lasso; when riding at full speed, they throw it over
the horns of the cattle, or the heads of the horses, and
can hold the strongest if sideways on.   But I have seen
some old bulls that knew how to get loose ; they would
run straight away from the vacquero in places where he
could not ride round them, and getting a straight pull
on the lasso, would break it, or draw it out of his hands.
There are no horses or mules, and very few cattle, however, that know how to do this, I was told by the
herdsmen.

     After crossing the river, we soon reached Pital, where
I had a cup of tea and got a fresh mule.   We now
turned nearly at right angles to our former course, and
struck into the dark forest, the road through which I
have already described.   It was very wet and muddy.
In some places, although it was only the commencement
of the wet season, the mules sank above their knees.
On this occasion, as on many others, I had often to
notice how well the mule remembered places where in
some former year it had avoided a particularly bad part
by making a detour.   I was riding a mule that had
tender feet, having just recovered from the bite of a
spider, that had occasioned the loss of one of its hoofs,
and when it came near to a place where it could escape
the deep mud by going over a stony part it would slacken
its pace and look first at the mud, then at the stones,
evidently balancing in its mind which was the lesser evil.
Sometimes, too, when it came to a very bad place, which
was better at the sides, I left it to itself, and it would
be so undecided which side was the best, that making

towards one it would look towards the other, and end by getting into the worst of the mud. It was just like many men who cannot decide which of two courses to take, and end by a middle one, which is worse than either. And just as in men, so in mules, there is every variety of disposition and ability. Some are easily led, others most obstinate and headstrong ; some wise and prudent, others foolish and rash. The memory of localities is much stronger in horses and mules than in man. When travelling along a road that they have been over only once, and that some years before, where there are numerous branch roads and turnings, they will never make a mistake, even in the dark ; and I have often, at night, when I could not make out the road myself, left them to their own guidance, and they have taken me safely to my destination. Only once was I misled, and that through the too good memory of my mule. Many years before it had been taken to a pasture of good grass, and recollecting this, it took me several miles out of my road towards its old feeding-ground, causing me to be benighted in consequence.

I reached the mines at nine o'clock, and found that during my absence it had been raining almost continuously, although at Juigalpa there had been only a few slight showers.

CHAPTER XI.

Start on journey to Segovia—Rocky mountain road—A poor lodging
—The rock of Cuapo—The use of large beaks in some birds—
Comoapa—A native doctor—Vultures—Flight of birds that soar
—Natives live from generation to generation on the same spot—
Do not give distinctive names to the rivers—Caribs barter guns
and iron pots for dogs—The hairless dogs of tropical America—
Difference between artificial and natural selection—The cause of
sterility between allied species considered—The disadvantages
of a covering of hair in a domesticated animal in a tropical country.

In July of the same year, 1872, I made the longest
journey of any I undertook in Nicaragua. It had been
for some time difficult to obtain sufficient native labourers
for our mines, and, as we contemplated extending our
operations, it was very important that it should be ascertained whether or not we could depend upon obtaining the additional workmen that would be required.
Nearly all our native miners came from the highlands
of the province of Segovia, near to the boundary of
Honduras. The inhabitants of the lower country are
mostly vacqueros, used to riding on horseback after
cattle, and not to be tempted, even by the much higher
wages they can obtain, to engage in the toilsome labour
of underground mining. The inhabitants of Segovia, on
the contrary, have been miners from time immemorial,
and it is work they readily take to. I had often desired
to see for myself what supply of labour could be ob-

tained, but the journey was a long and toilsome one, and it was not until the labour question became urgent that I resolved to undertake it.

Having determined on the journey, I soon completed my preparations. I took my Mestizo boy, Rito, with me ; Velasquez was to join me on the road ; a pack-mule carried our equipment, consisting of some bread, rugs, a large waterproof sheet, a change of clothes, and a hammock. We started at seven o'clock on the morning of the 11th July, and, as usual, made very slow progress through the forest as far as Pital, in consequence of the badness of the road, which was now worse than when I had passed over it a month before. After reaching the savannahs, we proceeded more rapidly. We followed the Juigalpa road until we got two leagues beyond Libertad, when we turned more to the north, taking a path that led over mountain ranges. This road was very rocky and steep; we were continually ascending or descending, and as it rained all the afternoon, the footing for our beasts was very bad. I was riding on a horse, and he not being so sure-footed or so cautious as a mule, often stumbled on the steep and slippery slopes. In some places the path led along the top of the narrow ridge of a long hog-backed hill ; in others, by a series of zigzags, we surmounted or came down the precipitous slopes. I nearly came to grief at one place. We had climbed up one of the steep hills, and at the top a rocky shelf or cap had to be leaped, at right angles to the narrow path that slanted up the face of the hill. I put my horse to it, but he slipped on the smooth rock and fell. If he had gone back over the narrow path, he must have rolled down the abrupt slope ; but he made another spring, fell again, but this time with his fore-feet over the rock, and on the third attempt scrambled over and landed me safely on the top, but, I confess, much shaken in my

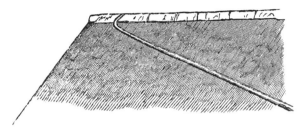

THE ROAD AND ROCKY LEDGE.

seat. My straw-hat came off in the struggle, and was rolling merrily down the hill, when it was caught in a low bush, much to Rito's satisfaction, who was antici-pating a long tramp after it. We had a fine view from the top of this range over a deep valley, bounded with precipitous cliffs and dark patches of forest. Over our heads floated drifting rain-clouds from the north-east that sometimes concealed the mountain tops, sometimes lifted and showed their craggy summits.

Our beasts were tired out with the rough travelling, and we moved along slowly. About five o'clock we came in sight of the rock of Cuapo, an isolated perpendicular cliff rising about 300 feet above the top of a hill that it crowns. After descending a long, steep range, we reached, near dusk, a small hut, called Tablasón, and here we determined to pass the night, although the accommodation was about the scantiest possible. A man and his wife, six children, and a woman to grind the maize for tortillas, lived in the hut. The greatest portion

N

of it was quite open at the sides, without even a fence to
keep out the pigs. At one end a place about ten feet
square was partitioned off from the rest, and surrounded
with mud-walls, and in this the whole family slept.
Both the people and the house were very dirty. The remains of a broken chair was the only furniture, excepting
the rough bedsteads made by inserting four sticks into
the ground, on which were laid two long poles, kept apart
by two shorter ones at the end, over which rude frame
a dry hide was stretched. I was offered one of these
couches for the night, and accepted it; though if it had
not been for the rain I would rather have slept outside,
but all around was sloppy and wet; night had set in;
our mules and horse were tired; we ourselves were
fatigued, and there was no other shelter within several
miles. They had no food to sell us, and appeared to
have nothing for themselves, excepting a few tortillas
and a little homemade cheese. We opened out some of
our preserved meats. Whilst I was eating, the whole
family crowded around me, apparently never having
seen any one eat with a fork before. Fortunately we
had brought candles with us, or we should have been
in darkness, for they had none; nor did they appear
to use them, as they had no candlesticks, and the
children and our host himself took it by turns to
hold our lights. All wore ragged, dirty cotton clothes,
that only half-covered them. They had four cows,
and pigs, dogs, and poultry. The land around was
fertile; they might take as much of it as they liked
to cultivate, and, with a little trouble, might have
grown almost anything; but the blight of Central
America—the curse of idleness, was upon them, and

they were content to live on in squalid poverty rather
than work.

We were so tired, that notwithstanding our miserable
and crowded quarters, we slept soundly, but were up at
daylight, and soon ready for our journey again, after
Rito had made a little coffee, and I had compensated
our host for our lodging. The scenery around was very
fine, and the place might have been made an earthly
paradise. To the north-east a spur of the forest came
down to within a mile of the house ; in front were grassy
hills and clumps of brushwood and trees, with a clear
gurgling stream in the bottom ; and beyond, in the
distance, forest-clad mountains. As usual, the family
had a pet animal. Before we left, a pretty fawn came
in from the forest to be fed, and eyed us suspiciously,
laying its head back over its shoulders, and gazing at us
with its large, dreamy-looking eyes. The woman told
us it had a wild mate in the woods, but came in daily to
visit them, the dogs recognising and not molesting it.
Our road still lay within a few miles of the dark Atlantic
forest, the clouds lying all along the first range, concealing more than they exposed. There was a sort of
gloomy grandeur about the view ; so much was hidden,
that the mind was left at liberty to imagine that behind
these clouds lay towering mountains and awful cliffs.
The road passed within a short distance of the rock of
Cuapo, and, leaving my horse with Rito, I climbed up
towards it. A ridge on the eastern side runs up to
within about 200 feet of the summit, and so far it is
accessible. Up this I climbed to the base of the brown
rock, the perpendicular cliff towering up above me ; here
and there were patches of grey, where lichens clung to

the rock, and orchids, ferns, and small shrubs grew in
the clefts and on ledges. There were two fine orchids in
flower, which grew not only on the rock, but on some
stunted trees at its base ; and beneath some fallen rocks
nestled a pretty club-moss, and two curious little ferns
(*Aneimea oblongifolia* and *hirsuta*), with the masses of
spores on stalks rising from the pinnules. The rock
was the same as that of Peña Blanca, but the vegetation was entirely distinct. To the south-west there was
a fine view down the Juigalpa valley to the lake, with
Ometépec in the distance, and some sugar-loaf hills
nearer at hand. The weather had cleared up, white
cumuli only sailed across the blue aerial ocean. The
scene had no feature in it of a purely tropical character,
excepting that three gaudy macaws were wheeling round
and round in playful flight, now showing all red on the
under surface, then turning all together, as if they were
one body, and exhibiting the gorgeous blue, yellow, and
red of the upper side gleaming in the sunshine; screaming meanwhile as they flew with harsh, discordant cries.
This gaudy-coloured and noisy bird seems to proclaim
aloud that it fears no foe. Its formidable beak protects
it from every danger, for no hawk or predatory mammal
dares attack a bird so strongly armed. Here the necessity for concealment does not exist, and sexual selection
has had no check in developing the brightest and most
conspicuous colours. If such a bird was not able to
defend itself from all foes, its loud cries would attract
them, its bright colours direct them, to its own destruction. The white cockatoo of Australia is a similar
instance. It is equally conspicuous amongst the dark-
green foliage by its pure white colour, and equally its

loud screams proclaim from afar its resting-place, whilst its powerful beak protects it from all enemies excepting man.   In the smaller species of parrots the beak is not sufficiently strong to protect them from their enemies, and most of them are coloured green, which makes them very difficult to distinguish amongst the leaves. I have been looking for several minutes at a tree, in which were scores of small green parrots, making an incessant noise, without being able to distinguish one ; and I recollect once in Australia firing at what I thought was a solitary " green leek " parrot amongst a bunch of leaves, and to my astonishment five " green leeks " fell to the ground, the whole bunch of apparent leaves having been composed of them.   The bills of even the smallest parrots must, however, be very useful to them to guard the entrances to their nests in the holes of trees, in which they breed.

I believe that the principal use of the long sharp bill of the toucan is also that of a weapon with which to defend itself against its enemies, especially when nesting in the hole of a tree.   Any predatory animal must face this formidable beak if seeking to force an entrance to the nest ; and I know by experience that the toucan can use it with great quickness and effect.   I kept a young one of the largest Nicaraguan species (*Ramphastus tocard*) for some time, until it one day came within reach of and was killed by my monkey.   It was a most comical-looking bird when hopping about, and though evidently partial to fruit, was eager after cockroaches and other insects ; its long bill being useful in picking them out of crevices and corners.   It used its bill so dexterously that it was impossible to put one's hand near it without being struck, and the blow would always draw blood. That in the tropics birds should have some special development for the protection of their breeding-places is not to be wondered at when we reflect upon the great number of predatory mammals, monkeys, raccoons, opossums, &c., that are constantly searching about for nests and devouring the eggs and young ones. I have already mentioned the great danger they run from the attacks of the immense armies of foraging ants, and the importance of having some means of picking off the scouts, that they may not return and scent the trail for the advance of the main body, whose numbers would overcome all resistance.

After examining round the rock without finding any place by which it could be ascended, I rejoined Rito in the valley below, and we continued our journey. We passed over some ranges and wide valleys, where there was much grass and a few scattered huts, but very little cattle; the country being thinly populated. On the top of a rocky range we stayed at a small house for breakfast, and they made us ready some tortillas. As usual, there seemed to be three or four families all living together, and there were a great number of children. The men were two miles away at a clearing on the edge of the forest, looking after their "milpas," or maize patches. The house, though small, was cleaner and tidier than the others we had seen, and in furniture could boast of a table and a few chairs, which showed we had chanced to fall on the habitation of one of the well-to-do class. The ceiling of the room we were in was made of bamboo-rods, above which maize was stored. The women were good-looking, and appeared to be of nearly pure Spanish descent ; which perhaps accounted for the chairs and table, and also for the absence of any attempt at gardening around the house —for the Indian eschews furniture, but is nearly always a gardener.

We finished our homely breakfast and set off again, crossing some more rocky ranges, and passing several Indian huts with orange trees growing around them, and at two o'clock in the afternoon reached the small town of Comoapa, where I determined to wait for Velasquez. Looking about for a house to stay at, we found one kept by a woman who formerly lived at Santo Domingo, and who was glad to receive us ; though we found afterwards she had already more travellers staying with her than she could well accommodate.

I had shot a pretty mot-mot on the road, and proceeded to skin it, to the amusement and delight of about a dozen spectators, who wondered what I could want with the " hide " of a bird, the only skinning that they had ever seen being that of deer and cattle. A native doctor, who was staying at the house, insisted on helping me, and as the mot-mot's skin is very tough, he did not do much harm. The bird had been shot in the morning, and some one remarking that no blood flowed when it was cut, the doctor said, with a wise air, that that class of birds had no blood, and that he knew of another class that also had none, to which his auditors gave a satisfied " Como no " (" Why not ? "). He also gave us to understand that he had himself at one time skinned birds, for being evidently looked up to as an authority on all subjects by the simple country people,

he was unwilling that his reputation should suffer by it
being supposed that a stranger had come to Comoapa
who knew something that he did not.   Having skinned
my bird and put the skin out in the sun to dry, I took a
stroll through the small town, and found it composed
mostly of huts inhabited by Mestizos, with a tumble-
down church and a weed-covered plaza.   Around some
of the houses were planted mango and orange trees, but
there was a general air of dilapidation and decay, and
not a single sign of industry or progress visible.

Velasquez arrived at dusk, having ridden from Libertad that day.   About a dozen of us slung our hammocks
in the small travellers' room, where, when we had all
gone to rest, we looked like a cluster of great bats
hanging from the rafters.   No one could get along the
room without disturbing every one else, and the next
morning all were early astir.   We got our animals
saddled as soon as possible, and set off on our journey.
It was a clear and beautiful morning, and a cool breeze
from the north-east fanned us as we rode blithely over
grassy savannahs and hills.   High up in the air soared
a couple of large black vultures, floating on the wind,
and describing large circles without apparent movement
or exertion, scanning from their airy height the country
for miles around, on the look-out for their carrion food.
Like all birds that soar, both over sea and land, when
it is calm the vultures are obliged to flap their wings
to fly; but when a breeze is blowing they are able to use
their specific gravity as a fulcrum, by means of which
they present their bodies and outstretched wings and
tails at various angles to the wind, and literally sail.
How often, when becalmed on southern seas, when not

a breath of air was stirring and the sails idly flapped against the mast, have I seen the albatross, the petrel, and the Cape-pigeon resting on the water, or rising with difficulty, and only by the constant motion of their long wings able to fly at all.   But when a breeze sprang up they were all life and motion, wheeling in graceful circles, now presenting one side, now the other, to view, descending rapidly with the wind, and so gaining velocity to turn and rise up again against it.   Then, as the breeze freshened to a gale, the petrels darted about, playing round and round the scudding ship, at home on the wings of the storm, poising themselves upon the wind as instinctively and with as little effort as a man balances himself on his feet.   The old times recurred as I rode over the savannah, and the soaring vultures brought back to my mind the wheeling stormy petrels that darted about whilst under close-reefed topsails we struggled against the gale, rounding the stormy southern cape ; when great blue seas, " green glimmering towards the summit," towered on every side, or struck our gallant ship like a sledge, making it shiver with the blow, and sending a driving cloud of spray from stem to stern.   Then the petrels were in their element; then they darted about—above, below, now here, now there—all life and motion ; as if their chief pleasure was, like Ariel, " to ride on the curled cloud " and " point the tempest." *

We were travelling nearly parallel with the edge of

* The Duke of Argyll, in his " Reign of Law," has some excellent remarks on the flight of birds that soar, or hover. My remarks, of which the above account is a paraphrase, were written out in my journal in 1852, but were not published.

the great forest which was two or three miles away on
our right; in all other directions the view was bounded
by ranges, some grassed to their tops, others with forests
climbing up their steep sides, excepting where white
cliffs gave no foothold for the trees. We passed several
grass-thatched huts inhabited by half-clad Indians or
Mestizos, who generally possess a few cows, and, away on
the edge of the forest, small clearings of maize. These
people, with unlimited fertile land at their disposal, were
all sunk in what looked like squalid poverty; but they
had a roof over their heads, and sufficient, though coarse,
food, and they cared for nothing more. Our road lay
a couple of miles to the north of the village of Huaco,
where much of the maize of the province is grown; the
road then led over many swampy valleys, and our beasts
had hard work plunging through the mud. We passed
through La Puerta, a scattered collection of Indian
huts; then over a river called the Aguasco, running to
the east, and probably emptying into the Rio Grande.
There were a few orange trees about some of the huts,
but most of the people were Mestizos, or half-breeds, and
nothing but weeds grew around their habitations. Their
plantations of maize were always some miles distant, and
they never seem to think of moving their houses nearer
to their clearings on the edge of the forest. Nearly
always when I asked the question, I found that the
grown-up people had been born on the spot where they
lived, and they are evidently greatly attached to the
localities where they have been brought up. Probably
when the settlements were first made, forest land lay
near, in which they made their clearings and raised their
crops of corn. Since then the edge of the forest has

been beaten back some miles to the north-east; but the
people cling to the old spots, where, generation after
generation, their ancestors have lived and died.   A
new house could be built in a few days, closer to the
forest; but they prefer travelling several miles every
day to and from their clearings, rather than desert
their old homes.

Beyond the Aguasco, we had to travel over a swampy
plain for about a mile, our animals plunging all the time
through about three feet of mud.   This plain was covered
with thousands of guayava trees, laden with sufficient
fruit to make guava jelly for all the world.   After floun-
dering through the swamp, we reached more savannahs,
and then entered a beautiful valley, well grassed, and
with herds of fine cattle, horses, and mules grazing on
it.   The grass was well cropped, and looked like pasture-
land at home.   The ground was now firmer, and we got
more rapidly across it.   A flock of wild Muscovy ducks
flew heavily across the plain, looking very like the tame
variety.   I do not wonder at sportsmen sometimes being
unwilling to fire at them, mistaking them for domestic
ducks.   The tame variety is very prolific, and sits better
on its eggs than the common duck.   I have seen twenty
ducklings brought out at a single hatching.   They are
good eating, and a large one has nearly as much flesh
upon it as an average-sized goose.

About dusk on these plains, which extended around
for several miles, we reached the cattle hacienda of
Olama, where was a large tile-roofed house, near a river
of the same name.   The natives of Nicaragua seldom
give distinctive names to their rivers, but call them after
the towns or villages on their banks.   Thus, at Olama,

the river was called the Olama river; higher up, at Matagalpa, the same stream is called the Matagalpa river; and at Jinotego the Jinotego river. The Caribs, however, who live on the rivers, and use them as highways, have names for them all; but to the agricultural Indians and Mestizos of the interior, they are but reservoirs of water, crossed at distant points by their roads, and everywhere amongst them I found the greatest ignorance prevailing as to the connection of the different streams, and their outflow to the ocean. All the streams about Olama flow eastward, and join together to form the Rio Grande, that reaches the Atlantic about midway between Blewfields and the river Wanks. It is very incorrectly marked on all the maps of Nicaragua that I have seen.

The Caribs from the lower parts of the river occasionally come up in their canoes to Olama, and bring with them common guns and iron pots that they have obtained from the mahogany cutters at the mouth of the river. These they barter for dogs. I could not ascertain what they wanted with the dogs, but both at this place and at Matagalpa I was told of the great value the Caribs put on them. Although the people of Olama expressed great surprise that the " Caritos," as they call the river Indians, should take so much trouble to obtain dogs, they had not had the curiosity to ask them what they wanted them for. Some people near the river have even commenced to rear dogs, to supply the demand. The Caribs had a special liking for black ones, and did not value those of any other colour so much. They would barter a gun or a large iron pot for a single dog, if it was of the right colour.

The common dogs of Central America are a mongrel breed—not differing, I believe, from those of Europe. There are usually a number of curs about the Indian houses that run out barking at a stranger, but seldom bite.

The hairless dogs, mentioned by Humboldt, as being abundant in Peru,* are not common in Central America, but there are a few to be met with. At Colon I saw several. They are of a shining dark colour, and are quite without hair, excepting a little on the face and on the tip of the tail. Both in Peru and Mexico this variety was found by the Spanish conquerors. It would be interesting to have these dogs compared with the hairless dogs of China, which Humboldt says have certainly been extremely common since very early times. Perhaps another link might be added to the broken chain of evidence that connects the peoples of the two countries.

A large naked dog-like animal is figured by Clavigero as one of the indigenous animals of Mexico. It was called *Xoloitzcuintli* by the Mexicans; and Humboldt considers it was distinct from the hairless dog, and was a large dog-like wolf. Its name does not support this view; *Xoloitzcuintli* literally means " a servant dog," from " *Xolotl*," a slave or servant, and *itzcuintli*, a dog ; and we find the word *Xolotl* in *Huexlotl*, the Aztec name of the common turkey, which was domesticated by them, and largely used as food. I am led to believe from this, that *Xolotl* was applied to any animal that lived in the house or was domesticated, and that the *Xoloitzcuintli* was merely a large variety of the hairless dog. Clavi-

" Aspects of Nature," vol. i. p. 109.

gero's description of it would fit the hairless dog of the present day very well, excepting the size; he says it was four feet long, totally naked, excepting a few stiff hairs on its snout, and ash coloured, spotted with black and tawny.

Tschudi makes two races of indigenous dogs in tropical America. 1. The *Canis caraibicus* (Lesson), without hair, and which does not bark. 2. The *Canis ingœ* (Tschudi), the common hairy dog, which has pointed nose and ears, and barks.* The small eatable dog of the Mexicans was called by them *Techichi;* and Humboldt derives the name from *Tetl*, a stone, and says that it means "a dumb dog," but this appears rather a forced derivation. *Chichi* is Aztec for "to suck;" and it seems to me more probable that the little dogs they eat, and which are spoken of by the Spaniards as making very tender and delicate food, were the puppies of the *Xoloitzcuintli*, and that *Techichi* meant "a sucker."

Whether the hairless dog was or was not the *Techichi* of which the Mexicans made such savoury dishes is an open question, but there can be no doubt that the former was found in tropical America by the Spanish conquerors, and that it has survived to the present time, with little or no change. That it should not have intermixed with the common haired variety, and lost its distinctive characters, is very remarkable. It has not been artificially preserved, for instead of being looked on with favour by the Indians, Humboldt states that in Peru, where it is abundant, it is despised and ill-treated. Under such circumstances, the variety can only have

* J. J. von Tschudi, quoted by Humboldt, "Aspects of Nature," English edition, vol. i. p. 111.

been preserved through not interbreeding with the common form, either from a dislike to such unions, or by some amount of sterility when they are formed. This is, I think, in favour of the inference that the variety has been produced by natural and not by artificial selection, for diminished fertility is seldom or never acquired between artificial varieties.

Man isolates varieties, and breeds from them, and continuing to separate those that vary in the direction he wishes to follow, a very great difference is, in a comparatively short time, produced.   But these artificial varieties, though often more different from each other than some natural species, readily interbreed, and if left to themselves, rapidly revert to a common type.   In natural selection there is a great and fundamental difference.   The varieties that arise can seldom be separated from the parent form and from other varieties, until they vary also in the elements of reproduction. Thousands of varieties probably revert to the parent type, but if at last one is produced that breeds only with its own form, we can easily see how a new species might be segregated.   As long as varieties interbreed together and with the parent form, it does not seem possible that a new species could be formed by natural selection, excepting in cases of geographical isolation.   All the individuals might vary in some one direction, but they could not split up into distinct species whilst they occupied the same area and interbred without difficulty. Before a variety can become permanent, it must be either separated from the others, or have acquired some disinclination or inability to interbreed with them.   So long as they interbreed together, the possible divergence is kept within narrow limits, but whenever a variety is produced, the individuals of which have a partiality for interbreeding, and some amount of sterility when crossed with the parent form, the tie that bound it to the central stock is loosened, and the foundation is laid for the formation of a new species. Further divergence would be unchecked, or only slightly checked, and the elements of reproduction having begun to vary, would probably continue to diverge from the parent form, for Darwin has shown that any organ in which a species has begun to vary, is liable to further change in the same direction.* Thus one of the best tests of the specific difference of two allied forms living together, is their sterility when crossed, and nearly allied species separated by geographical barriers are more likely to interbreed than those inhabiting the same area. Artificial selection is more rapid in its results, but less stable than that of nature, because the barriers that man raises to prevent intermingling of varieties are temporary and partial, whilst that which nature fixes when sterility arises is permanent and complete.

For these reasons I think that the fact that the hairless dog of tropical America has not interbred with the common form, and regained its hairy coat, is in favour of the inference that the variety has been produced by natural and not by artificial selection. By this I do not mean that it has arisen as a wild variety, for it is probable that its domestication was an important element amongst the causes that led to its formation, but that it has not been produced by man selecting the individuals to breed from that had the least covering

* See "Animals and Plants under Domestication," vol. ii. p. 241.

of hairs. I cannot agree with some eminent naturalists that the loss of a hairy covering would always be disadvantageous. My experience in tropical countries has led me to the conclusion that in such parts at least there is one serious drawback to the advantages of having the skin covered with hair. It affords cover for parasitical insects, which, if the skin were naked, might more easily be got rid of.

No one who has not lived and moved about amongst the bush of the tropics can appreciate what a torment the different parasitical species of *acarus* or ticks are. On my first journey in Northern Brazil, I had my legs inflamed and ulcerated from the ankles to the knees, from the irritation produced by a minute red tick that is brushed off the low shrubs, and attaches itself to the passer-by. This little insect is called the "Mocoim" by the Brazilians, and is a great torment. It is so minute that except by careful searching it cannot be perceived, and it causes an intolerable itching. If the skin were thickly covered with hair, it would be next to impossible to get rid of it. Through all tropical America, during the dry season, a brown tick (*Ixodes bovis*), varying in size from a pin's head to a pea, abounds. In Nicaragua, in April, they are very small, and swarm upon the plains, so that the traveller often gets covered with them. They get upon the tips of the leaves and shoots of low shrubs, and stand with their hind-legs stretched out. Each foot has two hooks or claws, and with these it lays hold of any animal brushing past. All large land animals seem subject to their attacks. I have seen them on snakes and iguanas, on many of the large birds, especially on the curassows.

O

They abound on all the large mammals, and on many of the small ones.   Sick and weak animals are particularly infested with them, probably because they have not the strength to rub and pick them off, and they must often hasten, if they do not cause their death. The herdsmen, or "vacqueros," keep a ball of soft wax at their houses, which they rub over their skin when they come in from the plains, the small "garrapatos" sticking to it, whilst the larger ones are picked off. How the small ones would be got rid of if the skin had a hairy coat I know not, but the torment of the ticks would certainly be greatly increased.

There are other insect parasites, for the increase and protection of which a hairy coating is even more favourable than it is for the ticks.   The *Pediculi* are specially adapted to live amongst hair, their limbs being constructed for clinging to it.   They deposit their nits or eggs amongst it, fastening them securely to the bases of the hairs.   Although the *pediculi* are almost unknown to the middle and upper classes of civilised communities, in consequence of the cleanliness of their persons, clothing, and houses, they abound amongst savage and half-civilised people.   A slight immunity from the attacks of *acari* and *pediculi* might in a tropical country more than compensate an animal for the loss of its hairy coat, especially in the case of the domesticated dog, which finds shelter with its master, has not to seek for its food at night, and is protected from the attacks of stronger animals.   In the huts of savages dogs are greatly exposed to the attacks of parasitical insects, for vermin generally abound in such localities.   Man is the only species amongst the higher primates that lives for

months and years—often indeed from generation to
generation—on the same spot. Monkeys change their
sleeping places almost daily. The ourang-outang, that
makes a nest of the boughs of trees, is said to con-
struct a fresh one every night. The dwelling-places
of savages, often made of, or lined with, the skins of
animals, with the dusty earth for a floor, harbour all
kinds of insect vermin, and produce and perpetuate
skin disease, due to the attacks of minute *sarcopti*. If
the dog by losing its hair should obtain any protection
from these and other insect pests, instead of wondering
that a hairless breed of dogs has been produced in a
tropical country, I am more surprised that haired ones
should abound. That they do so must, I think, be
owing to man having preferred the haired breeds for
their superior beauty and greater variety, and en-
couraged their multiplication.

CHAPTER XII.

WE rode up to the large hacienda at Olama, and were asked to alight by a man whom I at first took to be the proprietor, but afterwards discovered to be a traveller like ourselves, buying cattle for the Leon market. The owner of the house and his sister were away at a little town three or four miles distant; and I was a little nervous about the reception we should have when they returned and found us making ourselves at home at their house. Velasquez had, however, no apprehensions on that score, as he knew that throughout the central departments of Nicaragua it is the custom for travellers to expect and to receive a welcome at any house they may arrive at by nightfall. Excepting in the towns, and on some of the main roads, there are no houses where travellers can stop and pay for a night's lodging. Every one expects to be called on at any time to give a night's shelter. This is all that is afforded, as travellers carry with them their hammocks and food. About an

hour after dark, the owner and his sister returned on
mules, and the gentleman seemed pleased at finding us
at his house.   I was about to offer a chair to the sister;
but Velasquez told me it was not the custom to show any
civilities to the ladies, as they would probably be mis-
construed.   After a while, the master had some chocolate

THE "SANATÈ," OR QUISCALUS.

brought to him by his sister, who waited upon him.   The
wife, the sister, and the daughter in the departments
seldom sit down to their meals with the master of the
house, but attend upon him like servants.

Whilst coffee was preparing next morning, I strolled
about the outbuildings, and was much amused at the
antics of the jet black *Quiscalus*, called " sanate " by the

natives. They are about the size of a magpie, with much of the active movements of that bird. They are generally seen about cattle, sometimes picking the garrapatos off them, but more often one on each side, watching for the grasshoppers and other insects, that are frightened up as the cattle feed. On this morning, there were several of them on the top of a shed. Every now and then one would ruffle out its feathers, open its wings a little, give a step or two forward towards another, stretch out its neck, open its bill, and then give rather a long squeak-like whistle. As soon as it had done this, it would hurriedly close its feathers and wings, and hold its head straight up, with its bill pointing to the sky. All its movements were grotesque; and its sudden change in appearance after delivering its cry was ludicrous. It appeared as if it was ashamed of what it had done, and was trying to look as if it had not done it—just as I have seen a schoolboy throw a snowball, and then stand rigidly looking another way. After a few moments, the "sanate" would lower its head, and, in a short time, go through the same performance again, repeating every movement automatically.

Bidding adieu to our host, we rode over grassy savannahs, with much cattle feeding on them, and in about five miles reached a small village called Muy-muy, which means "very-very." I think it is a corruption of an old Indian word "Muyo," met with in other Indian names of towns, as, for instance, in Muyogalpa. After riding all round the plaza, which formed three-fourths of the town, we at last found a house where they consented to make us some tortillas, on condition that we would buy some native cheese also.

The land around was fertile, but the people too lazy to cultivate it. Many of the houses were dilapidated huts. The place altogether had a most depressing aspect of poverty and idleness. I asked one man what the people worked at. He said, "Nada, nada, señor," that is, "Nothing, nothing, sir." Some of them possess cattle; and those that have none sometimes help those that have, and get enough to keep them alive. The principal subject of interest seemed to be the " caritos," who had come up the river, and given them guns and iron pots for their black dogs; but no one had had the curiosity to ask what they wanted the dogs for. It was Sunday, and many of the country people from around had come into the village. All that had any money were at the estanco, drinking aguardiente. The men were dressed alike, with palm-tree hats, white calico jackets and trousers, the latter often rolled up to the thigh on one leg, as is the fashion in this part of the world. Nearly all were barefooted.

Having breakfasted off tortillas and cheese, we continued our journey, and crossed two rivers running to the eastward; then ascended a high and rocky range, along the top of which the path lay. We took this mountain-path to avoid some very bad swamps that we were told we should encounter if we went by the main road. The mountain range was bare and bleak, but we had a fine view over the surrounding country. Opposite to us, on the other side of a wide valley, was a similar range to that along which we were travelling, the sides partly wooded and partly cleared for planting maize. We passed several Indian huts with grass-thatched roofs, and met a party of Indians travelling down the mountain in single file, each man carrying his bow and arrows. They were going down to Huaco to buy corn, the maize crop having failed around Matagalpa the last season. The mountain road, though dry, was rocky, with steep ascents, and our mules got very tired. About five o'clock we descended from the hills into the valley of Ocalca, near to which there had been some gold workings, now abandoned. Here we came in sight, for the first time, of the pine forests, a high range a few miles to the north being covered with them.

About dusk, we reached an Indian hut, and proposed staying there for the night. The owners were pure Indians; the women, engaged as usual in grinding maize, were naked to the waist. There was an old man and his son, and some children. The old Indian looked distressed at our proposal to take up our quarters there for the night, but he made no objection. The accommodation was very poor, there being no hammocks or bedsteads; and I think all the inmates must have slept above on some bamboos that were laid across the beams. Learning from the old man that there was a larger and better house a little further on, we relieved him of our company, and crossing a river, reached a cattle hacienda owned by a very stout native named Blandon, who made us welcome. The house was a large one; and there were a number of mozos and women-servants about. We asked if we could buy anything to eat, and Señor Blandon said he would get supper prepared, at which we were much pleased, as we had had nothing all day excepting a drink of coffee at daylight, and some tortillas and cheese at Muy-muy. After waiting a long time, we were invited to our supper; and on going into an inner room, found it consisted only of coffee and two small cakes called " roskears " for each of us; and we were told they had nothing else to offer us. So, munching our dry roskears, we mumbled over them as long as we could, and did not waste a crumb, wondering how our host got so fat on such fare. We were as hungry when we finished as when we began, and soon laid down on our hard couches to forget our hunger in sleep.

We started off early the next morning, as we were within a few leagues of the town of Matagalpa, and knew when we got there we should obtain plenty of provisions. About a league before arriving at Matagalpa there is a high range, with perpendicular cliffs near the summit. Rito told us that near the base of these cliffs there was a carving of a bull, and that the place was enchanted. I had heard in other parts stories of bulls being engraved or painted on rocks, but was very doubtful about their being true, as, up to the advent of the Spaniards, the Indians of Central America had never seen any cattle; and since the conquest they appear to have entirely given up their ancient practice of carving on stone, whilst the Spaniards and half-breeds have not learnt the art; so that I have never seen a single carving in the central departments that could be ascribed to a later period than the Spanish conquest.

Tired and hungry though we were, I was determined to put this story to the test; so Velasquez and I climbed up to the cliffs, and searched all round them, but could find no carving. At one place there was a large black stain on the cliff, produced by the trickling down of water from above, and I afterwards learnt that this stain at a distance somewhat resembled a bull, and

a little imagination completed the likeness.   The lady
of the house where we stayed at Matagalpa assured us
she had seen it, and that everything appertaining to a
bull was there.   This she insisted on with a minuteness
of detail rather embarrassing to a fastidious auditor.

Clambering down the rocks, we reached our horse
and mule, and started off again, passing over dry weedy
hills.   One low tree, very characteristic of the dry
savannahs, I have only incidentally mentioned before.

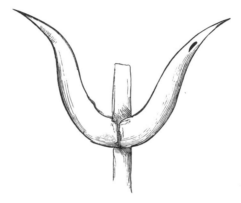

THE BULL S-HORN THORN.

It is a species of acacia, belonging to the section *Gum-
miferæ*, with bi-pinnate leaves, growing to a height of
fifteen or twenty feet.   The branches and trunk are
covered with strong curved spines, set in pairs, from
which it receives the name of the bull's-horn thorn,
they having a very strong resemblance to the horns of
that quadruped.   These thorns are hollow, and are
tenanted by ants, that make a small hole for their
entrance and exit near one end of the thorn, and also

burrow through the partition that separates the two horns ; so that the one entrance serves for both. Here they rear their young, and in the wet season every one of the thorns is tenanted ; and hundreds of ants are to be seen running about, especially over the young leaves. If one of these be touched, or a branch shaken, the little ants (*Pseudomyrma bicolor*, Guer.) swarm out from the hollow thorns, and attack the aggressor with jaws and sting. They sting severely, raising a little white lump that does not disappear in less than twenty-four hours.

These ants form a most efficient standing army for the plant, which prevents not only the mammalia from browsing on the leaves, but delivers it from the attacks of a much more dangerous enemy—the leaf-cutting ants. For these services the ants are not only securely housed by the plant, but are provided with a bountiful supply of food, and to secure their attendance at the right time and place, the food is so arranged and dis-tributed as to effect that object with wonderful perfec-tion. The leaves are bi-pinnate. At the base of each pair of leaflets, on the mid-rib, is a crater-formed gland, which, when the leaves are young, secretes a honey-like liquid. Of this the ants are very fond ; and they are constantly running about from one gland to another to sip up the honey as it is secreted. But this is not all ; there is a still more wonderful provision of more solid food. At the end of each of the small divisions of the compound leaflet there is, when the leaf first unfolds, a little yellow fruit-like body united by a point at its base to the end of the pinnule. Examined through a microscope, this little appendage looks like a golden pear. When the leaf first unfolds, the little

pears are not quite ripe, and the ants are continually
employed going from one to another, examining them.
When an ant finds one sufficiently advanced, it bites
the small point of attachment; then, bending down the
fruit-like body, it breaks it off and bears it away in
triumph to the nest. All the fruit-like bodies do not
ripen at once, but successively, so that the ants are
kept about the young leaf for some time after it unfolds.
Thus the young leaf is always guarded by the ants;
and no caterpillar or larger animal could attempt to
injure them without being attacked by the little warriors.
The fruit-like bodies are about one-twelfth of an inch
long, and are about one-third of the size of the ants;
so that an ant carrying one away is as heavily laden as
a man bearing a large bunch of plantains. I think
these facts show that the ants are really kept by the
acacia as a standing army, to protect its leaves from
the attacks of herbivorous mammals and insects.

The bull's-horn thorn does not grow at the mines in
the forest, nor are the small ants attending on them
found there. They seem specially adapted for the tree,
and I have seen them nowhere else. Besides the
Pseudomyrma, I found another ant that lives on these
acacias; it is a small black species of *Crematogaster*,
whose habits appear to be rather different from those
of *Pseudomyrma*. It makes the holes of entrance to
the thorns near the centre of one of ·each pair, and not
near the end, like the *Pseudomyrma ;* and it is not so
active as that species. It is also rather scarce; but
when it does occur, it occupies the whole tree, to the
exclusion of the other. The glands on the acacia are
also frequented by a small species of wasp (*Polybia*

occidentalis).   I sowed the seeds of the acacia in my
garden, and reared some young plants.   Ants of many
kinds were numerous; but none of them took to the
thorns for shelter, nor the glands and fruit-like bodies
for food; for, as I have already mentioned, the species
that attend on the thorns are not found in the forest.
The leaf-cutting ants attacked the young plants, and
defoliated them, but I have never seen any of the trees
out on the savannahs that are guarded by the *Pseudomyrma* touched by them, and have no doubt the acacia
is protected from them by its little warriors.   The
thorns, when they are first developed, are soft, and
filled with a sweetish, pulpy substance; so that the
ant, when it makes an entrance into them, finds its
new house full of food.   It hollows this out, leaving
only the hardened shell of the thorn.   Strange to say,
this treatment seems to favour the development of the
thorn, as it increases in size, bulging out towards the
base; whilst in my plants that were not touched by
the ants, the thorns turned yellow and dried up into
dead but persistent prickles.   I am not sure, however,
that this may not have been due to the habitat of the
plant not suiting it.

These ants seem at first sight to lead the happiest of
existences.   Protected by their stings, they fear no foe.
Habitations full of food are provided for them to commence housekeeping with, and cups of nectar and
luscious fruits await them every day.   But there is a
reverse to the picture.   In the dry season on the plains,
the acacias cease to grow.   No young leaves are produced, and the old glands do not secrete honey.   Then
want and hunger overtake the ants that have revelled

in luxury all the wet season ; many of the thorns are depopulated, and only a few ants live through the season of scarcity. As soon, however, as the first rains set in, the trees throw out numerous vigorous shoots, and the ants multiply again with astonishing rapidity.

Both in Brazil and Nicaragua I paid much attention to the relation between the presence of honey-secreting glands on plants, and the protection the latter secured by the attendance of ants attracted by the honey. I found many plants so protected ; the glands being specially developed on the young leaves, and on the sepals of the flowers. Besides the bull's-horn acacias, I, however, only met with two other genera of plants that furnished the ants with houses, namely the *Cecropiæ* and some of the *Melastomæ*. I have no doubt that there are many others. The stem of the Cecropia, or trumpet-tree, is hollow, and divided into cells by partitions that extend across the interior of the hollow trunk. The ants gain access by making a hole from the outside, and then burrow through the partitions, thus getting the run of the whole stem. They do not obtain their food directly from the tree, but keep brown scale-insects (*Coccidæ*) in the cells, which suck the juices from the tree, and secrete a honey-like fluid that exudes from a pore on the back, and is lapped up by the ants. In one cell eggs will be found, in another grubs, and in a third pupæ, all lying loosely. In another cell, by itself, a queen ant will be found, surrounded by walls made of a brown waxy-looking substance, along with about a dozen *Coccidæ* to supply her with food. I suppose the eggs are removed as soon as laid,

for I never found any along with the queen-ant. If
the tree be shaken, the ants rush out in myriads, and
search about for the molester. This case is not like
the last one, where the tree has provided food and
shelter for the ants, but rather one where the ant has
taken possession of the tree, and brought with it the
Coccidæ; but I believe that its presence must be beneficial. I have cut into some dozens of the Cecropia trees,

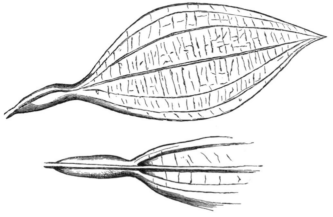

LEAF OF MELASTOMA.

and never could find one that was not tenanted by ants.
I noticed three different species, all, as far as I know,
confined to the *Cecropiæ*, and all farming scale-insects.
As in the bull's-horn thorn, there is never more than
one species of ant on the same tree.

In some species of *Melastomæ* there is a direct provision of houses for the ants. In each leaf, at the base
of the laminæ, the petiole, or stalk, is furnished with a

couple of pouches, divided from each other by the mid-rib, as shown in the figure. Into each of these pouches there is an entrance from the lower side of the leaf. I noticed them first in Northern Brazil, in the province of Maranham ; and afterwards at Pará. Every pouch was occupied by a nest of small black ants, and if the leaf was shaken ever so little, they would rush out and scour all over it in search of the aggressor. I must have tested some hundreds of leaves, and never shook one without the ants coming out, excepting on one sickly-looking plant at Pará. In many of the pouches I noticed the eggs and young ants, and in some I saw a few dark-coloured *Coccidæ* or aphides ; but my attention had not been at that time directed to the latter as supplying the ants with food, and I did not examine a sufficient number of pouches to determine whether they were constant occupants of the nests or not. My subsequent experience with the Cecropia trees would lead me to expect that they were. If so, we have an instance of two insects and a plant living together, and all benefiting by the companionship. The leaves of the plant are guarded by the ants, the ants are provided with houses by the plant, and food by the *Coccidæ* or aphides, and the latter are effectually protected by the ants in their common habitation.

Amongst the numerous plants that do not provide houses, but attract ants to their leaves and flower-buds by means of glands secreting a honey-like liquid, are many epiphytal orchids, and I think all the species of *Passiflora*. I had the common red passion-flower growing over the front of my verandah, where it was continually under my notice. It had honey-secreting glands

on its young leaves and on the sepals of the flower-buds.
For two years I noticed that the glands were constantly
attended by a small ant (*Pheidole*), and, night and day,
every young leaf and every flower-bud had a few on
them.   They did not sting, but attacked and bit my
finger when I touched the plant.   I have no doubt that
the primary object of these honey-glands is to attract
the ants, and keep them about the most tender and
vulnerable parts of the plant, to prevent them being
injured ; and I further believe that one of the principal
enemies that they serve to guard against in tropical
America is the leaf-cutting ant, as I have observed that
the latter are very much afraid of the small black ants.

On the third year after I had noticed the attendance
of the ants on my passion-flower, I found that the
glands were not so well looked after as before, and soon
discovered that a number of scale-insects had established
themselves on the stems, and that the ants had in a
great measure transferred their attentions to them.   An
ant would stand over a scale-insect and stroke it alternately on each side with its antennæ, whereupon every
now and then a clear drop of honey would exude from a
pore on the back of the latter and be imbibed by the
ant.   Here it was clear that the scale-insect was com-
peting successfully with the leaves and sepals for the
attendance and protection of the ants, and was successful either through the fluid it furnished being more
attractive or more abundant.*   I have, from these facts,
been led to the conclusion that the use of honey-secreting
glands in plants is to attract insects that will protect

* I have since observed ants attending scale-insects on a large plant
of *Passiflora macrocarpa* in the palm-house at Kew.

the flower-buds and leaves from being injured by herbivorous insects and mammals, but I do not mean to infer that this is the use of all glands, for many of the small appendicular bodies, called "glands" by botanists, do not secrete honey. The common dog-rose of England is furnished with glands on the stipules, and in other species they are more numerous, until in the wild *Rosa villosa* of the northern counties the leaves are thickly edged, and the fruit and sepals covered with stalked glands. I have only observed the wild roses in the north of England, and there I have never seen insects attending the glands. These glands, however, do not secrete honey, but a dark, resinous, sticky liquid, that probably is useful by being distasteful to both insects and mammals.

If the facts I have described are sufficient to show that some plants are benefited by supplying ants with honey from glands on their leaves and flower-buds, I shall not have much difficulty in proving that many plant-lice, scale-insects, and leaf-hoppers, that also attract ants by furnishing them with honey-like food, are similarly benefited. The aphides are the principal ant-cows of Europe. In the tropics their place is taken in a great measure by species of *Coccidæ* and genera of *Homoptera*, such as *Membracis* and its allies. My pine-apples were greatly subject to the attacks of a small, soft-bodied, brown coccus, that was always guarded by a little, black, stinging ant (*Solenopsis*). This ant took great care of the scale-insects, and attacked savagely any one interfering with them, as I often found to my cost, when trying to clear my pines, by being stung severely by them. Not content with watching over their cattle, the ants brought up grains of damp earth, and built domed galleries over them, in which, under the vigilant guard of their savage little attendants, the scale-insects must, I think, have been secure from the attacks of all enemies.

Many of the leaf-hoppers—species, I think, of *Membracis*—were attended by ants. These leaf-hoppers live in little clusters on shoots of plants and beneath leaves, in which are hoppers in every stage of development —eggs, larvæ, and adults. I believe it is only the soft-bodied larvæ that exude honey. It would take a volume to describe the various species, and I shall confine my remarks to one whose habits I was able to observe with some minuteness. The papaw trees growing in my garden were infested by a small brown species of *Membracis*—one of the leaf-hoppers—that laid its eggs in a cottony-like nest by the side of the ribs on the under part of the leaves. The hopper would stand covering the nest until the young were hatched. These were little soft-bodied dark-coloured insects, looking like aphides, but more robust, and with the hind segments turned up. From the end of these the little larvæ exuded drops of honey, and were assiduously attended by small ants belonging to two species of the genus *Pheidole,* one of them being the same as I have already described as attending the glands on the passion-flower. One tree would be attended by one species, another by the other; and I never saw the two species on the same tree. A third ant, however—a species of *Hypoclinea*— which I have mentioned before as a cowardly species, whose nests were despoiled by the *Ecitons,* frequented all the trees, and whenever it found any young hoppers unattended, it would relieve them of their honey, but would scamper away on the approach of any of the *Pheidole*. The latter do not sting, but they attack and bite the hand if the young hoppers are interfered with. These leaf-hoppers are, when young, so soft-bodied and sluggish in their movements, and there are so many enemies ready to prey upon them, that I imagine that in the tropics many species would be exterminated if it were not for the protection of the ants.

Similarly as, on the savannahs, I had observed a wasp attending the honey-glands of the bull's-horn acacia along with the ants, so at Santo Domingo another wasp, belonging to quite a different genus (*Nectarina*), attended some of the clusters of frog-hoppers, and for the possession of others a constant skirmishing was going on. The wasp stroked the young hoppers, and sipped up the honey when it was exuded, just like the ants. When an ant came up to a cluster of leaf-hoppers attended by a wasp, the latter would not attempt to grapple with its rival on the leaf, but would fly off and hover over the ant; then when its little foe was well exposed, it would dart at it and strike it to the ground. The action was so quick that I could not determine whether it struck with its fore-feet or its jaws, but I think it was with the feet. I often saw a wasp trying to clear a leaf from ants that were already in full possession of a cluster of leaf-hoppers. It would sometimes have to strike three or four times at an ant before it made it quit its hold and fall. At other times one ant after the other would be struck off with great celerity and ease, and I fancied that some wasps were much cleverer than others. In those cases where it succeeded in clearing the leaf, it

was never left long in peace.   Fresh relays of ants were
continually arriving, and generally tired the wasp out.
It would never wait for an ant to get near it, doubtless
knowing well that if its little rival once fastened on
its leg, it would be a difficult matter to get rid of it
again.   If a wasp first obtained possession, it was able
to keep it; for the first ants that came up were only
pioneers, and by knocking these off it prevented them
from returning and scenting the trail to communicate
the intelligence to others.

Before leaving this subject, I may remark that just as
in plants some glands secrete honey that attracts insects,
others a resinous liquid that repels them, so the secre-
tions of different genera of the homopterous division of the
Hemiptera are curiously modified for strikingly different
useful purposes.   We have seen that by many species of
plant-lice, scale-insects, and leaf-hoppers, a honey-like
fluid is secreted that attracts ants to attend upon them.
Other species of aphides (*Eriosoma*) that have no honey-
tubes, and many of the Coccidæ, secrete a white, flocculent,
waxy cotton, under which they lie concealed.   In many
of the Homoptera, this secretion only amounts to a white
powder covering the body, as in some of the Fulgoridæ.
In others it is more abundant, and it reaches its extreme
limit in a species of *Phenax* that I found at Santo
Domingo.   The insect is about an inch in length, but
the waxy secretion forms a long thick tail of cotton-like
fibres, two inches in length, that gives the insect a most
curious appearance when flying.   This flocculent mass
is so loosely connected with the body that it is difficult
to catch the insect without breaking the greater part of
it off.   Mr. Bates has suggested that the large brittle

wings of the metallic Morphos may often save them from
being caught by birds, who are likely to seize some portion
of the wide expanse of wing, and this, breaking off, frees
the butterfly.   Probably the long cumbersome tail of
the *Phenax* has a similar use.   When flying, it is the
only portion of the insect seen ; and birds trying to capture it on the wing are likely to get only a mouthful of
the flocculent wax.   The large Homoptera are much
preyed upon by birds.   In April, when the Cicadæ are
piping their shrill cry from morning until night, individuals are often seen whose bulky bodies have been
bitten off from the thorax by some bird.   The large
and graceful swallow-tailed kite at that time feeds on
nothing else.   I have seen these kites sweeping round in
circles over the tree-tops, and every now and then
catching insects off the leaves, and on shooting them I
have found their crops filled with Cicadæ.

The frog-hoppers, besides exuding honey in some
genera and wax in others, in a third division emit, when
in the larval state, a great quantity of froth, in which
they lie concealed, as in the common "cuckoo-spit" of
our meadows.

CHAPTER XIII.

AT noon we arrived at Matagalpa, the capital of the
province of the same name. The town contains about
three thousand inhabitants ; the province, or department, about thirty thousand. Matagalpa is built
close to the river, on a rocky surface, with stony
knolls rising up in some parts amongst the houses. It
contains three churches, and the usual large square or
plaza. Around, the country appeared very dry and
barren, and there is scarcely any cultivation in the
immediate neighbourhood. We put up at one of the
best houses in the town. The family consisted of a
stout lady about fifty and her husband, their daughter
and her husband, and an unmarried son. The two
younger men appeared to do nothing ; the elder one
had a contract with the government to manufacture
aguardiente for three towns, and spent nearly all his
time at a small hacienda, a league distant, where he
grew sugar-cane and maize, and distilled the spirit.

There is a great deal of aguardiente, an inferior kind
of rum, sold throughout Nicaragua, and most of the
Indians make it a point to get drunk on their feast-

days, but at other times are a sober race.   They do not owe the introduction of intemperance to the Spaniards, though they can now obtain stronger liquor than in the old times, as the ancient Indians do not appear to have known how to distil, but they made several kinds of fermented liquors.   In Mexico the chief drink was " pulque," the fermented juice of the agave or maguey plant.   In Nicaragua " chicha," a kind of light beer, made from maize, is still the favourite Indian beverage. On the warmer plains, the wine-palm (*Cocos butyracea*) is grown.   I saw many of them near San Ubaldo. The wine is very simply prepared.   The tree is felled, and an oblong hole cut into it, just below the crown of leaves.   This hole is eight inches deep, passing nearly through the trunk.   It is about a foot long and four inches broad ; and in this hollow the juice of the tree immediately begins to collect, scarcely any running out at the butt where it has been cut off.   This tendency of the sap to ascend is well shown in another plant, the water liana.   To get the water from this it must be cut first as high as one can reach ; then about a foot from the ground, and out of a length of about seven feet, a pint of fine cool water will run ; but if cut at the bottom first, the sap will ascend so rapidly that very little will be obtained.   In three days after cutting the wine-palm the hollow will be filled with a clear yellowish wine, the fermented juice of the tree, and this will continue to secrete daily for twenty days, during which the tree will have yielded some gallons of wine. I was told that a very large grove of these trees was cut down by the Government near Granada, on account of the excesses of the Indians, who used to assemble there on their festivals, and get drunk on the palm-wine. The Indians of Nicaragua, when the Spaniards first came amongst them, objected to the preaching of the padres against intemperance. They said "getting drunk did no man any harm."

The manufacture of aguardiente is a Government monopoly, which is farmed out to contractors. The

NATIVE STILL.

contracts are always given to the political supporters of the party in power.

There are many private illegal stills in the mountains. They are generally amongst thick forest, near a small brook, with some dense brushwood close at hand, for the distiller to slip into if any Government officers should come up. One day, when rambling in the woods near Santo Domingo, I came across one of these "sly grog" manufactories. The apparatus was very simple. It consisted of two of the common earthenware pots of the country, one on the top of the other, the top one having had the bottom taken out and luted to the lower one with clay. This was put on a fire with the fermented liquor. The spirit condensed against the flat bottom of a tin dish that covered the top vessel, and into which cold water was poured, and fell in drops on to a board, that conducted it into a long wooden tube, from which it dropped directly into bottles.

Matagalpa does not rise above the dulness of other Nicaraguan towns; and there is a stagnation about it, and utter absence of aim or effort in the people, that are most distressing to a foreigner used to the bustle, business, and diversions of European cities. A few women washing in the river, or making tortillas or cigars in the houses, was all I saw going on in the way of work. The men, as usual, lolled about in hammocks, smoking incessantly. A few houses were in process of building, or, rather, were standing half finished. Now and then, a little is done to them; and so they take months and years to finish; and men will show you, with the greatest complacency, a half-built house on which nothing has been done for two years, telling you they are so busy with it that they cannot undertake anything else. There are no libraries, theatres, nor concert-rooms : no public meetings nor lectures. Newspapers do not circulate amongst the people, nor books of any kind. I never saw a native reading, in the central provinces, excepting the lawyers turning over their law books, or some of the functionaries in the towns looking up the Government gazette, or children at their lessons. Night sets in at six o'clock. A single dim dip candle is then lighted, in the better houses, set up high, so as to shed a weak, flickering light over the whole room, not sufficient to read by. The natives sit about and gossip till between eight and nine, then lie down to sleep.

A single billiard-table, in a dimly-lighted room, at which three or four play all the evening, until the closing hour, at nine, and a dozen others sit round the walls on benches; a gambling room, licensed by the Government, where only the smallest sums are staked; cock-fighting on Sundays; a feast day; and perhaps a bull-fight once or twice a year; private gambling carried on to a considerable extent by the higher classes, and aguardiente-drinking by the lower, complete the list of Nicaraguan diversions.

On entering the Matagalpa district, we had found the roads dry and dusty; and we now learnt that whilst at Santo Domingo the season had been unusually wet, near Matagalpa it had been so dry that the maize crops were suffering greatly from the drought. We had been travelling nearly north-west, and were getting gradually further and further away from the Atlantic, into a region where the north-east trade wind, having to travel over a greater stretch of land, gets drained of its moisture.

Our mules and horse were completely tired out; and we expected to have been able, without difficulty, to hire fresh animals to take us on to Ocotal in Segovia; but we were disappointed. We lost the afternoon by depending upon a man who undertook to get us some. He went away, saying he was going after them. Hour after hour passed, and he did not return. We went to his house; and his wife told us that he was getting the mules for us. Night set in, and still he came not. At last, about nine o'clock, we found him at the billiard-room. He said he thought, when he did not return, we would take it for granted that he had not been able to find the mules. I believe he had never been further than the billiard-saloon looking for them. These people get through the days with such *ennui* and difficulty, that they have no idea of people economising time. A story is told about them which, whether true or not, illustrates this. When the steamboats were first put on the Lake of Nicaragua, the natives complained that they were charged as much as they were in the bungoes, although they got sometimes a week's sailing in the latter, and only one day in the steamboat. We were in a dilemma about mules. I wished to push on, as I found the journey was a longer one than I expected when I set out; and it was important that I should get back to the mines by the end of the month. At last, our host offered us mules to take us as far as Jinotega, charging us three times as much as was usual; and we determined to go on there, and seek animals to continue our journey. We got our own mules put into a good portrero of Pará grass just below the town, resisting our host's invitation to leave them with him, fearing he might use them instead of feeding them. He had to send out to his hacienda for the fresh ones; and although he promised them at seven, it was ten o'clock the next day before they arrived; and the delay in waiting for them quickened my appreciation of the laziness and want of punctuality of the people of Matagalpa.

On leaving the town, we crossed the river, and ascended a range on the other side. Here, for the first time, I got amongst pine trees in the tropics; and they

gave a very different aspect to the country from what I
had before seen.   No brushwood grows under them, and
they stand apart at regular intervals, not shouldering
each other, as in the Atlantic forest, where the trees
crowd together, each trying to overtop its neighbour.
No lianas hang from the trees, and, excepting a few
narrow-leaved Tillandsias, no epiphytes nestle on the
branches and trunks.   Below, instead of shrubby palms,
large-leaved heliconias, and curious melastomæ, the
ground was bare and brown from the fallen leaves of
the pines, excepting that in some places light grass had
sprung up; in others the common bracken-fern of
Europe.   All that I thought characteristic of a tropical
forest had disappeared ; and the whistling of the wind
through the pine-tops, which I had not heard for years,
carried me back in imagination amongst the Canadian
forests.   The road was rocky, and to the left rose
mountains of nearly bare cliffs, up which clung strag-
gling pines, reaching to the summits, relieving, but
not concealing, their nakedness.   Clumps of evergreen
oaks were the only other trees ; and these, like the
pines, grew in social groups on the hills.   In the valleys,
the oaks and pines gave place to a variety of trees and
brushwood, different species of acacia being the most
abundant.   Occasionally a tree-cactus appeared, its
curious flattened, kite-shaped joints, covered with
prickles, looking like great leaves, and its stem, formed
of the same, thickened at the bottom into a round fili-
form trunk, not differing much from the trees around,
but in the branches showing all the gradations by which
the flat constricted joints thicken out into stems.   In
some parts, as we travelled on, we found the oak trees

and many of the pines completely draped with hanging festoons of the grey moss-like *Tillandsia usneoides*, or " old man's beard." Not a bough but had a great fringe hanging down, sometimes as much as six feet long, like a grey veil swaying in the breeze, and giving the trees a strange and venerable look. The ride was delightful after the stagnation at Matagalpa : everything was fresh and new to me. The aspect of the country, the trees, shrubs, and flowers, the birds and insects, the aromatic perfume from the pines, claimed my attention every minute.

After four hours' riding across the pine-clad ranges, we reached a gorge leading up to the heights overlooking the valley of Jinotega. The path was along the steep side of this gorge, often along the side of a precipice, where a few logs were laid to prevent the mules going over, but really increasing the danger, for they were old and rotten. Large boulders, imbedded in dark-coloured earth, lay on the steep slopes, and about these grew small herbaceous ferns in the greatest variety and profusion —a very paradise for a fern-collector. In some parts a light green maiden-hair fern covered the ground with its beautifully tender foliage, reminding me of shady banks in the north of England, covered with the equally lovely oak-fern. Every few yards discovered some new species, filling the mind with delight at their beauty and variety. In dryer and more stony places, a pinnatifid club-moss stood up amongst the stones in crisp tufts, like the parsley fern on mountain-sides at home. A black and blue bird (*Cyanocitta melanocyanea*), about the size of a jackdaw, flew in small noisy flocks ; and I noticed a beautiful trogon, with burnished green back, and rose-

coloured breast. The highest points of the ranges enclosing this ravine were covered with pine trees (*Pinus
tenuifolia*); lower down grew evergreen oaks, and lower
still a variety of small trees, shrubs, and herbaceous
plants, reaching to the dry bed of the brook.

After a steep and rocky ascent, we reached the top of
the range, and before us lay the upper end of the valley
of Jinotega. Here it was very narrow, hemmed in by
rocky ranges capped with pine forests. Descending the
steep and rocky slope, we soon left the pines and oaks
above us, and came down on a narrow alluvial flat,

NATIVE PLOUGH.

gradually widening out as we proceeded down the valley.
On each side of the road were fields of maize, suffering
greatly from the drought. The soil was a fine deep, dark
loam, and for the first time in Nicaragua I found they
ploughed their land, and made permanent fences. The
plough was a primitive implement, not unlike some of
those still in use in parts of Spain. It was entirely of
wood, excepting that the point was shod with an iron
plate. Many of the fences were hedges, amongst which
grew the lovely creeper (*Antigonon leptopus*), with festoons of pink and rose-coloured flowers. The Indian

and Mestizo girls bind it in their hair, and call it "la vegessima," "the beautiful." It does not wither for some time after being cut, and so is very suitable for garlands and bouquets. It has been carried to Grey-town and the West Indies; and wherever it flourishes, it is a great favourite.

About a mile down the valley we reached the small town of Jinotega, and put up at the estanco kept by a very polite and dignified elderly gentleman, who, in the customary phrase of the country, placed himself, his house, and all he possessed, at our service. His wife, a bustling young woman, not more than half the age of her husband, set to work at once to get our dinner ready. There were several women-servants and many children about the house. It was kept cleaner than is usual in Nicaragua, and I noticed in the yard behind that some attempt at drainage had been made. Our host appeared to be in comfortable circumstances. Outside the town he had a small farm where he grew maize and wheat. He complained greatly of the drought, and said it had never occurred before in his recollection that the maize had failed in Jinotega for want of rain. He found us a man who promised to supply us with mules or horses to take us to Ocotal, but as they had to be brought up from the "Campos" or plains he could not let us have them early, and it was ten o'clock the next day before we started again.

Whilst waiting for the mules we strolled around the town. In the centre most of the houses are substantially built and tiled; on the outskirts there are small grass-thatched huts with high-pitched roofs. Wheat, maize, potatoes, and beans are the principal things grown.

Many of the people have light sandy-coloured hair and blue eyes, and I thought at first they might be the off-spring of a number of Americans that settled in Jino-tega during the civil war in the States, but afterwards abandoned the place. I found, however, some elderly people with the same distinctive marks of ancestry other than the Spaniards, Indians, or Negroes, and I am in-clined to believe that on the breaking up of the bands of buccaneers by Morgan, at the end of the seventeenth century, many of them found a refuge up the Rio Grande and Rio Wanks. They were well acquainted with these rivers, and made many forays up them to harry the Spanish settlements on the Pacific slope. In 1688 a body of about three hundred French and English pirates abandoned their ships in the Gulf of Fonseca, forced their way across the country, and descended the Rio Wanks to the Atlantic. The fair-haired and blue-eyed natives of Matagalpa and Segovia are probably the descendants of the outlaws who made these provinces their highway from one ocean to another.

Jinotega is pleasantly situated, and has many advan-tages over other Nicaraguan towns. The climate is temperate and moderately dry, the land very fertile. Pine trees on the surrounding ranges furnish fuel and light. Pasture is abundant; for two miles below the town the valley opens out into wide "campos" covered with grass, on which a large number of horses, cattle, and mules are reared.

Our road lay down the valley. On the sides of the enclosing ranges there were many cultivated patches, and we saw whole families, men, women, and children, weed-ing amongst the maize. A few showers had fallen during

Q

the night and given them some hopes of saving their crops. We passed a village called Apanás and then struck across the plains, and on the other side reached low flat-topped ranges covered with small trees and brushwood, amongst which were many clearings well fenced and planted with maize. Passing over an undulating country, the hills covered with oak forests, the lowlands well grassed, we reached about two o'clock San Rafael, a small town that has used up all its houses in forming the plaza in front of a barn-like church. As usual, the half-breed population were sunk in idleness and poverty.

We stopped at one of the houses to get a drink of "tiste," and were visited by a fussy little man who told us that he was secretary to the judge and keeper of the "estanco," and in fact the ruling power in the town, which he placed at our disposal. We, however, wanted nothing but our "tiste," and to get some information about a cave we had heard was in the neighbourhood. Our friend knew all about it, and got a boy to show us the way for a couple of dimes. Under his guidance we crossed a brook, and passing through a pine forest soon reached the cave, which was on the side of the precipitous bank of a small stream. It was only a small one, extending for about twenty feet back, hollowed out of a sandy conglomerate, probably by the action of the brook when it ran at a higher level. I dug a little into the floor, but had not time to do much, and found nothing. There were signs of its having been recently occupied, the walls and roof were blackened with smoke, and numerous shells of the common fresh-water melania were lying about. We were told that the Indians when travelling used it, and that during the last revolution the inhabitants of San Rafael hid their valuables in it, though what they consisted of I am at a loss to say.

On leaving the cave our guide put us on the wrong road, and we did not discover the mistake until we had travelled a couple of miles. We then arrived at some huts in the pine forest, where we were told that the road to Ocotal was half a mile distant, across a stream and a high steep range opposite. We had either to return to San Rafael to take the right road or to cross the range. The latter looked rather formidable, but we determined to try it. It was very steep and rocky, but amongst the pines there was no underwood, so, after some stumbling and slipping, our beasts managed to scramble to the top, and we soon after regained the road.

We now travelled over steep ranges, composed of great moraine-like heaps of clay, with large angular boulders. Pine and oak trees covered the heights, shrouded with long fringes and festoons of the moss-like Tillandsia. Many epiphytes grew on the oaks, amongst which the mottled yellow flower of an orchid hung down in spikes six feet long.

Five miles after regaining the road we reached the top of a high range of hills, and found a single hut on the summit. Night was coming on, it was raining, and we were told that there was a very bad road before us over mountains, and no other house for three leagues. We determined to stay at the hut, although the prospect of our night's entertainment was a most cheerless one. The hut was about twenty feet square, with a small attached shed for a kitchen. The floor was the natural earth, littered with corn husks and other refuse.

There was not a bit of furniture, excepting some rough
sleeping-places made of hides stretched over poles.
There was not a stool nor even a log of wood to sit
down upon. In this miserable hut dwelt three families, consisting of nine individuals; men, women, and
children.

The land around appeared to be poor. A patch of
the forest in front of the house, sloping down the side
of a steep valley, had been cleared, and planted with
maize and wheat. We were told that there were a few
other houses down this valley. The people in the hut
seemed miserably poor. I said to Velasquez that they
must have been born on the settlement, as I could not
imagine any one coming from outside the mountains to
live at such a spot, and on inquiry we found that every
one was a native, born within a mile of the hut. It
was perhaps bleaker than usual that evening, a continuous rain was falling, and a high wind whistling
through the pine-tops. Pigs, dogs, and fowls were
constantly in one's way, and the only cheering sign
was the bright blaze and fragrant smell of the burning
pine splinters. I asked one of the men if he preferred
this place to Jinotega, where the fertile slopes and
grassy plains had so pleased our eyes. He answered
he did, the air was fresher and there was less fever.

They made for us some tortillas, and we had tea with
us. The only ingenious thing about the place was a
sort of stove, dome-shaped, made of clay, with two
holes through the top like a cooking-stove, on which
they put their earthenware cooking vessels. I turned
into my hammock early, with all my clothes and my
boots on, and my coat buttoned tightly round me,

as the bleak wind found many a crevice to whistle through, and the open network of the hammock, agreeable enough in the warm lowlands, was too slight a protection against the cold of the mountains. A few poles placed across the doorway partially closed it, but some of the smallest pigs got through, and were rooting and grunting amongst our baggage all night.

As soon as daylight broke next morning we were up, stiff, chilled, and cramped, and got some hot coffee made, which warmed us a little. We then had a better look round than we had had the night before. It was a most desolate spot, with scarcely any grass; and a poor half-starved horse came up to get a small feed of maize.

The people of the mountain regions of Europe cannot, if they would, take up land in the fertile lowlands, as they are already occupied, but in the central provinces of Nicaragua the greater part of the land is unappropriated, and these people might, if they liked, make their homesteads where, with one-half the labour they spend on their barren mountain ridge, they might live in abundance. But they have been born and bred where they live, and knowing how strong is the force of custom and how attached the Indians are to their homes, I do not wonder that they stay from generation to generation on this bleak range. I can imagine that if removed to the lowlands they would sigh for their mountain home, to smell the fragrance of the pine trees, and to hear once more the wind whistling through their branches. I have already noticed how the Indians cling generation after generation to the same spot, even when a short removal would be manifestly to their advantage. I fear there is a more ignoble reason that has as much to do with this as their love of home, their confirmed and innate laziness. They shrink from any labour that they are not forced to undertake. As an instance, no one during at least two generations that the house had been occupied had brought in even a log of wood for a seat, and a table would, I fancy, be beyond their wildest dreams of comfort. An Avocado tree grew before their door, the only fruit tree to be seen, and it was nearly destroyed by being deeply cut into. I asked why they had injured it, and they said they fired at it as a target, and, lead being scarce, they dug out the bullets with their knives; yet within thirty paces of their hut there were plenty of pine trees that would have done equally well as a target, but then they would have had to walk a few yards from their door.

How was such a spot first chosen for settlement? All the names of the places around are Indian, and probably in the old times when there was continual warfare amongst the tribes, the remnants of one, conquered and nearly extirpated, fled to the mountains, and occupied a locality from necessity and for safety that they would not otherwise have chosen. Afterwards when a new generation arose they looked on the pine-clad hills as their home and birthright.

CHAPTER XIV.

BIDDING adieu to our hosts, we mounted our mules and
descended the ridge on which their hut is built. The
range was very steep, and fully 1200 feet high, composed entirely of boulder clay. This clay was of a
brown colour, and full of angular and subangular blocks
of stone of all sizes up to nine feet in diameter. The
hill on the slope that we descended was covered with a
forest resembling that around Santo Domingo, though
the trees were not so large ; but tree-ferns, palms,
lianas, and broad - leaved Heliconiæ and Melastomæ
were again abundant. In these forests, I was told, the
" Quesal," the royal bird of the Aztecs (*Trogon resplen-
dens*), is sometimes found.

After descending about 1000 feet, we issued from
the forest and passed over well - grassed savannahs

surrounded by high ranges, on the eastern slopes of which were forests of pine-trees. The ground was entirely composed of boulder clay, and not until we had travelled about five miles did we see any rock *in situ*. This boulder clay had extended all the way from San Rafael, and ranges of hills appeared to be composed entirely of it. The angular and subangular stones that it contained were an irregular mixture of different varieties of trap, conglomerate, and schistose rocks. In the northern states of America such appearances would be unhesitatingly ascribed to the action of ice, but I was at the time unprepared to believe that the glacial period could have left such a memorial of its existence within the tropics, at no greater elevation above the sea than 3000 feet.

Riding on without stopping, we passed through Yales, a small village of scattered huts, and reached a river flowing north through a fine alluvial plain almost uninhabited. After crossing the river three times, we turned off to the north-west, and passed over low grassy ranges with scattered pine-trees, and in the hollows a few clearings for growing maize, wheat, and beans. At noon we halted for an hour to let our mules feed on a small alluvial flat, for they had had nothing to eat the night before on the bleak mountain summit.

Continuing our journey, we arrived at Daraily, where was a fine large clearing, with stone walls and a sugar-mill. The house was about half a mile from the road, at the foot of a hill covered with scattered pine-trees, forming a fine background to the scene. The farm was well cultivated, and kept clean from weeds. Altogether the scene was a most unusual one for the central pro-

vinces of Nicaragua, and reflected great credit on the
proprietor, Don Estevan Espinosa.   Had Nicaragua
many such sons they would soon change the face of
the country, and turn many a wilderness into a fruitful
garden.

Passing over a stony range, we descended by a steep
pass into the valley of the Estelý, and followed it down
to the westward across low dry hills with prickly bushes
and scrub.   About five o'clock we reached an extensive
plain, covered with prickly trees and shrubs, and pressed
on to get to the village of Palacaguina, where we proposed to pass the night.   There were many paths leading
across the plain, and there was no person to be seen to
direct us which to take; whilst the scrubby trees inter-
rupted our view in every direction.   Rito had once
before been in the neighbourhood, and thought he knew
the way, so we submitted ourselves to his guidance; but,
as it proved, he took a path which led us past, instead
of to, the town.   Night set in as we were pushing across
dry weed-covered hills, destitute of grass or water, every
minute expecting to meet some one who could tell us
about the road.   Rito was still confident that he was
right, although both Velasquez and myself had concluded
we must have got on the wrong road.   The only animal
we met with was a black and white skunk, with a young
one following it.   The mother ran too fast up a rocky
slope for the young one, which was left behind, and
came towards us.   It was very pretty, with its snow-
white bushy tail laid over its black back.   We were, however, afraid to touch it, fearing that, young as it was, it
might have a supply of that fœtid fluid that its kind
discharge with too sure an aim at any assailant.   The

skunks move slowly about, and their large white tails render them very conspicuous. Their formidable means of defence makes for them the obscure colouration of other dusk-roaming mammals unnecessary, as they do not need concealment.

Hour after hour passed, and we reached no house, nor met any one on the road; and at last, about nine o'clock, we determined to stop at a spot where there was a little grass, but no water, as the poor jaded mules had been ridden since daylight, excepting for an hour at midday. We spread our waterproof sheet from the branch of a tree, and lay down dinnerless and supperless, having had nothing but a little sweet bread and native cheese all day; we were now too thirsty to eat even that. Hearing some frogs croaking in the distance, Velasquez went away in the direction from whence the sound came, hoping to find some water: but there was none, the frogs being in damp cracks in the ground. About eleven we heard the noise of men talking; and holloaing to them, our shouts were returned. We ran across the plain, through the bushes, and found two Indians, who were returning from some plantations of maize to their home, several miles distant. Both were nearly naked, the youngest having only a loin-cloth on. When talking to us, they shouted as if we were many yards distant; and as soon as one began to answer a question, the other went on repeating, in a higher key, what the first said.

They told us that we had come two leagues past Palacaguina, and were on the road to a small town called Pueblo Nuevo, and directed us how we should find the right track in the morning for continuing our journey to Ocotal. They were highly amused at our

misadventure, and laughed and talked to each other
about it. Rito also laughed much at the mistake he
had made, and though disposed to be angry at his
obstinacy in bringing us several miles out of our course,
we knew that he had done his best. All the native
servants, when they make a mistake, or do any damage
accidentally, treat it as a joke ; and it is best, under
such circumstances, to be good-humoured with them, as,
if reproved, they are very likely to turn sulky, and do
some more damage. They are independent, and care
nothing about being discharged, as any one can live
in Nicaragua without working much. Rito was an
active, merry fellow, and might every now and then be
observed laughing to himself; if asked what it was
about, he was sure to answer that he was thinking
about some little accident that had occurred. I once,
when trying to loop up the side of my hammock, fell
out of it, and next day Rito could not control himself,
but was continually exploding in a burst of laughter ;
and for days afterwards any allusion to it would set
him into convulsions. When we returned to Santo
Domingo, it was one of his stock stories. He used to
say he wanted very much to come to my assistance,
but could not for laughing.

Next morning we started at daylight, and soon found
the path the Indians had told us about, which took us
to a place called Jamailý (pronounced Hamerlee), where
was an extensive indigo plantation. About 100 men
were employed weeding and clearing the ground. No
fences are required for indigo growing, as neither horses
nor cattle will eat the plant. A mile beyond Jamailý
we saw, amongst some bushes, a poor-looking, grass-

thatched hut, with the sides made of an open work of
branches and leaves.   We went up to it to try to buy
something to eat, but found only three children in it;
the oldest, a very dirty little girl of about five years of
age, with a piece of cloth worn like a shawl, her only
clothing, and the two younger quite naked.   A little
boy, about three years old, was very talkative, and
prattled away all the time we were there.   He said that
some people living near had four cows, but that they
had none; that his father shot deer and sold their
skins, and that two days before he fired at a rock,
thinking it was a deer.

We heated some water and made tea, and with some
sweet bread and native cheese managed to allay our
hunger, the little boy amusing us all the time with
his prattle.   Pointing to a mangy dog lying on the
floor covered with some old rags, he said it had fever,
and that at night it threw off the rags, and the fleas got
at it, but that during the day he kept it well covered
up.   I was amused with the little fellow, who in that
squalid hut, without a scrap of clothing, and fed with
the coarsest food, was as happy as, if not happier than
any child I had seen.   By-and-by an elder girl came
along from some other hut, and told us that the man
was away hunting for deer, and that his wife had gone
to her mother's, about a mile distant.   She also informed
us that the hunter had not a gun of his own, but gave
half the meat of the deer he killed for the loan of one.
He had a trained ox, which, as soon as it saw a deer,
commenced eating, and walking gradually towards it;
whilst the man followed, concealed, and thus got within
distance to shoot it.   He generally got two when he

went out, and sold the hides for twenty cents per
pound, the skins averaging five pounds' weight each.
It is astonishing that deer should be so little afraid of
man as they are, after having been objects of chase for
probably thousands of years. Sometimes when one is
encountered in the forest it will stand within twenty
yards stupidly gazing at a man, or perhaps striking
the ground impatiently with its forefoot, and often
waiting long enough for an unloaded gun to be charged.
The woman of the house came in before we left, and
we paid her for the use of her fire. She did not know
how old her children were, and Velasquez told me that
very few of the lower classes in Nicaragua knew either
their own age or that of their children.

The soil about here, for many leagues, was full of
small angular fragments of white quartz. They had
attracted my attention the day before, and I now found
they were derived from thick beds of conglomerate, the
decomposition of which released the fragments of quartz,
of which it was mainly composed. Many of these beds
of conglomerate were inclined at high angles. I noticed
also some contorted, highly-inclined talcose schists, full
of small quartz veins, generally running between the
laminæ of the schists. Probably the conglomerates had
been produced by the wearing down of these schists.

We passed through two Indian towns—the first
Yalaguina, the second Totagalpa. At the last the
church looked very clean and pretty, and was ornamented with a single square tower, built of rough stones,
and covered with white cement that glistened like
marble at a short distance. The peculiar shining appearance of the cement is due to the admixture of a fine

black sand in the whitewash used. The cement itself is strong and durable, and its manufacture was known to the Indians long before the advent of the Spaniards. Bernal Diaz de Castillo, one of the followers of Cortez, often speaks, in his history, of the houses built of stone and lime, and covered with cement. On their march to Mexico, when they arrived at Cempoal, he says, " Our advanced guard having gone to the great square, the buildings of which had been recently plastered and whitewashed, in which art the people are very expert, one of our horsemen was so struck with the splendour of their appearance in the sun that he came back in full speed to Cortez to tell him that the walls of the houses were of silver." We also learn from the same historian that the city of Cholula " had at that time above 100 lofty white towers, which were the temples of their idols."

Between Yalaguina and Totagalpa there was much of the conglomerate rock that I have already mentioned. Over this the soil was dry and stony, and filled with small quartz pebbles. The vegetation was scanty, principally thorny shrubs and trees. Amongst the former the Pinuela, a plant closely allied to the pine-apple, and used to make fences, was the most abundant. In the alluvial flats were many fine patches of maize looking extremely well, for in Segovia the crops had not been injured by drought. The low hills were very sandy and dry, and the beds of the brooks waterless, but a little beyond Totagalpa we found a small running stream, and stopped an hour to refresh our mules and to eat some provisions we had bought at Yalaguina.

All through Segovia the country is divided into townships, embracing an area of from twenty to twenty-five square leagues. Over each of these there is an alcalde, living in the small central town, and elected by the inhabitants of the townships. The boundaries are marked by heaps of stones surmounted by wooden crosses, set up on the roads leading from one town to another.

After riding a few more leagues over rocky hills with scanty vegetation, we came in sight, from the top of one of the ranges, of the town of Ocotal, the capital of Segovia, with its white walls and red-tiled roofs. Descending a long rocky slope we forded one of the affluents of the Rio Wanks, and half a mile further on arrived at the town, situated on a dry plain. A heavy thunderstorm broke over us as we entered the town, and the rain came down in torrents whilst we were searching for a house to put up at. In answer to our inquiries we were directed to the best house in the town. It was situated at the corner of the plaza, had lofty well-built walls, large doors and gateway, clean tiled floors, and in the courtyard behind a pretty flower garden, with a tank to hold rain water. We were received by two elderly ladies, the sisters of the owner Don Pedro, who made us welcome in a stately sort of way, and got some dinner prepared, consisting of beans, tortillas, avocados, and coffee.

We learnt that the present town was about seventy years old and not very flourishing, as the land around was dry and sterile. The old capital of Segovia was situated five leagues further down the river, where the land around was fertile. But the buccaneers came up the river in their boats and sacked the town, and the site was deserted for one more difficult of access, the river being much shallower and obstructed by rapids higher up. At the site of the old town the church still stands, but only a few poor negroes live there now. Two branches of the river unite a little below the present town, and following it down for about four days' journey a place named Cocos is reached, which is the furthest settlement of the Spaniards towards the Atlantic. To this point large bungoes come up the river, and Don Pedro had been very wishful to get it opened out above for navigation, but had not succeeded.

There were very few men to be hired at Ocotal, and we determined to go on to Depilto, a small mining town near the Honduras boundary, where we were assured there were plenty to be obtained. We had only engaged the mules to come as far as Ocotal, and had great difficulty in getting others to go on with. I think the people at first were afraid that we might cross the boundary and never return. We afterwards learnt that robberies of mules often took place; some rogues making a business of stealing mules out of Honduras, bringing them into Nicaragua, selling them, and stealing others to return with. There were, however, some people in Ocotal who had worked at the mines and knew us, and when this information spread we had the offer of several animals. If we had known the cause of the reluctance of the people to let us have mules at first, we should easily have got over the difficulty by leaving the value of the animals in the hands of some responsible person, but the owners had made all sorts of excuses for not lending them, and we had not suspected the true cause. We had been travelling continually for nine days, and looked more like brigands than honest travellers, and the good easy-going people of Ocotal had their suspicions about us.

As I have said, when satisfied of our good faith, the mule owners soon offered us the use of their beasts, and next morning Velasquez and I started at seven o'clock on two fine fresh mules and rode merrily up the valley of the Depilto. The river rises in the high ranges that form the boundary between Honduras and Nicaragua, and running down past Depilto joins the Ocotal river a little below the capital. Our road lay up the valley close to the river, which we crossed and recrossed several times. The vegetation was scanty, but the morning was a lovely one after the thunderstorm of the night before, and we greatly enjoyed our ride. We did not see many birds, a pretty hawk that I shot being the most noticeable. Hawks of various kinds are very abundant in the tropics, and if the small birds had to personify death, they would certainly represent him as one, for this is the form in which he must generally appear to them. Towards evening the hawk glides noiselessly along and alights on a bough, near where he hears the small birds twittering amongst the bushes. Perhaps they see him and are quiet for a little, but he sits motionless as the sphinx, and they soon get over their fear and resume their play or feeding. Then suddenly a dark mass swoops down and rises again. It is the hawk, with a small bird grasped in his strong talons, gasping out its last breath. Its comrades are terror-struck for a moment and dash madly into the thickets, but soon forget their fear. They chirp to each other, the scattered birds reunite; there is a fluttering and twittering, a rearranging of

R

mates, then again songs, feeding, love, jealousy, and bickerings.

The banks of the river were sandy and sterile, and the soil contained much small quartz. The bed rock was a talcose schist near to Ocotal, but higher up the river it changed to gneissoid and quartz rocks, the latter in hard and massive beds. As we ascended the valley, the ranges bounding it got higher and steeper, the soil more sandy and barren, with scattered pine trees growing amongst the rocks. Great, bare, rounded masses of hard quartzite protruded through the scanty soil, and in the river were enormous boulders of granite-like gneiss.

Depilto is only nine miles from Ocotal, but we took three hours to reach it, as I made many stoppages to examine the rocks and to catch fleet-limbed speckled tiger-beetles on the sandy roads. The little town was not half populated, the silver-mines had been closed for some time, most of the houses were empty, and the people still clinging about the place seemed to have nothing to do, for the land is too barren for cultivation. We made known our requirements for labourers, and were assured that plenty would be glad to go to Santo Domingo. They would not, however, bind themselves there, but preferred to go down untrammelled with any conditions about pay or work, and I may anticipate here by saying that the result of our visit was very satisfactory, numbers of workmen having been obtained for the mines.

After getting some breakfast at a house that seemed to be the hotel of Depilto, we set out to visit a silver-mine named "El Coquimba." We had to ascend a high range opposite the town, and found riding over the steep bare exposures of quartz rock so difficult and dangerous

that about half way up we tied our mules to some young
pine trees and proceeded on foot. The mine was abandoned, and the shafts and levels were closed by falls
of rock. Some of the ore, sulphide of silver, was lying
at the mouth of one of the old shafts. Our guide told us
that the lode was two feet wide. Both it and the containing rock was very hard, and the miners had also water
to contend against. I do not think from what I saw that
the mine could be made to pay on a large scale, though
next the surface small remunerative deposits of ore had
been found. In depth the hardness of the rocks would
make the sinking of shafts and driving of levels, the
" dead work " of the miners, very costly.

We started on our return down the valley at three
o'clock, and took particular note of the succession of
the rocks, as I had become much interested in finding
these quartz and gneissoid beds, which I had no doubt
were the same Laurentian rocks that I had seen in
Canada and Brazil—the very backbone of the continent,
ribbing America from Patagonia to the Canadas—the
fundamental gneiss which is covered, in other parts of
Central America that I had visited, by strata of much
more recent origin. Going down the valley of the
Depilto the massive beds of quartz and gneiss are soon
succeeded by overlying, highly inclined, and contorted
schists, and as far as where the road from Ocotal to
Totagalpa crosses the river, the exposures of bed rock
were invariably these contorted schists, with many small
veins of quartz running between the laminæ of the rock.
On the banks of the river, from about a mile below
Depilto, unstratified beds of gravel are exposed in
numerous natural sections. These beds deepen as the

river is descended, until at Ocotal they reach a thickness
of between two and three hundred feet, and the undulating plain on which Ocotal is built is seen in sections
near the river to be composed entirely of them.   These
unstratified deposits consist mostly of quartz sand with
numerous angular and subangular blocks of quartz and
talcose schist.   Many of the boulders are very large, and
in some parts great numbers have been accumulated in
the bed of the river by the washing away of the smaller
stones and sand.   Some of these huge boulders were
fifteen feet across, the largest of them lying in the bed of
the river two miles below Depilto.   Most of them were
of the Depilto quartz rock and gneiss, and I saw many in
the unstratified gravel near Ocotal fully eight miles from
their parent rock.   Near Ocotal this unstratified formation is nearly level, excepting where worn into deep
gulches by the existing streams.   The river has cut
through it to a depth of over two hundred feet, and
there are high precipices of it on both sides, similar to
those near streams in the North of England that cut
through thick beds of boulder clay.

The evidences of glacial action between Depilto and
Ocotal were, with one exception, as clear as in any Welsh
or Highland valley.   There were the same rounded and
smoothed rock surfaces, the same moraine-like accumu-
lations of unstratified sand and gravel, the same transported boulders that could be traced to their parent
rocks several miles distant.   The single exception was,
I am convinced, one of observation and not one of fact,
viz., I saw no glacial scratches on the rocks; but geologists know how rare these are on natural exposures in
some districts that have certainly been glaciated, and

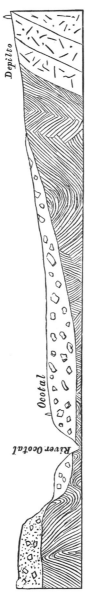

SECTION OF STRATA

between Depilto and the hill three miles south-west of Ocotal.

Gravel with boulders of trap
and conglomerate.

Contorted schists.

Gravel with boulders of gneiss
and quartz rock.

Quartz rock and gneiss.

will not be surprised that in a hurried visit of only a few hours I should not have discovered any. Glacial scratches are seldom preserved on rock surfaces exposed to the action of the elements. Even in Nova Scotia, where scratches and grooves are met with wherever the rock surface has been recently laid bare, I do not remember having ever seen any on natural exposures. It is only where protected by a covering of clay or gravel from the action of the elements, that they have been preserved through the ages that have passed since the glacial epoch, and as I did not see any rock surfaces near Depilto that had been recently bared, it is not surprising that, notwithstanding the other proofs of glacial action, I should not have seen any ice scratches or grooves.

I could no longer withstand the evidence that had been gradually accumulating of the presence of large glaciers in Central America during the glacial period, and these, once admitted, afforded me a solution of many phenomena that had before been inexplicable. The immense ridges of boulder clay between San Rafael and Yales, the long hog-backed hills near Tablason, the great transported boulders two leagues beyond Libertad on the Juigalpa road, and the scarcity of alluvial gold in the valleys of Santo Domingo, could all be easily explained on the supposition that the ice of the glacial period was not confined to extra-tropical lands, but in Central America covered all the higher ranges, and descended in great glaciers to at least as low as the line of country now standing at two thousand feet above the sea.

In my description of the mines of Santo Domingo I have only briefly alluded to the scarcity of alluvial gold in the valleys. It may be correlated with a similar scarcity in the glaciated valleys of Nova Scotia and North Wales, in the neighbourhood of auriferous quartz veins, and is probably due to the same cause. Glacier ice scoops out all the contents of the valleys, and in deepening them does not sort the materials like running water or the action of the waves upon the sea coast. I have in another place * shown that in Nova Scotia, in the neighbourhood of rich auriferous quartz veins that have been greatly denuded, grain gold is only sparingly disseminated throughout the drifts of the valleys, whilst in Australia every auriferous quartz vein has been the source of an alluvial deposit of grain gold, produced by the denudation and sorting action of running water. When the denuding agent was water, the rocks were worn away, and the heavier gold left behind at the bottom of the alluvial deposits ; but when the denuding agent was glacier ice the stony masses and their metallic contents were carried away, or mingled together in the unassorted moraines.

That the transportation of boulders in Nicaragua was due to glaciers, and not to floating icebergs, may be argued on zoological grounds. The transported boulders, near Ocotal, are about three thousand feet above the sea, those near Libertad about two thousand feet. The low pass between the Atlantic and the Pacific oceans, through the valley of the San Juan and the Lake of Nicaragua, is less than two hundred feet above the sea,† and to allow for the flotation of icebergs at

* "The Glacial Period in North America," by Thos. Belt. Published in Trans. Nova Scotian Institute of Natural Science, 1886, p. 93.
† See ante, p. 35.

the lower of the two places named, a channel of more
than eighteen hundred feet in depth would have connected the two oceans. This supposition is negatived
by the fact that the mollusca on the two coasts, separated by the narrow Isthmus of Darien, are almost
entirely distinct, whilst we know that since the glacial
period there has been little change in the molluscan
fauna, nearly, if not all, the shells found in glacial
deposits still existing in neighbouring seas. In the
Caribbean province, which includes the Gulf of Mexico,
the West Indian islands, and the eastern coast of South
America as far as Rio de Janeiro, the number of marine
shells is estimated by Professor C. B. Adams at not
less than 1500 species. From the Panamic province,
which, on the western coast of America, extends from
the Gulf of California to Payta in Peru, there has been
catalogued 1341 distinct species of marine molluscs.
Out of this immense number of species, less than fifty
occur on both sides of the narrow Isthmus of Darien.
So remarkably distinct are the two marine faunas, that
most zoologists consider that there has been no
communication in the tropics between the two seas
since the close of the miocene period, whilst the
connection that is supposed to have existed at that
remote epoch, and to account for the distribution of
corals, whilst advocated by Professor Duncan and other
eminent men, is disputed by others equally eminent.
No zoologist of note believes that there has been a
submergence of the land lying between the Pacific
and the Atlantic since the pliocene period, and icebergs
could not have floated without such submergence,
so that, in the cases I have mentioned, the boulders,

if ice-borne, have been carried by glaciers and not by floating ice.

Whilst I thus found evidence of the ice of the glacial period reaching, in the northern hemisphere, to within the tropics; in the southern hemisphere Professor Hartt has found glacial drift extending from Patagonia, all through Brazil to Pernambuco, and Agassiz has even announced the discovery of glacial moraines up to the equator. I have myself seen, near Pernambuco, and in the province of Maranham, in Brazil, a great drift deposit that I believe to be of glacial origin; and I think it highly probable that the evidence that is accumulating will force geologists to the conclusion that the ice of the glacial period was not only more extensive than has been generally supposed, but that it existed at the same time in the northern and southern hemispheres, leaving, at least, on the American continent, only the lower lands of the tropics free from the icy covering.

I shall not enter upon the question of the cause of the cold of the glacial period. It is probably closely connected with the cause of an exactly opposite state of things, the heat of the miocene period, when the beech, the hazel, and the plane, lived and flourished in Spitzbergen, as far north as latitude 78°, and, according to Heer, firs and poplars reached to the North Pole, if there was then land there for them to grow upon. I consider that the great extension of the ice in the glacial period supports the conclusion of Professor Heer, founded on the northern extension of the miocene flora, that these enormous changes of climate cannot be explained by any rearrangement of the relative positions of land and water, and that "we are face to face with a problem whose solution must be attempted and doubtless completed by the astronomer." *

There is another branch of the subject that I cannot so easily leave. It is the answer to the question, What became of the many peculiar tropical American genera of animals and plants, when a great part of the tropics was covered with ice, and the climate of the lower lands much colder than now? For instance, the Heliconii and Morphos are a group of butterflies peculiar to tropical America, containing many distinct genera which, on any theory of descent from a common progenitor, must have originated ages before the glacial period. How is it that such peculiarly tropical groups were not exterminated by the cold of the glacial period, or if able to stand the cold, that they did not spread into temperate regions on the retreat of the ice? I believe the answer is, that there was much extermination during the glacial period, that many species and some genera, as, for instance, the American horse, did not survive it, and that some of the great gaps that now exist in natural history were then made; but that a refuge was found for many species, on lands now below the ocean, that were uncovered by the lowering of the sea caused by the immense quantity of water that was locked up in frozen masses on the land.

Mr. Alfred Tylor considers that the ice cap of the glacial period was the cause of a great reduction of the level of the sea, amounting to at least 600 feet.† But

* I have since discussed this question in the *Quarterly Journal of Science* for October 1874.

† *Geological Magazine*, vol. ix. p. 392.

if we admit that the ice existed in both hemispheres at the same time, we shall have to speculate on a lowering of the level of the sea to at least 1000 feet. We have many facts tending to prove that during the extreme extent of the glacial period the land stood much higher relatively to the sea than it now does. Professor Hartt believes that during the time of the drift, Brazil stood at a much higher level than at present,* and we can, on the supposition of a general lowering of the sea all over the world, account for the distribution of animal life over islands now separated by shallow seas. Thus Mr. Bland, in a paper read before the American Philosophical Society, on "The Geology and Physical Geography of the West Indies, with reference to the distribution of Mollusca," states his opinion that Porto Rico, the Virgins, the Anguilla group, Cuba, the Bahamas, and Hayti, once formed continuous dry land that obtained its land molluscs from Central America, and Mexico. The land molluscs of the islands to the south, on the contrary, from Barbuda and St. Kitt's down to Trinidad, are of two types, one Venezuelan, the other Guianian; the western side of the supposed continuous land, namely, Trinidad, Tobago, Grenada, the Grenadines, St. Vincent, and St. Lucia, belonging to the first type; the eastern side, from Barbados to Antigua, to the second.†

Commenting on Mr. Bland's valuable communication, Mr. Kingsley justly says: " If this be so, a glance at the map will show the vast destruction of tropic land during

---

* "Geology and Physical Geography of Brazil," by Ch. Fred. Hartt, p. 573.

† Quoted in "At Last," by Charles Kingsley, p. 305.

almost the very latest geological epoch; and show, too, how little, in the present imperfect state of our knowledge, we ought to dare any speculations as to the absence of man, as well as of other creatures, on those great lands destroyed. For, to supply the dry land which Mr. Bland's theory needs, we shall have to conceive a junction, reaching over at least five degrees of latitude, between the north of British Guiana and Barbados; and may freely indulge in the dream that the waters of the Orinoco, when they ran over the lowlands of Trinidad, passed east of Tobago, then northward between Barbados and St. Lucia, afterwards turning westward between the latter island and Martinique, and that the mighty estuary—for a great part at least of that line—formed the original barrier which kept the land shells of Venezuela apart from those of Guiana." *

A very similar theory has been propounded by Mr. Wallace to account for the distribution of the faunas of the Malay Archipelago, in his admirable work on the natural history of that region.† Java, Sumatra, and Borneo are separated from each other, and from the continent of Asia, by a shallow sea less than six hundred feet in depth, and must at one time have been connected by continuous land to allow of the elephant and tapir of Sumatra and Borneo, the rhinoceros of Sumatra and Java, and the wild cattle of Borneo and Java, to spread from the continent to these now sea-surrounded lands, as none of these large animals could have passed over the arms of the sea that now separate them. The smaller mammals, the birds, and insects, all illustrate this view,

* Loc. cit., p. 306.
† "The Malay Archipelago," vol. i. p. 11.

almost all the genera found in any of the islands occurring also on the Asiatic continent, and the species being often identical. On the other hand, the fauna of islands to the eastward are more closely connected with Australia, and must at one time have been joined to it by nearly continuous land. Honeysuckers and lories take the place of the woodpeckers, barbets, trogons, and fruit thrushes of the western islands, and the many mammals belonging to Asiatic genera are no more seen.

Mr. Wallace ascribes the present isolation of the islands, and their separation from the adjoining continents, to the submergence of the channels between them caused by the abstraction of matter thrown out by the numerous volcanoes. Looking, however, at the fact that at the time when these islands were probably connected with the continents of Asia on the one side and Australasia on the other, namely, at the close of the pliocene period, England was connected with the continent; Malta, as shown by its fossil elephants, with Africa; the West Indies with Yucatan and Venezuela; it seems to me more probable that the cause was not a local one, but a general lowering of the waters of the ocean all over the world to at least one thousand feet,—produced by the prodigious quantity of water locked up in the frozen masses that covered a great part of both hemispheres.

The wide diffusion of the Malayan dialects over the Pacific, reaching as far as the Sandwich Islands, shows the great extension of that race in former times. On numerous islands in Polynesia there are cyclopean ruins utterly out of keeping with their present size and population. Who can look at the pictures of little Easter

Island, with its gigantic images standing up in unworshipped solitude, without feeling that that insignificant islet could never have supported the race that reared the monuments. But if that and other islands were once hills overlooking peopled lowlands, the sense of incongruity vanishes. We see the images, not gazing gloomily over the ocean that narrowly circles them in, but proudly looking across wide plains peopled by their worshippers, who from their villages and fields behold the gods they adore, and implore their protection and support.

Was the fabled Atlantis really a myth, or was it that great continent in the Atlantic laid bare by the lowering of the ocean, on which the present West Indian islands were mountains, rising high above the level and fertile plains that are now covered by the sea? Obscurely the accounts of it have come down to us from the dim past, but there is a remarkable coincidence between the traditions that have been handed down on the two sides of the Atlantic.

In a fragment of the works of Theopompus, who lived in the fourth century before the Christian era, is an account of a conversation between Silenus and Midas, the king of Phrygia, in which the former tells the king that Europe, Asia, and Africa were surrounded by the sea, but that beyond them was an island of immense size, in which were many great cities, and nations with laws and customs very different from theirs. Plato, in his " Timæus and Critias," relates that Solon was told by a priest of Sais, from the sacred inscriptions in the temple, how Solon's country " once opposed a power

which with great arrogance pushed its way into Europe
and Asia from the Atlantic Ocean. Beyond the entrance
which you call the Pillars of Hercules there was an
island larger than Libya and Asia together. From it
navigation passed to the other islands, and from them
to the opposite continent which surrounded that ocean.
On this great Atlantic island there was a powerful and
singular kingdom, whose dominion extended not only
over the whole island, but over many others, and parts
of the continent. It ruled also over Libya as far as
Egypt, and over Europe as far as Tyrrhenia. This
kingdom with the whole of its forces united tried to
subjugate in one campaign your country and ours, and
all the country within the strait. At that time, O
Solon, your nation shone out from all others by bravery
and power. It was placed in great danger, but it de-
feated the attacking army, and erected triumphal monuments. But when at a later period earthquakes and
great floods took place, the whole of your united army
was swallowed up during one evil day and one evil
night, and at the same time the island of Atlantis sank
into the sea." Crantor, quoted by Proclus, corroborates
the account by Plato, and says that he found this same
story retained by the priests of Sais, three hundred
years after the period of Solon, and that he was shown
the inscriptions on which it was recorded.

Turning to the western side of the Atlantic, we find
in the "Teo Amoxtli," as translated by the Abbé Brasseur de Bourburg, an account of the overwhelming of a
country by the sea, when thunder and flames came out
of it, and "the mountains were sinking and rising."
Everywhere throughout America there are traditions of

a great catastrophe, in which a whole country was submerged, and only a few people escaped to the mountains; and the Spanish conquerors relate with wonder the accounts they found amongst the Indians of a universal deluge. Amongst the modern Indians the traveller, Catlin, relates that in one hundred and twenty different tribes that he had visited in North, and South, and Central America, " every tribe related, more or less distinctly, their tradition of the deluge, in w֫֗ ᴸ one, or three, or eight persons were saved ab֝ᵧ.   waters on the top of a high mountain." *

If Atlantis were lowlands connecting the West Indian islands with America, the other islands mentioned by Plato may have been the Azores, also greatly increased in extent by the lowering of the ocean; and the overwhelming of this lowland, on the melting of the ice at the close of the glacial period, may be that great catastrophe that is recorded on both sides of the Atlantic, but is more clearly remembered in the traditions of America, because all the highlands there had been covered with ice, and the inhabitants were restricted to those that were overwhelmed by the deluge.

I approached this subject from the side of Natural History. I was driven to look for a refuge for the animals and plants of tropical America during the glacial period, when I found proofs that the land they now occupy was at that time either covered with ice or too cold for genera that can now only live where frost is unknown. I had arrived at the conclusion that they must have inhabited lowlands now submerged, and following up the question, I soon saw that the very

* "Lifted and Subsided Rocks in America," by G. Catlin, p. 182.

accumulation of ice that made their abode impossible provided another for them by the lowering of the sea. Then pursuing the subject still further, I saw that all over the world curious questions concerning the distribution of races of mankind, of animals, and of plants, were rendered more easy of solution on the theory that land was more continuous once than now; that islands now separated were then joined together, and to adjacent continents; and that what are now banks and shoals . . . . the sea were then peopled lowlands.

I have said that during the glacial period, if, as I believe, it was contemporaneous in the two hemispheres, the sea must have stood at least 1000 feet lower than it now does. It may have been much lower than this, but I prefer to err on the safe side. When geologists have mapped out the limits of ancient glacier and continental ice all over the world, it will be possible to calculate the minimum amount of water that was abstracted from the sea; and if by that time hydrographers have shown on their charts the shoals and submerged banks that would be laid dry, fabled Atlantis will rise before our eyes between Europe and America, and in the Pacific the Malay Archipelago will give place to the Malay Continent. Here is a noble inquiry, an unexplored region of research, at the entrance of which I can only stand and point the way for abler and stronger minds; an inquiry that will lead to the knowledge of the lands where dwelt the peoples of the glacial period who lived before the flood.

Vague and visionary as these speculations must seem to many, to others who are acquainted with the enormous glaciation to which America has been subjected they

S

will appear to be based on substantial truths.   The immense accumulation of ice over both poles, reaching far down into the temperate zones, in some meridians encroaching on the tropics, and in Equatorial America certainly all the land, lying 2000 feet above the level of the sea, supporting great glaciers, involve conditions which must have greatly drained the sea.   Lands now submerged must have been uncovered, and on the return of the waters at the close of the glacial period many a peopled lowland must have been overwhelmed in the nearly universal deluge.

CHAPTER XV.

A Nicaraguan criminal—Geology between Ocotal and Totagalpa—Preparations at Totagalpa for their annual festival—Chicha-drinking
—Piety of the Indians—Ancient civilisation of tropical America
—Palacaguina—Hospitality of the Mestizos—Curious custom at
the festival at Condego—Cross range between Segovia and Matagalpa—Sontuli—Birds' nests.

WE got back to Ocotal, from Depilto, before dark, and
made arrangements for setting out on our return to
the mines the next morning. Whilst sitting under the
corridor, looking across the pretty flower-garden at the
glowing western sky, illumined by the last rays of the
setting sun, a poor fettered criminal, holding up by
means of a string the thick chain that bound together
his ankles, came limping along, with a soldier behind
him armed with gun and bayonet. He had been brought
out of prison to beg. In most of the towns of Nicaragua
no food is given to the prisoners, whether convicted, or
merely charged with crime. Those that have no money
to buy food are sent out every day with an armed escort
to beg. The prisoner that hobbled up to me was under
twenty years of age, and had been convicted of murder
and condemned to death. He had appealed against the
sentence to a higher court, but I was told that there
was scarcely any chance of a decision in his favour, and
that he would probably be shot in a day or two. Not-

withstanding his critical position, he was lively and
cheerful, and when I gave him a small piece of silver
was as overjoyed as if he had got news of his reprieve.
Jumping away, his clanking fetters making ghastly
music, he gleefully showed to his guard the coin that
would probably procure him food the few days he had
to live. His wretched appearance, impending fate, and
shocking levity, had chased away the peaceful feelings
with which I had watched the quiet sunset; but as he
hobbled off, night, like a pall, fell over the scene ; the
trembling stars peeped out from the vault of heaven,
and soon a million distant orbs proclaimed that the
world was but a grain of dust in the vast universe, that
the things of earth were but for a moment, and, as a
shadow, would pass away.

Next morning, when we wished to settle up with our
kind entertainers, they absolutely refused to accept any
payment. We had been recommended to the house,
and told that we could pay for what we got ; but we
now learnt that no one was ever refused entertainment,
and that no charge was made. We were total strangers,
nor should I have any opportunity of returning their
hospitality, as I had determined shortly to return to
Europe; but all I could prevail upon them to accept
was a present to a little girl that lived with the ladies,
and of whom they were very fond, calling her "the
daughter of the house." Leaving the hospitable Señoras
Rimirez with many thanks, we started on our return
journey about seven o'clock.

After crossing the river, I noticed boulders of conglomerate in the drift, none of which had occurred in

the valley of Depilto.   The bed rock was still contorted
schists, with many quartz veins.   At the top of a steep
rise, beyond the river, is a small plateau, or level
terrace, fringing the range, formed of a gravelly boulder
deposit ; then another steep ascent led us to a second
higher plateau, like the first, covered with boulders,
lying on the level surface.   The first beds of the quartz-
conglomerate occurred about half-way between Ocotal
and Totagalpa.   Between it and the contorted schists
we passed over some soft, decomposing trap-rocks,
which, both here and elsewhere, appeared to intervene
between these two formations.   Over the whole country
between Ocotal and Totagalpa were spread many large
boulders, great blocks of conglomerate, and of a hard
blue trap-rock that I did· not see *in situ*, lying on the
upturned edges of the schistose rocks.   I should have
liked to have worked out the exact relative positions of
the quartz conglomerate and the contorted schists, for
I have no doubt that a day or two's search amongst the
ravines would have shown many natural sections that
would have thrown great light upon the subject ; but
I had no time to devote to it.   We were hurrying on
every day as far as our mules could carry us, as it was
important that I should get back to the mines before
the end of the month, and I was only able to note down
the exposures that occurred within sight of the road.
These, however, were sufficient to show me that the
gneiss of Depilto was overlain conformably by the
contorted schists ; that the latter were followed by soft
trappean beds, and these by thick beds of quartz conglomerate, apparently derived from the degradation of
the schistose rocks, with their numerous quartz veins.

We reached Totagalpa about eleven o'clock, and
remained there some time engaging labourers. We
stayed at the house of a man who made the common
palm-leaf hats, worn throughout the central provinces
by both men and women. The palm-leaves are first
boiled, then bleached in the sun, split into small strips,
and platted together like straw. It was Sunday, and
most of the people were in town, sitting at the doors of
their huts, or under their verandahs. Nearly all the
inhabitants of Totagalpa are pure Indians, and are
simple and inoffensive people. They sat listening to
three men, one with a whistle, the others with drums,
each striving to make as much noise as possible,
without any attempt at harmony or tune, whilst an
enthusiast in discord kept clanging away at the bells
of the church.

They had no padre of their own, but one occasionally
came over from Somoti, four leagues distant, to celebrate
services, or visit the sick. The next day was the great
feast of Totagalpa, and they were preparing for it. As
we sat under a verandah opposite the church, a procession of the town authorities issued from it, bearing a
table and all the silver and brass ornaments. The
principal officials each carried his stick of office, but
none, excepting the Alcalde, could boast a pair of shoes.
Their looks of importance and gravity showed, however,
that they considered themselves the chief actors in an
important ceremony. The procession slowly traversed
half the round of the plaza, whilst the bells clanged,
the whistle squeaked, and the drummers thumped their
loudest. Stopping at a house at the corner of the
plaza, the officials seated themselves on a bench outside.

Then was brought out to them in bowls, nearly as large
as wash-hand basins, the old Indian drink, " chicha,"
made from fermented corn and sugar. Each man had
one of the great bowls and a napkin ; the latter they
spread over their knees, and rested the bowl on it, taking
long sips every now and then with evident signs of
satisfaction. Little have these people changed from
the times of the Conquest. Pascual de Andagoya,
writing of the people of Nicaragua when they were
first subjugated by Hernandez de Cordova, in 1520,
says, " The whole happiness of the people consists in
drinking the wine they make from maize, which is like
beer, and on this they get as drunk as if it was the
wine of Spain ; and all the festivals they hold are for
the purpose of drinking.*

The cross, candlesticks, and other ornaments were
arranged on a table, and were each carefully and
solemnly washed with hot water. This they do every
year the day before their feast, and it makes the occasion for the procession and chicha-drinking. Most of the
men of the township were gathered around, and in all,
the straight coarse black hair and Indian features were
unmistakable. The chicha-drinking was too long a
business for our patience, and we went over to the church,
where we found a number of the Indian women with
great baskets full of most beautiful and sweet-smelling
flowers, making garlands and bouquets to decorate the
holy images and church. The beautiful flowers were
twined in wreaths, or stuck on prepared stands and
shapes, and their fragrance filled the church. The love

* Hakluyt Society. " Narrative of Pascual de Andagoya." Trans.
by C. R. Markham, p. 34.

of flowers is another beautiful trait of the old Indians that their descendants have not lost. The ancient Mexicans decorated their altars and temples with flowers, and in their festivals crowned themselves with garlands.

I mentioned the glistening white tower of the church in the account of our journey out. I now learnt that it was only finished the year before our visit, and had cost these poor people over 700 dollars in money, besides gifts of stone, wood, and labour amounting to more than as much again. At other Mestizo towns, where the churches were like dilapidated barns, we heard much of the religious fervour of the Indians of Totagalpa. At one time, when building the tower, both their funds and the lime were exhausted. In this strait the Alcalde called the people of the town together, and told them that the tower, on the building of which they had already spent so much, could not be finished without lime. Then and there they determined themselves to carry the limestone from the quarries, near Ocotal, ten miles distant. Next morning, before daylight, the whole village set out, and at night a long line of men, women, and children came staggering back into Totagalpa, every one with a block of limestone ; and so zealous were they to bring as large stones as they could carry, that some of them had great sores worn between their shoulders where they carried their loads, slung, Indian fashion, from their foreheads. Here survives the same old Indian spirit, only turned in another direction, that impelled their forefathers, with great labour and patience, to bring from a distance and pile up great cairns of stones over the graves of their chieftains.

This care of their church is quite spontaneous on their part, as they have no padre ; indeed, from my experience of the priests in other towns, I think it likely that if they had one, he would intercept most of the offerings expended on the church and images.   There are exceptions, but generally the padres of Central America are rapacious and immoral.   They are much now as they were in Thomas Gage's time, more than two hundred years ago, and the poor Indians are just as humble and respectful to them.   In his quaint book, " A New Survey of the West Indies," he says : " Above all, to their priest they are very respectful ; and when they come to speak to him put on their best clothes and study their words and compliments to please him.   They yielded to the popish religion, especially to the worshipping of saints' images, because they look upon them as much like their forefathers' idols.   Out of the smallest of their means they will be sure to buy some of these saints, and bring them to the church that they may stand and be worshipped by them and others.   The churches are full of them, and they are placed upon stands, gilded and painted, to be carried in procession on their proper day. And hence comes no small profit to the priests ; for on such saints' days the owner of the saint makes a great feast in the town, and presents the priest sometimes two or three, sometimes four or five crowns for his mass and sermon, besides a turkey and three or four fowls, with as much cacao as will make him chocolate for all the octave or eight days following.   The priest, therefore, is very watchful over these saints' days, and sends warning beforehand to the Indians of the day of their saint.   If they contribute not bountifully, then the priest will chide and threaten that he will not preach." *

When we left Totagalpa, they were still drinking "chicha;" and I shall not forget the solemn satisfied look of the shoeless corporation, as they sipped their drink in sight of their townspeople, now and then singling out some friend, to whom they signed to come and quaff at the big bowl. The warm drink had loosened the tongue of the solemn alcalde. He came, and with many compliments, wished us a good journey. He, good man, had reached the summit of his ambition—he was the chief of his native town; he wore shoes; and what more could he hope for or desire?

The central Government interferes but little with the local officials; and the small towns in the interior are almost self-governed. Neither do they pay any direct taxes, the only contributions to the national exchequer being fees for killing cattle, selling land or houses, and making agreements, and a Government monopoly in the sale of tobacco and spirits. So the country folks lead an easy life, excepting in times of revolution, when they are pressed into the army. The Indian townships are better managed than those of the Spaniards and Mestizos; the plazas are kept freer from weeds, and the roads in good order. Probably nowhere but in tropical America can it be said that the introduction of European civilisation has caused a retrogression; and that those communities are the happiest and the best-governed who retain most of their old customs and habits. Yet there it is so. The civilisation that Cortez overthrew was more suitable for the Indians than that which has

* Loc. cit., pp. 332–334.

supplanted it. Who can read the accounts of the populous towns of Mexico and Central America in the time of Montezuma, with their magnificent buildings and squares; their gardens both zoological and botanical; their markets, attended by merchants from the surrounding countries; their beautiful cloth and feather work, the latter now a lost art; their picture writing; their cunning artificers in gold and silver; their astronomical knowledge; their schools; their love of order, of cleanliness, of decency; their morality and wonderful patriotism, without feeling that the conquest of Mexico was a deplorable calamity; that if that ancient civilisation had been saved, it might have been Christianised and purified without being destroyed, and to-day have stood one of the wonders and delights of the world. Its civilisation was self-grown, it was indigenous, it was unique : a few poor remnants of its piety, love of order, and self-government still remain in remote Indian townships; but its learning, magnificence, and glory have gone for ever.

On leaving Totagalpa, we took the road for Yalaguina. About a mile from the first-named town, the contorted schists cropped up again, and were followed, as before, by beds of soft decomposing trap, and these again by thick beds of quartz conglomerate. This succession was repeated two or three times during the day's journey. The trap beds formed, by decomposition, a dark fertile soil. Wherever maize was planted on it, it was thriving greatly. We reached Yalaguina about two o'clock, and pushed on for Palacaguina, four leagues further on, passing for a considerable part of the road along the banks of a small stream, by the side of which were some large and fine fields of maize and beans.

We reached Palacaguina an hour before dark, and on asking for lodging for the night, were directed to a small poor-looking house.   The front door of this was closed when we rode up, but was opened with haste, and about a dozen young men rushed out, who, it turned out afterwards, had been gambling, and hence the closed doors. We were asked to alight ; one man took the gun ; others offered to take our hats, to unload the pack-mule, &c. Two or three of them were Zambeses, and not very good-looking ; they made themselves so officious, that Velasquez confessed to me afterwards that he was rather afraid of them, and thought they were too pressing in their attentions, and meant to rob us.   Our fears were groundless; they had been suddenly startled in the midst of an illegal game, and were glad to find that we were not Government officers pouncing upon them. The house itself was dirty and small, with one hammock and one chair for its furniture ; we should have fared badly if one of the men, Don Trinidad Soso, had not recollected having once seen Velasquez before, and on the strength of that considered himself bound to take our entertainment into his own hands.   He was the nephew of the padre, who was absent, and he invited us to his uncle's house, where we were soon installed, and found much more comfortable quarters.   The padre had a good-looking house-keeper, who was also an excellent cook ; and she got us ready a supper of venison, tortillas, eggs, and chocolate, to which we did not fail to do justice.   Then the padre's bedstead was placed at my disposal, so that altogether we had been most fortunate in meeting with our good friend Don Trinidad.

Most of the people living at Palacaguina were half-breeds with a large infusion of negro blood ; and the weed-covered streets and plaza and dilapidated church compared unfavourably with the not far distant Indian town of Totagalpa. The Mestizos are a thriftless, careless people, but I care not here to dilate on their shortcomings. Let only the hospitality and kindness I experienced in Palacaguina live in my mind, and let regret draw a veil over their failings, and censure forget to chide.

Next morning Don Trinidad went himself to get us milk for our chocolate, three or four others assisted us as kindly on our departure as they had welcomed us on our arrival, and we rode away with more pleasant recollections of the weedy-looking town than if we had been entertained by grandees ; for these people were poor, and had assisted us out of pure good-nature. The country at first was level, and the roads smooth and dry. The morning was delightfully cool ; and as we trotted along our spirits were high and gay, and snatches of song sprang unbidden to our lips. How delightful these rides in the early morning were ! how all nature seemed to be in accord with our feelings ! Every bush and tree was noted, every bird-call heard. We would shout to one another, " Do you see this or that ? " or set Rito off into convulsions with some thin joke. Every sense was gratified ; it was like the youth of life. But as the day wore on, the sun would shine hotter and hotter, what had been a pleasure became a' toil, and we would push on determinedly but silently. The day would age, and our shadows come again and begin to lengthen ; the heat of the day was past, but our spirits would not mount to their morning's height. The beautiful flowers, the curious thorny bushes, the gorgeous butterflies, and many-coloured birds were all there ; but our attention

could only be called unwillingly to them. Our jaded
animals trudged on with mechanical steps, and, tired
ourselves, we thought of nothing but getting to the end
of our day's journey, and resting our weary frames.

We did not return from Palacaguina by the road we
had come, but took one much more to the westward.
This we did, not only to see a fresh line of country, but
to gratify Rito with a visit to his relations, whom he had
not seen for two years. Two miles beyond Palacaguina,
we crossed a river, beyond which I saw no more of the
quartz conglomerate that I have so often mentioned
whilst passing through Segovia. From this place to the
mines the rocks were soft decomposing dolerites, with
many harder bands of felsite, and, occasionally, plains
composed of more recent trachytic lavas.

We passed through another weedy, dilapidated town,
called Condego, where they have a singular custom at
their annual festival held on the 15th of May. For some
weeks before this date, they catch all the wild beasts and
birds they can, and keep them alive. During the night
preceding the feast-day they plant the plaza in front of
the church with full-grown plants of maize, rice, beans,
and all the other vegetables that they cultivate; and
amongst them they fasten the wild beasts and birds that
have been collected; so that the sun that set on a bare,
weedy plaza rises on one full of vegetable and animal
life. The year before, a young jaguar that had been
caught was the great attraction. It has now grown so
large, that they are afraid of it, and do not know what
to do with it. It is kept in an empty house at Pueblo
Nuevo, along with a dog, to which it is greatly attached,
although it is the one that caught it when young. The
custom of planting the square with vegetables, and

bringing together all the wild animals that can be collected, is doubtless an Indian one. The ancient Nicaraguans are said to have worshipped maize and beans, but the service may not have had more significance than our own harvest feasts.

We reached the edge of the savannahs of the plain of Segovia and began to ascend the high ranges that divide it from the province of Matagalpa, and soon entered a mountainous country. Our course at first lay up the banks of a torrent that had cut deeply into beds of boulder clay filled with great stones. The lower part of the range was covered with trees of various kinds, but none of them growing to a great height; higher up we reached the sighing pine trees, and higher still, the hills were covered with grass, and supported herds of cattle. About noon, we arrived at a poor-looking hacienda near the top of the range. The proprietor owned about two hundred cattle, and lived in a house, mud-walled and grass-thatched, consisting of one room and a kitchen. Round the sides of the room were crowded eight rude bedsteads, and hammocks were slung across the centre. A mob of twenty-one men, women, and children, lived at the house, and must have herded together like cattle at night. There were a great number of half-clothed and naked children running about. The women, of whom there were six, made us some chocolate and tortillas ready, and we rested awhile. Before we left, the men came in with the milking cows and calves. There were two men on horseback, but as the country was too rough for riding fast, they were accompanied by three boys on foot, who were sweating profusely with running after the cattle. The calves were separated from the cows and fastened up. The cows would keep near the corral until the next morning, when they would be milked, and the calves turned out with them again.

We continued to ascend for a mile further, and then reached the top of the range, which was bare of trees and covered with sedgy grass. Heavy rain came on, with tremendous gusts of wind, and as the path lay along the very crest of the mountain range, we were exposed to all the fury of the storm. In some places the cargo mule was nearly blown down the steep slope, and the one I was riding had to stop sometimes to keep its feet. The wind was bleak, and we were drenched with rain, and very cold. Fortunately the storm of rain did not last for more than half-an-hour, but the high cold wind continued all the time we were on the ridge, which was several miles long, with steep slopes on either side. We were glad when we got to a more sheltered spot, where some mountain oak trees protected us from the wind, and at four o'clock, reaching a small scattered settlement called Sontúli, we determined, although early in the day, to stay there, as it was Rito's birthplace, and his only sister, whom he had not seen for two years, lived there. All the hamlet were Rito's friends, and he had soon a crowd about him talking and laughing.

None of the lands around were enclosed—all seemed to be common property; and every family had a few cows and two or three brood mares. A little maize was grown, but the climate was rather too bleak and wet for it. We were now close to the boundary of the province of Matagalpa, and began again to hear of the drought that had destroyed most of the maize crop in that province, although in Chontales, on one side of it, we had had rather more rain than usual, and in Segovia, on the other, we had seen that the crops were excellent. Probably the high ranges that bound Matagalpa on every side had intercepted the rains and drained the winds of their moisture.

Having made such an early halt, we intended to have made up for it by an equally early start the next morning, but were detained by our mules having strayed during the night, and it was seven o'clock before they could be found. We had a long day's journey before us, during which we should not be able to buy any provisions, so, over night, Rito's sister had cooked a fowl for us to take with us. She had married one of the settlers of Sontúli, and, although still young and fresh-looking, had already three lusty children. The great number of children at all the houses had surprised me greatly, as I had been told that the country was decreasing in population. This, I have no doubt, is a mistake, and the inhabitants, if the country should remain at peace, would multiply rapidly.

On leaving Sontúli, the road led over mountain pastures and through woods of the evergreen oak draped from top to bottom with the grey moss-like *Tillandsia*, which hung in long festoons from every branch, and was wound around the trunks, like garlands, by the wind : the larger masses, waving in the breeze, hung down for four or five feet below the branches. The small birds build in them, and they form excellent hiding-places for their nests, where they are tolerably secure from the attacks of their numerous enemies. I had often, when in the tropics, to notice the great sagacity or instinct of the small birds in choosing

T

places for their nests. So many animals—monkeys, wild-cats, raccoons, opossums, and tree-rats—are constantly prowling about, looking out for eggs and young birds, that, unless placed with great care, their progeny would almost certainly be destroyed. The different species of Oropendula or Orioles (*Icteridæ*) of tropical America choose high, smooth-barked trees, standing apart from others, from which to hang their pendulous nests. Monkeys cannot get at them from the tops of other trees, and any predatory mammal attempting to ascend the smooth trunks would be greatly exposed to the attacks of the birds, armed, as they are, with strong sharp-pointed beaks. Several other birds in the forest suspend their nests from the small but tough air roots that hang down from the epiphytes growing on the branches, where they often look like a natural bunch of moss growing on them. The various prickly bushes are much chosen, especially the bull's-horn thorn, which I have already described. Many birds hang their nests from the extremities of the branches, and a safer place could hardly be chosen, as with the sharp thorns and the stinging ants that inhabit them, no mammal would, I think, dare to attempt the ascent of the tree. Stinging ants are not the only insects whose assistance birds secure by building near their nests. A small parrot builds constantly on the plains in a hole made in the nests of the termites, and a species of fly-catcher makes its nest alongside of that of one of the wasps. On the savannahs, between Acoyapo and Nancital, there is a shrub with sharp curved prickles, called *Viena paraca* (come here) by the Spaniards, because it is difficult to extricate oneself from its hold

when the dress is caught, for as one part is cleared
another will be entangled. A yellow and brown fly-
catcher builds its nest in these bushes, and generally
places it alongside that of a banded wasp, so that with
the prickles and the wasps it is well guarded. I
witnessed, however, the death of one of the birds from
the very means it had chosen for the protection of its
young. Darting hurriedly out of its domed nest as we
were passing, it was caught just under its bill by one
of the curved hook-like thorns, and in trying to extricate itself got further entangled. Its fluttering disturbed the wasps, who flew down upon it, and in less
than a minute stung it to death. We tried in vain to
rescue it, for the wasps attacked us also, and one of our
party was severely stung by them. We had to leave
it hanging up dead in front of its nest, whilst its mate
flew round and round screaming out its terror and
distress. I find that other travellers have noted the
fact of birds building their nests near colonies of wasps
for protection. Thus, according to Gosse, the grassquit
of Jamaica (*Spermophila olivacea*) often selects a shrub
on which wasps have built, and fixes the entrance to
its domed nest close to their cells. Prince Maximilian
Neuwied states in his "Travels in Brazil," that he
found the curious purse-shaped nest of one of the Todies
constantly placed near the nests of wasps, and that the
natives informed him that it did so to secure itself from
the attacks of its enemies. I should have thought that
when building their nests they would be very liable to
be attacked by the wasps. The nests placed in these
positions appear always to be domed, probably for
security against their unstable friends.

CHAPTER XVI.

SOME of the ranges were very craggy, and one was so steep and rocky that we had to dismount and lead our mules, and even then one of them fell several times. These craggy ranges were covered with the evergreen oaks, and we saw but few pine trees. Now and then we passed over the tracks of the leaf-cutting ants, who were hurrying along as usual, laden with pieces of foliage about the size of a sixpence. There were but few birds, and insects also were scarce, the bleak wet weather doubtless being unsuitable for them.

We now began to descend on the Matagalpa side of the elevated ranges we had been travelling over, and crossed many small valleys and streams, the latter everywhere cutting through boulder clay, with very few exposures of the bed rock. In the lower lands were many patches cultivated with maize and beans, but the country was very sparsely inhabited. At noon, we reached a small town called Concordia, where the houses were larger and better built than those in the small towns of Segovia. The church, on the other hand, was an ugly barn-like building, apparently much neglected.

The rocks were trachytes, and the soil seemed fertile,
but there was very little of it cultivated. Many of the
men we met wore long swords instead of the usual
machetes. There is a school for learning fencing at
Concordia, and the people of the district are celebrated
for being expert swordsmen. They have often fencing
matches. The best man is called the champion, and he
is bound to try conclusions with every one that chal-
lenges him.

After leaving Concordia we had only one more range
to cross, then began to descend towards the plains
below Jinotega, and about dusk reached that town
and were kindly received by our former entertainers.
Doubtless much European blood runs in the veins of
the inhabitants of Jinotega, but in their whole manner
of living they follow the Indian ways, and it is the
same throughout Nicaragua, excepting amongst the
higher classes in the large towns. All their cooking
vessels are Indian. Just as in the Indian huts, every
pot or pan is of coarse pottery, and each dish is cooked
on a separate little fire. The drinks in common use
are Indian, and have Indian names ; tiste, pinul, pinullo,
and chicha, all made from maize, sugar, and chocolate.
As before observed, whatever was new to the Spaniards
when they invaded the country retained its Indian
name. It is so with every stage of growth of the maize
plant, chilote, elote, and maizorca. The stone for
grinding the maize is exactly the same as those found in
the old Indian graves, and it is still called the metlate.
All the towns we passed through in Segovia retained
their Indian names, though their present inhabitants
know nothing of their meaning. The old names of

many of the towns are probably remnants of a language
earlier than that of the inhabitants at the time of the
conquest, and their study might throw some light on
the distribution of the ancient peoples. Unfortunately
the names of places are very incorrectly given in the
best maps of Central America, every traveller having
spelt them phonetically according to the orthography
of his own language. Throughout this book I have
spelt proper names in accordance with the pronuncia-
tion of the Spanish letters.

Many of the names of towns in Nicaragua and
Honduras end in " galpa," as Muyogalpa, Juigalpa,
Totagalpa, and Matagalpa. Places apparently of less
consequence in Segovia often end in the termination
" lee " strongly accented, as Jamailý, Esterlý, Darailý,
&c., and in " guina " pronounced " weena," as in Palacaguina and Yalaguina. In Chontales many end in
"apa," or "apo," as Cuapo, Comoapa, Comelapa, Acoyapo,
and others.

The Spaniards, whenever they gave a name to a town,
either named it after some city in Spain or after their
Saints. There are dozens of Santo Rosas, San Juans,
and San Tomases. Even some of the towns, which
have well-known Indian names, are called officially
after some Spanish saint, but the common people stick
to the old names, and they are not to be thrust aside.

We had a long talk with our courteous host of the
estanco at Jinotega. He had a small library of books,
nearly all being missals and prayer-books. He had a
little knowledge of geography and was wishful to learn
about Europe, and at the same time most desirous that
we should not think that he, one of the chief men of

the town, did not know all about it. That England
was a small island he admitted was new to him, as he
thought it was part of the United States or at least
joined to them. He asked if it was true that Rome
was one of the four quarters of the globe. We explained
that it was only a large city, to which he replied gravely
that he knew it was so, but wished to have our opinion
to confirm his own.

No newspapers come to Jinotega, excepting occasionally a Government gazette, and only a few of the
grown-up people are able to read. News travel quickly
from one town to another, but every incident is greatly
exaggerated; and many extravagant stories are set
afloat with no other foundation than the inventive
faculties of some idle brain. To appreciate what an
immense aid a newspaper press is to the dissemination
of truth one must travel in some such country as Nicaragua where newspapers do not circulate. It is impossible to get trustworthy intelligence about any event
that has happened a hundred miles away, and stories
of murders and robberies that were never committed
are widely circulated amongst the credulous people.
As far as my experience goes highway robbery is unknown in Nicaragua. Foreigners entrusted with money
have stated they have been robbed, but there has always
been suspicions that they themselves embezzled the
money that they said they lost. Personally I never
carried arms for defence in the country, and was never
molested nor even insulted, though I often travelled
alone. The only dangerous characters in the country
are the lower class of foreigners, and these are not
numerous. Petty thefts are common enough, and at

the mines we found that none of the labouring class were to be trusted; but robberies of a daring character or accompanied by violence were never committed by the natives to my knowledge.

In their drinking bouts they often quarrel among themselves, and slash about with their long heavy knives, inflicting ugly gashes and often maiming each other for life. One-armed men are not uncommon; and I knew of two cases where an arm was chopped off in these encounters. Nearly every pay-week our medical officer was sent for to sew up the wounds that had been received. Fortunately even at these times they do not interfere with foreigners, their quarrels being amongst themselves, and either faction fights or about their women, or gambling losses. Many of the worst cases of cutting with knives were by the Honduraneans employed at the mines, who generally got off through the mountains to their own country. One who was taken managed to escape by inducing the soldiers who had him in charge to take him up to the mines to bring out his tools. He went in at the level whilst they guarded the entrance. Hour after hour passed without his returning, and at last they learnt that he had got through some old workings to another opening into the mine and had started for Honduras. Once in the bush pursuit is hopeless, as the undergrowth is so dense that it is impossible to follow by sight.

We left Jinotega at seven in the morning, passed over the pine-clad ranges again, and at one o'clock came in sight of the town of Matagalpa. At the river a mill was at work grinding wheat. I went into the shed that covered it and found it to be simple and ingenious. Below the floor was a small horizontal water-wheel driven by the stream striking against the inclined floats. The shaft of the wheel passed up through the floor and the lower stone, and was fixed to the upper one, which turned round with it without any gearing. The flour made is dark and full of impurities, as no care is taken to keep it clean.

We found the mules and horses we had left at Matagalpa in good condition, and after getting some dinner started again, taking the road towards Teustepe instead of that by which we had come, as we were told we should avoid the swamps by so doing, for more to the westward they had had no rain. We rode down the valley below the town and found it very dry and barren, the only industry worth naming being a small indigo plantation. Indigo seems to have been more cultivated formerly than now. In many parts I saw the deserted vats in which the plants were steeped to extract the dye. We ascended a high range to the left of the valley, on the top of which were a few pine trees. These we were told were the last we should see on the road to Chontales. On the other side of the range the descent was very steep, and the road was carried down the precipitous and rocky slope in a series of zigzags, so that we saw the mules a few score yards in advance directly under our feet.

From the hill we had seen a house in the valley, and as night was setting in we sought for it, but the whole district was so covered with low scrubby trees with many paths running in various directions that it was long before we found it. When at last we discovered it,

the prospect before us of a night's lodging was so dis-
couraging that had it not then been getting quite dark,
and being told that we should have to travel several miles
before coming to another house, we should have sought
for other shelter. The small hut was as usual filled
with men, women, and children. Two of the women
were lying ill, and one seemed to be dying. There was
no room for us in the hut if we had been willing to
enter it. We slung our hammocks under a small open-
sided shed near by and passed a miserable night. A
strong cold wind was blowing, and the swinging of the
hammocks caused by it kept a number of dogs continually barking and snapping at our hammocks and
boots. We rose cold and cramped at daylight, and
without waiting to make ready any coffee, saddled our
beasts and rode away.

A little maize was grown about this place, and the
people told us that sugar thrived, but the plantations
of it were small and ill-kept, and everything had a look
of poverty and decadence. They said that twenty years
ago there was no bush growing around their house. The
country was then open grassed savannahs, and there was
less fever.   Now the bush grows up to their very doors,
and they will not take the trouble to cut it down even
to save themselves from the attacks of fever.   Here, as
everywhere throughout the central provinces, deep in-
grained indolence paralyses all industry or enterprise,
and with the means of plenty and comfort on every
side, the people live in squalid poverty.

For four leagues we rode over high ranges with very
fine valleys separating them, containing many thatched
houses and fields of maize, sugar, and beans.   Where

not now cultivated the sides of the ranges were covered
with weedy-looking shrubs and low trees, proving that
all the land had at one time been cropped, and this was
further shown by the old lines of pinuela fences and
ditches that were seen here and there amongst the
brushwood. As we got further south the alluvial flats
in the valleys increased in size and fertility, and the
cultivated fields were enclosed with permanent fences.
On some of the ranges we crossed, the rocks were amyg-
daloidal, containing nests of a white zeolite, the fractured
planes of which glittered like gems on the pathway.

Eight leagues from Matagalpa we reached the small
town of Tierrabona, where, as the name implies, the land
is very good. Every house had an enclosure around
it, planted with maize and beans : and though it was
evident that the land was cropped year after year, it still
seemed to bear well. We stopped at a small brook just
outside the town, and ate some provisions we had brought
from Matagalpa. Some speckled tiger-beetles ran about
the dusty road, and on wet muddy places near the
stream groups of butterflies collected to suck the moisture. Amongst them were some fine swallow-tails
(*Papilio*), quivering their wings as they drank, and
lovely blue hair-streaks (*Theclæ*). The latter, when they
alight, rub their wings together, moving their curious
tail-like appendages up and down. Great dragon-flies
hawked after flies; while on the surface of still pools
"whirligigs" (*Gyrinidæ*) wheeled about in mazy gyra-
tions, just as they are seen to do at home.

Savannahs, sparingly timbered, were next crossed ;
then we reached one of those level plains, with black
soil and blocks of porous trachyte lying on the surface,

which are swamps in the rainy season, and have for
vegetation sedgy grasses and scattered jicara trees,
cactuses and thorny acacias. Up to the time we passed,
there had been no rain in these parts, and the plain
was dry and bare, with great cracks in the black soil.
The grass had not sprung up, not a breath of air was
stirring, and the heated air quivered over the parched
ground, forming in the distance an imperfect mirage.

Directly overhead the noonday sun hung hot in the
hazy sky. As we moodily toiled over the plain, my
attention was arrested by a dust whirlwind that suddenly
sprang up about fifty yards to our left. The few dry
leaves on the ground began to whirl round and round,
and to ascend. In a minute a spiral column was
formed, reaching, perhaps, to the height of fifty feet, consisting of dust and dry dead leaves, all whirling round
with the greatest rapidity. The column was only a few
yards in diameter. It moved slowly along, nearly
parallel with our course, but only lasting a few minutes.
Before I could point it out to Velasquez, who had
ridden on ahead, it had dissolved away. I had been
very familiar with these air eddies in Australia, and
had hoped to carry on some investigations concerning
them, begun there, in Central America; but, though
common on the plains of Mexico and of South America,
this was the only one I witnessed in Central America.

The interest with which I regarded these miniature
storms was due to the assistance that their study was
likely to give in the discussion of the cause of all
circular movements of the atmosphere, including the
dreaded typhoon and cyclone. The chief meteorologists who have discussed this difficult question have

approached it from the side of the larger hurricanes.
There is a complete gradation from the little dust eddies
up through larger whirlwinds and tornadoes to the awful
typhoons and cyclones of China and the West Indies;
and it has long been my opinion that if meteorologists
devoted their attention to the smaller eddies that can
be looked at from the outside, and their commencement,
continuance, and completion watched and chronicled,
they could not fail to obtain a large amount of information to guide them in the study of cyclonic movements
of the atmosphere.

Unless the smaller whirlwinds are quite distinct from
the larger ones in their origin, the theories advanced
by meteorologists to account for the latter are certainly
untenable.   According to the celebrated M. Dove,
cyclones owe their origin to the intrusion of the upper
counter trade-wind into the lower trade-wind current.*
More lately, Prof. T. B. Maury has stated that "the
origin of cyclones is found in the tendency of the south-
east trade-winds to invade the territory of the north-east
trades by sweeping over the equator into our hemisphere, the lateral conflict of the currents giving an
initial impulse to bodies of air by which they begin to
rotate." Cyclones having thus originated, Prof. Maury
considers that they are continued and intensified by the
vapour condensed in their vortex forming a vacuum.†

Humboldt had long ago ascribed whirlwinds to the
meeting of opposing currents of air.‡ There is this
dynamical objection to the theory. The movements of

---

* "Law of Storms," p. 246.
† *Quarterly Journal of Science*, 1872, p. 418.
‡ "Aspects of Nature," vol. i. p. 17.

the air in whirlwinds are much more rapid than in any
known straight current, such as the trade winds ; and it
is impossible that two opposing currents should generate
between them one of much greater force and rapidity
than either. If force A joins with force B, surely
force C, the product, must have the power of both A and
B. But even if this fundamental objection to the
theory could be set aside, the small whirlwinds could
not thus arise, as they are most frequent when the air
is nearly or quite motionless.

Then, again, when we turn to Prof. Maury's theory
that the cyclones, having been initiated by the conflict
of contrary currents, are continued and intensified by
the condensation of vapour in their vortex forming a
vacuum, we find it negatived by the fact that in the
smaller whirlwinds the air is dry, and there is conse-
quently no condensation of vapour ; yet, in comparison
with their size, they are of as great violence as the
fiercest typhoon. Tylor describes the numerous dust
whirlwinds he saw on the plains of Mexico,* Clarke
those on the steppes of Russia, and Bruce those on the
deserts of Africa, and nowhere is there mention made
of any condensation of vapour. I have seen scores of
whirlwinds in Australia, many rising to a height of
over one hundred feet; yet there was never any perceptible condensation of vapour, though some of them
were of sufficient force to tear off limbs of trees, and
carry up the tents of gold-diggers into the air. Franklin
describes a whirlwind of greater violence than any of
these. It commenced in Maryland by taking up the
dust over a road in the form of an inverted sugar-loaf, and

* " Anahuac," by E. B. Tylor, p. 21.

soon increased greatly in size and violence. Franklin followed it on horseback, and saw it enter a wood, where it twisted and turned round large trees: leaves and boughs were carried up so high that they appeared to the eye like flies. Again there was no condensation of vapour.

We thus see that whirlwinds of great violence occur when the air is dry, and there can be no condensation. When, however, they are formed at sea, and occasionally on land, the air next the surface is saturated with moisture; and this moisture is condensed when it is carried to a great height, forming clouds, or falling in showers of rain and hail. This condensation of vapour is an effect, and not a cause, and takes place, not in the centre, but at the top or at the sides of the ascending column. This is well shown in an account, by an eye-witness, of a whirlwind that did great damage near the shore of Lough Neagh, in Ireland, in August 1872.* It was about thirty yards in diameter. It destroyed several hay-stacks, and carried the hay up into the air out of sight. It partially unroofed houses, and tore off the branches of trees. The railway station at Randalstown was much injured; great numbers of slates, and two and a half hundredweight of lead were torn from the roof. When passing over a portion of the lake, it presented the appearance of a water-spout. On land everything that it lapped up was whirled round and round, and carried upwards in the centre, whilst dense clouds surrounded the outside and came down near to the earth.

As above mentioned, I had in Australia many opportunities of studying the dust whirlwinds; and as I looked upon them as the initial form of a cyclone, I

* "Nature," vol. vi. p. 541.

paid much attention to them. On a small plain, near to Maryborough, in the province of Victoria, they were of frequent occurrence in the hot season. This plain was about two miles across, and was nearly surrounded by trees. In calm, sultry weather, during the heat of the day, there were often two at once in action in different parts of it. They were only a few yards in diameter, but reached to a height of over one hundred feet, and were often, in their higher part, bent out of their perpendicular by upper aërial currents. The dust and leaves they carried up rendered their upward spiral movement very conspicuous. No one who studied these whirlwinds could for a moment believe that they were caused by conflicting currents of air. They occurred most frequently when there was least wind; and this particular plain seemed to be peculiarly suitable for their formation, because it was nearly surrounded by trees, and currents of air were prevented. They lasted several minutes, slowly moving across the plain, like great pillars of smoke.*

When attentively watched from a short distance, it was seen that as soon as one was formed, the air immediately next the heated soil, which was before motionless, or quivering as over a furnace, was moving in all directions towards the apex of the dust-column. As these currents approached the whirlwind, they quickened and carried with them loose dust and leaves

* A friend of mine tells me that he saw a similar whirlwind rise at noon one still summer day, and traverse the dusty road on the Chesil Bank between Portland and Weymouth. It travelled fully half a mile, about as fast as he could walk; and the point where it met the ground was not thicker than his walking stick. By-and-by it swept out to sea, where the dust gradually fell.

into the spiral whirl. The movement was similar to that which occurs when a small opening is made at the bottom of a wide shallow vessel of water : all the liquid moves towards it, and assumes a spiral movement as it is drawn off.

The conclusion I arrived at, and which has since been confirmed by further study of the question, was, that the particles of air next the surface did not always rise immediately they were heated, but that they often remained and formed a stratum of rarefied air next the surface, which was in a state of unstable equilibrium. This continued until the heated stratum was able, at some point where the ground favoured a comparatively greater accumulation of heat, to break through the over-lying strata of air, and force its way upwards. An opening once made, the whole of the heated air moved towards it and was drained off, the heavier layers sinking down and pressing it out. Sir George Airey has sug-gested to me that the reason of the particles of air not rising as they are heated, when there is no wind blow-ing, may be due to their viscosity : and this suggestion is correct. That air does not always rise when heated, appears from the hot winds of Australia, which blow from the heated interior towards the cooler south, instead of rising directly upwards. Sultry, close weather, that sometimes lasts for several days, would also be impossible on the assumption that air rises as soon as it is heated.

This explanation supplies us with the force that is necessary to drive the air with the great velocity with which it moves in whirlstorms. The upper, colder, and heavier air is pressing upon the heated stratum, and the

U

greater the area over which the latter extends, the greater will be the weight pressing upon it, and the greater the violence of the whirlwind when an opening is formed for the ascent of the heated air.   There is a gradual passage, from the small dust eddies, through larger whirlstorms such as that at Lough Neagh, to tornadoes and the largest cyclone; every step of the gradation might be verified by numerous examples; and if this book were a treatise on meteorology, it might be admissible to give them; but to do this would take up too much of my space, and I shall only now make some observations on the largest form of whirlstorm—the dreaded cyclone.

Just as over the little plain at Maryborough, protected by the surrounding forest from the action of the wind, the heated air accumulates over the surface until carried off in eddies, so, though on a vastly larger scale, in that great bight formed by the coasts of North and South America, having for its apex the Gulf of Mexico, there is an immense area in the northern tropics, nearly sur-rounded by land, forming a vast oceanic plain, shut off from the regular action of the trade-winds by the great islands of Cuba and Hayti, where the elements of the hurricane accumulate, and at last break forth.   In this and such like areas, the lower atmosphere is gradually heated from week to week, and, as in Australia the quivering of the air over the hot ground foreshadows the whirlwind, and in Africa the mirage threatens the simoom, so in the West Indies a continuance of close, sultry weather, an oppressive calm, precedes the hurri-cane.   When at last the huge vortex is formed, the heated atmosphere rushes towards it from all sides, and is drained upwards in a spiral column, just as in the dust-eddy, on a gigantic scale. Unlike the air of the dust-eddy, that of the hurricane coming from the warm surface of the ocean is nearly saturated with vapour, and this, as it is carried up and brought into contact with the colder air on the outside of the ascending column, is condensed and falls in torrents of rain, accompanied by thunder and lightning.

I advanced this theory to account for the origin of whirlwinds in a paper read before the Philosophical Institute of Victoria, in 1857. It was afterwards communicated by the Astronomer-Royal to the *London Philosophical Magazine*, where it appeared in January 1859. A suggestion that I at the same time offered, that the opposite rotation of cyclones in the two hemispheres was due to the same causes as the westerly deflection of the trade-winds from a direct meridional course, has been generally adopted by physicists, and I am not without hopes that the main theory may also yet be accepted; but whether or not, I am confident that a study of the smaller eddies of air is the proper way to approach the difficult question of the origin of cyclones.

CHAPTER XVII.

AFTER crossing the trachytic plain, we reached a large
cattle hacienda, and beyond, the river Chocoyo, on the
banks of which was some good, though stony, pasture
land. We saw here some fine cattle, and learnt that a
little more care was taken in breeding them than is usual
in Nicaragua. The country, with its rolling savannahs,
covered with grass, is admirably suited for cattle-raising,
and great numbers are exported to the neighbouring
country of Costa Rica. Scarcely any attention is, however, paid to the improvement of the breeds. Few
stations have reserve potreros of grass. In consequence,
whenever an unusually dry season occurs, the cattle die
by hundreds, and their bones may be seen lying all over
the plains. Both Para and Guinea grass grow, when
planted and protected, with the greatest luxuriance ;
and the latter especially forms an excellent reserve, as
it grows in dense tufts that cannot be destroyed by the
cattle. When not protected by fencing, however, the
cattle and mules prefer these grasses so much to the
native ones, that they are always close-cropped, and

when the natural pasturage fails there is no reserve of
the other to fall back on. I planted both the Para and
Guinea grasses largely at the mines and at Pital, and
we were able to keep our mules always in good condition with them.

About four o'clock in the afternoon our animals were
getting tired, and we ourselves were rather fatigued,
having been in the saddle since daylight, with the exception of a few minutes' rest at Tierrabona. We halted at a
thatched cottage on some high stony savannah land, and
were hospitably received by the peasant proprietor, Don
Filiberto Trano. He informed us that we had entered
the township of Teustepe, and that the town itself was
eight leagues distant. The family consisted of Don
Filiberto, his wife, and four or five children. They had
just prepared for their own dinner a young fowl, stewed
with green beans and other vegetables, and this they
placed before us, saying that they would soon cook something else for themselves. We were too hungry to make
any scruples, and after the poor, coarse fare we had been
used to, the savoury repast seemed the most delicious I
ever tasted. I think we only got two meals on the whole
journey that we really enjoyed. This was one, the other
the supper that the padre's housekeeper at Palacaguina
cooked for us, and I have recorded at length the names
of the parties to whom we were indebted for them.

Don Filiberto had about twenty cows, all of which that
could be found were driven in at dusk, and the calves
tied up. As they came in, the fowls were on the look-out
for the garrapatos, or ticks ; and the cows, accustomed
to the process, stood quietly, while they flew up and
picked them off their necks and flanks. The calves are

always turned out with the cows in the morning, after
the latter are milked, so that if not found again for
some days, as is often the case in this bushy and unen-
closed country, the cows are milked by them and do
not go dry. They give very little milk, probably due
to the entire want of care in breeding them. It is at
once made into cheese, which forms a staple article of
food amongst the poorer natives.

The small house was divided into three compartments,
one being used as a kitchen. It was in rather a dilapidated condition, and Don Filiberto told me that he was
busy building a new residence. I was curious to see
what progress he was making with it, and he took me
outside and showed me four old posts used for tying
the cows to, which had evidently been in the ground for
many years. "There," he said, "are the corner-posts,
and I shall roof it with tiles." He was quite grave, but
I could not help smiling at his faith. I have no doubt
that, as long as he lives, he will lounge about all day,
and in the evening, when his wife and children are milking the cows, will come out, smoke his cigarette, leaning
against the door-post of his patched and propped-up
dwelling, and contemplate the four old posts with a
proud feeling of satisfaction that he is building a new
house. Such a picture is typical of Nicaragua.

Don Filiberto told us that there was a limestone
quarry not far from his house; and as I wished to learn
whether it occurred in beds or veins, I proposed next
morning to walk over to it, but he said we should need
the mules to cross the river. Thinking, from his description, that it was only about a mile distant, I started on
mule-back with him; but after riding fully a league, dis-

covered that he actually did not know himself where it was, but was seeking for another man to show him. We at last arrived at the house of this man. He was absent. A boy showed us a small piece of the limestone. It was concretionary, and I learnt from him that it occurred in veins. I was vexed about the time we had lost, and the extra work we had given the poor mules; my only consolation was that as we rode back I picked a fine new longicorn beetle off the leaves of an overhanging tree.

When we came to settle up with our host he proposed to charge us twenty-five cents, just one shilling, or fourpence each. They had given us a good dinner and put themselves to much inconvenience to provide me with a bedstead, and this was their modest charge. Nor did they make it with any expectation that we would give more. It is the universal custom amongst the Mestizo peasantry to entertain travellers; to give them the best they have and to charge for the bare value of the provisions, and nothing for the lodging. We could so depend upon the hospitality of the lower classes that every day we travelled on without any settled place to pass the night, convinced that we should be received with welcome at any hut that we might arrive at when our mules got tired or night came on. The only place in the whole journey where we had been received with hesitation was at the Indian house a day's journey beyond Olama. There the people were pure Indians, and other circumstances made me conclude that the Indians were not so hospitable as the Mestizos.

We finally started about nine o'clock and rode over dry savannahs, where, although there was little grass, I was told that cattle did well browsing on the small brushwcod with which the hills were covered. All the forenoon we travelled over stony ranges and dry plains and savannahs. At noon we reached the dry bed of a river and crossed it several times, but could find no water to quench our thirst, whilst the sun shone down on us with pitiless heat. About one o'clock we came to some pools where the bed of the river was bare rock with rounded hollows containing water, warm but clean, as the cattle could not walk over the smooth slopes to get at it. Here we halted for an hour and had some tiste and maize cakes, and cut some Guinea grass that grew amongst the rocks for our mules. Over the heated rocks scampered brown lizards, chasing each other and revelling in the sunshine. Butterflies on lazy wings came and settled on damp spots, and the cicada kept up his shrill continuous monotone, but not so loudly as he would later on when it got cooler. The cicada is supposed by some to pipe only during mid-day, but both in Central America and Brazil I found them loudest towards sunset, keeping up their shrill music until it was taken up by night-vocal crickets and locusts.

We were returning parallel to our course in going to Segovia, but several leagues to the westward, and this made a wonderful difference in the climate. There we were wading through muddy swamps and drenched with continual rains. Here the plains were parched with heat, vegetation was dried up, and there was scarcely any water in the river beds. The north-east trade-wind, before it reaches thus far, gives up its moisture to the forests of the Atlantic slope, and now passed over without even a cloud to relieve the deep blue of the sky or temper the rays of the sun.

The vegetation on the plains was almost entirely composed of thorny plants and shrubs; acacias, cacti, and bromeliæ were the most abundant. Animal life was scarce; there were a few flycatchers amongst the birds, and armadilloes were the only mammals. Horse-flies (*Tabanus*) were too numerous, and drops of blood trickled down our mules' faces where they had feasted. In some parts large, banded black and yellow wasps (*Monedula surinamensis*, Fabr.) came flying round us and had a threatening look as they hovered before our faces, but they were old acquaintances of mine in Brazil, and I knew that they were only searching about for the horse-flies with which they store their nests, just as other wasps do with spiders, first benumbing them with their sting. I noted here another instance of the instinctive dread that insects have of their natural enemies. The horse-flies were so bloodthirsty that we could kill them with the greatest ease with our hands on the mules' necks, or if we drove them away they would return immediately. As soon, however, as a wasp came hawking round, the flies lost their sluggish apathy and disappeared amongst the bushes, and I do not think that excepting when gorged with blood they would easily fall a prey to their pursuers.

We were joined on the road by a storekeeper on his way to Teustepe. He was armed with pistols, which it is the fashion to carry in Nicaragua, though many travellers have nothing more formidable in their holsters than a spirit flask and some biscuits. He talked as usual of threatened revolutionary risings, but these form the staple conversation throughout Central America amongst the middle classes, and until they really do break out it is best not to believe in them. He told us also that the drought had been very great around Teustepe, and that the crops were destroyed by it.

About three we reached the town, and after buying some provisions to take with us, pushed on again. Below Teustepe we crossed the river Malacatoyo which empties into the Lake of Nicaragua, and beyond it the road passed over a wild alluvial flat with high trees, amongst which we saw a troop of white-faced monkeys.

On the leaves of the bushes there were many curious species of Buprestidæ, and I struck these and other beetles off with my net as I rode along. After one such capture I observed what appeared to be one of the black stinging ants on the net. It was a small spider that closely resembled an ant, and so perfect was the imitation that it was not until I killed it that I determined that it was a spider and that I had needlessly feared its sting. What added greatly to the resemblance was that, unlike other spiders, it held up its two fore-legs like antennæ, and moved them about just like an ant. Other species of spiders closely resemble stinging ants ; in all of them the body is drawn out long like an ant, and in some the maxillary palpi are lengthened and thickened so as to resemble the head of one.

Ant-like spiders have been noticed throughout tropical America and also in Africa.* The use that the deceptive resemblance is to them has been explained to be the facility it affords them for approaching ants on

* See "Nature," vol. iii. p. 508.

which they prey. I am convinced that this explanation is incorrect so far as the Central American species are concerned. Ants, and especially the stinging species, are, so far as my experience goes, not preyed upon by any other insects. No disguise need be adopted to approach them, as they are so bold that they are more likely to attack a spider than a spider them. Neither have they wings to escape by flying, and generally go in large bodies easily found and approached. The real use is, I doubt not, the protection the disguise affords against small insectivorous birds. I have found the crops of some humming-birds full of small soft-bodied spiders, and many other birds feed on them. Stinging ants, like bees and wasps, are closely resembled by a host of other insects; indeed, whenever I found any insect provided with special means of defence I looked for imitative forms, and was never disappointed in finding them.

Stinging ants are not only closely copied in form and movements by spiders but by species of Hemiptera and Coleoptera, and the resemblance is often wonderfully close.* All over the world wasps are imitated in form and movements by other insects, and in the tropics these mimetic forms are endless. In many cases the insect imitating is so widely removed, in the normal form of the order to which it belongs, from that of the insect imitated, that it is difficult to imagine how the first steps in the process of imitation took place. Looking however at the immense variety of insect life in the

* Amongst the longicorn beetles of Chontales, *Mallocera spinicollis*, *Neoclytus Œsopus*, and *Diphyrama singularis*, Bates, all closely resemble stinging ants when moving about on fallen logs.

tropics, and remembering that in early tertiary times, nearly the whole world was in the same favourable condition as regards temperature (vegetation, according to Heer, extending to the poles), and must have supported a vast number of species and genera that were destroyed during the glacial period, we must suppose, that, in that great variety of forms, it sometimes occurred that two species belonging to distinct orders somewhat resembled each other in form or colouration, and that the resemblance was gradually increased, when one species had special means of protection, by the other being benefited the more nearly it approached it in appearance.

It is to be remarked that the forms imitated have always some kind of defence against insectivorous birds or mammals ; they are provided with stings or unpleasant odours or flavours, or are exceedingly swift in flight ; excepting where inanimate nature is imitated for concealment. Thus I had an opportunity of proving in Brazil that some birds, if not all, reject the Heliconii butterflies, which are closely resembled by butterflies of other families and by moths. I observed a pair of birds that were bringing butterflies and dragon-flies to their young, and although the Heliconii swarmed in the neighbourhood and are of weak flight so as to be easily caught, the birds never brought one to their nest. I had a still better means of testing both these and other insects that are mimicked in Nicaragua. The tame white-faced monkey I have already mentioned was extremely fond of insects, and would greedily munch up beetle, or butterfly, given to him, and I used to bring to him any insects that I found imitated by others to see whether they were distasteful or not. I found he would never eat the Heliconii. He was too polite not to take them when they were offered to him, and would sometimes smell them, but invariably rolled them up in his hand and dropped them quietly again after a few moments. There could be no doubt, however, from the monkey's actions, that they were distasteful to him. A large species of spider (*Nephila*) also used to drop them out of its web when I put them into it. Another spider that frequented flowers seemed to be fond of them, and I have already mentioned a wasp that caught them to store its nest with.

Amongst the beetles there is a family that is just as much mimicked as the Heliconii are amongst the butterflies. These are the Lampyridæ, to which the fireflies belong. Many of the genera are not phosphorescent, but all appear to be distasteful to insectivorous mammals and birds. I found they were invariably rejected by the monkey, and my fowls would not touch them.

The genus Calopteron belonging to this family is not phosphorescent. In some of the species, as in *C. basalis*, (Klug), the wing-covers are widened out behind in a peculiar manner. This and other species of Calopteron are not only imitated in their colour and markings by other families of beetles but also in this peculiar widening of the elytra. Besides this, the Calopteron when walking on a leaf raises and depresses its wing cases, and I observed exactly the same movement in a longicorn beetle (*Evander nobilis*, Bates), which is evidently a mimetic form of this genus. In addition to being mimicked by other families of beetles, Calopteron is closely resembled by a species of moth (*Pionia lycoides*, Walker). This

moth varies itself in colour; in one of the varieties it has
a central black band across the wings, when it resembles
Calopteron vicinum (Deyrolle), in another this black band
is wanting, when it resembles *C. basalis*. Professor Westwood has also pointed out to me that the resemblance to
the beetle is still further increased in the moth by raised
lines of scales running lengthwise down the thorax.

The phosphorescent species of Lampyridæ, the fireflies,
so numerous in tropical America, are equally distasteful,
and are also much mimicked by other insects. I found
different species of cockroaches so much like them in
shape and colour that they could not be distinguished
without examination. These cockroaches, instead of
hiding in crevices and under logs like their brethren,
rest during the day exposed on the surface of leaves, in
the same manner as the fireflies they mimic.

Protective resemblances amongst insects are so numerous and wide-spread, and they have been so ably
described by Bates and Wallace, that I shall only
mention a few of the most noticeable examples that
came under my attention, and which have not been
described by other authors. Amongst these were the
striking modifications of some beetles belonging to
the Mordellidæ. These, in their normal form, are
curious wedge-shaped beetles, which are common on
flowers, and leap like fleas. In some of the Nicaraguan
species the body is lengthened, and the thorax and elytra
coloured, so as to resemble wasps and flies. In the
Mordellidæ the head is small, and nearly concealed
beneath the large thorax; and in the mimetic forms the
latter is coloured so as to resemble the large head and
eyes of the wasp or fly imitated. The species that

resembles a wasp moves its antennæ restlessly, like the latter insect.

The movements, as well as the shape and colour of the insect imitated, are mimicked. I one day observed what appeared to be a hornet, with brown semi-transparent wings and yellow antennæ. It ran along the ground vibrating its wings and antennæ exactly like a

HORNET AND MIMETIC BUG.

hornet, and I caught it in my net, believing it to be one. On examining it, however, I found it to belong to a widely different order. It was one of the Hemiptera, *Spiniger luteicornis* (Walk.), and had every part coloured like the hornet (*Priocnemis*) that it resembled. In its vibrating, coloured wing-cases it departed greatly from the normal character of the Hemiptera, and assumed that of the hornets.

All the insects that have special means of protection, by which they are guarded from the attacks of insectivorous mammals and birds, have peculiar forms, or strongly contrasted, conspicuous colours, and often make odd movements that attract attention to them. There is no attempt at concealment, but, on the contrary, they appear to endeavour to make their presence known. The long narrow wings of the Heliconii butterflies, banded with black, yellow, and red, distinguish them from all others, excepting the mimetic species. The banded bodies of many wasps, or the rich metallic colours of others, and their constant jerky motions, make them very conspicuous. Bees announce their presence by a noisy humming. The beetles of the genus Calopteron have their wing-cases curiously distended, and move them up and down, so as to attract attention; and other species of Lampyridæ are phosphorescent, holding out danger signals that they are not eatable. The reason in all these cases appears to be the same as Mr. Wallace has shown to hold good with banded, hairy, and brightly coloured caterpillars. These are distasteful to birds, and, in consequence of their conspicuous colours, are easily known and avoided. If they were like other caterpillars, they might be seized and injured before it was known they were not fit for food.*

Amongst the mammals, I think the skunk is an example of the same kind. Its white tail, laid back on its black body, makes it very conspicuous in the dusk

* In a paper on "Mimicry, and other Protective Resemblances amongst Animals," first published in the *Westminster Review*, July 1867, afterwards in "Natural Selection," Wallace has elaborately discussed this question. My observations are supplemental to his and to the original ones of Bates.

when it roams about, so that it is not likely to be pounced upon by any of the carnivora mistaking it for other night-roaming animals. In reptiles, the beautifully banded coral snake (*Elaps*), whose bite is deadly, is marked as conspicuously as any noxious caterpillar with bright bands of black, yellow, and red. I only met with one other example amongst the vertebrata, and it was also a reptile. In the woods around Santo Domingo there are many frogs. Some are green or brown, and imitate green or dead leaves, and live amongst foliage. Others are dull earth-coloured, and hide in holes and under logs. All these come out only at night to feed, and they are all preyed upon by snakes and birds. In contrast with these obscurely coloured species, another little frog hops about in the daytime dressed in a bright livery of red and blue. He cannot be mistaken for any other, and his flaming vest and blue stockings show that he does not court concealment. He is very abundant in the damp woods, and I was convinced he was uneatable so soon as I made his acquaintance and saw the happy sense of security with which he hopped about. I took a few specimens home with me, and tried my fowls and ducks with them, but none would touch them. At last, by throwing down pieces of meat, for which there was a great competition amongst them, I managed to entice a young duck into snatching up one of the little frogs. Instead of swallowing it, however, it instantly threw it out of its mouth, and went about jerking its head as if trying to throw off some unpleasant taste.*

* Probably the strongly contrasted colours of the spotted salamander of Southern Europe and the warning noise made by the rattlesnake may be useful in a similar manner, as has been suggested by Darwin.

After travelling three leagues beyond Teustepe, we reached, near dusk, a small house by the roadside, at which had put up for the night a party of muleteers, with their mules and cargoes. Our beasts were too tired to go further, so we determined to take our chance of finding room for our hammocks. Soon after we alighted, as I sat on a stone near the door of the house, a gun went off close to us, and my horse sprang forward, nearly upon me. We soon found it was our own gun, which had been given to Rito to carry. He had strapped it behind his saddle, and one of the other mules had come up, rubbed against it, and let it off. The poor horse was only four feet from the muzzle, and the contents were lodged in its loin. A large wound was made from which the blood flowed in a great stream, until Velasquez got some burnt cloth and stanched it. Fortunately the charge in the gun was a very light one, and no vital part was touched. We arranged with the muleteers to take our cargo to Juigalpa for us, and determined to leave Rito behind to lead the horse gently to Pital. The horse, which was a very good one, ultimately recovered.

At this house the woman had eight children, the eldest, I think, not more than twelve years of age. The man who passed as her husband was the father of the youngest only. Amongst the lower classes of Nicaragua men and women often change their mates. In such cases the children remain with the mother, and take their surname from her. Baptism is considered an indispensable rite, but the marriage ceremony is often dispensed with; and I did not notice that those who lived together without it suffered in the estimation of

their neighbours. The European ladies at Santo Domingo were sometimes visited by the unmarried matrons
of the village, who were very indignant when they found
that there were scruples about receiving them. They
were so used to their own social observances, that
they thought those of the Europeans unwarrantable
prudery.

Before turning out the mules, Rito got some limes and
squeezed the juice out upon their feet, just above the
hoof. He did this to prevent them from being bitten by
the tarantula spider, a species of Mygale that makes its
nest in the ground, and is said to abound in this locality.
Many of the mules are bitten in the feet on the savannahs by some venomous animal. The animal bitten
immediately goes lame, and cannot be cured in less
than six months, as the hoof comes off, and has to
be renewed. The natives say that the Mygale is the
aggressor; that it gets on the mule's foot to bite off the
hairs to line its nest with, and that if not disturbed it
does not injure the mule, but that if the latter tries to
dislodge it, it bites immediately. I do not know whether
this story be true or not, and I had no opportunity of
examining a Mygale's nest to see if it was lined with
hairs, but Professor Westwood informs me that all that
he knows are lined with fine silk. Possibly the mules,
when rambling about, step on the spider, and are then
bitten by it. Velasquez told me that when he was a
boy he and other children used to amuse themselves by
pulling the Mygale out of its hole, which is about a foot
deep in the ground. To get it out they fastened a small
ball of soft wax to a piece of string, and lowered it down
the hole, jerking it up and down until the spider got

exasperated so far as to bury its formidable jaws in the wax, when it could be drawn to the surface.

We had part of the kitchen to sleep in, and were so tired, and getting so accustomed to sleep anywhere, that we had a good night's rest, rose early next morning, and were soon on the road again, leaving Rito to bring on the lamed horse. We had a good view of the rock of San Lorenzo, a high cliff capping a hill, and resembling the rocks of Cuapo and Peña Blanca, but with less perpendicular sides. About this part, which lay high, as well as where we stayed the night before, there had been rains; but on the lowlands lying between the two places there had been none. Our road again lay over grassy plains and low, lightly-timbered hills, with very few houses—probably not more than one in a league. The country was now greener; they had had showers of rain, and fine grass had sprung up. Passing as we did from a dried-up district into one covered with verdure, feelings were awakened akin to those with which in the temperate zone we welcome the spring after a long winter.

As we rode on, the grass increased; there were swampy places in the hollows, and now and then very muddy spots on the road. On every side the prospect was bounded by long ranges of hills—some of them precipitous, others covered to the summits with dark foliaged trees, looking nearly black in the distance. About noon we came in sight of the Amerrique range, which I recognised at once, and knew that we had reached the Juigalpa district, though still several leagues distant from the town. Travelling on without halting we arrived at the hacienda of San Diego at four o'clock.

Velasquez expected to find in the owner an old acquaintance of his, and we had intended staying with him for
the night, as our mules were tired out; but on riding up
to the house we found it untenanted, the doors thrown
down, and cattle stabling in it.   We pushed on again.
I thought I could make La Puerta, a hacienda three
leagues nearer Libertad than Juigalpa, and as the road
to it branched off from that to Juigalpa soon after passing San Diego, and Velasquez had to go to the latter
place to make arrangements for getting our luggage
sent on, I parted with him, and pushed on alone.   Soon
after, I crossed rather a deep river, and in a short time
my mule, which had shown symptoms of distress, became
almost unable to proceed, so that it was only with the
greatest difficulty I could get along at all.   After leading—almost dragging—it slowly for about a mile I
reached a small hut, where they told me that it was
three leagues to La Puerta, and only one to Juigalpa.
The road to Puerta was all up hill, and it was clearly
impossible for me to reach it that night, so I turned off
across the savannahs, in the direction of Juigalpa, wishing that I had not separated from Velasquez.   My poor
beast was dragged along with much labour, and I was
getting thoroughly knocked up myself.   Several small
temporary huts were passed, in which lived families that
had come down from the mountains, bringing with them
their cows to feed on the plains during the wet season.
I was tempted to put up at one of these, but all were
full of people, and I persevered on until it got quite dark.
Just then I arrived at a hacienda near the river, and
engaged a young fellow to get his horse and ride with
me to the town.   When my mule had a companion it

went better, and being very tired I got on its back again. It was extremely dark, and I should not have found the road without a guide. We passed over the small plain, where the broken statues lie, but my guide, who had lived all his life within a mile of them, had never heard of them. My mule fell heavily with me in a rocky pass, but I escaped with a slight bruise. We had great trouble to get it on its legs again, and ultimately reached Juigalpa about nine o'clock.

Next morning I awoke with a dreadful headache and pain in my back, brought on either by the fatigue of the day before, or by having been tempted to eat some half-ripe guayavas when coming across the plains tired and hungry. I lay in the hammock until ten o'clock, and then feeling a little better, got on my mule and started. I was so ill as to be obliged to hold on to the pommel of my saddle, and several times to get off and lie down. We had brought some " tiste " with us made from choco-late and maize, and drinks of this relieved me. I at last reached Libertad at four o'clock, and went to bed imme-diately. Having fasted all day in place of taking medi-cine, I rose pretty well next morning, and we rode through the forest to the mines, reaching them at noon on the 29th July, after an absence of nineteen days.

CHAPTER XVIII.

Division of Nicaragua into three zones—Journey from Juigalpa to lake
of Nicaragua—Voyage on lake—Fresh-water shells and insects—
Similarity of fresh-water productions all over the world—Distribution of European land and fresh-water shells—Discussion of the
reasons why fresh-water productions have varied less than those
of the land and of the sea.

I SHALL ask my readers to accompany me on one more
journey. I have described the great Atlantic forest that
clothes the whole of the eastern side of Nicaragua. I
have gone through the central provinces, Chontales,
Matagalpa, and Segovia; from the San Juan river, the
south-eastern boundary of Nicaragua, away to the confines of Honduras on the north-west. I now propose
to leave the central provinces, amongst which we have
so long lingered, and to describe one of my journeys to
those lying between the great lakes and the Pacific.

Whilst the country to the north-east of the lakes is
mostly composed of rocks, of great age, geologically, such
as schists, quartzites, and old dolerytic rocks, with newer
but still ancient trachytes, that to the south-west of
them is formed principally of recent volcanic tufas and
lavas, the irruption of which has not yet ceased. Most
of the land, resulting from the decomposition of the
tufas, is of extreme fertility; and, therefore, we find on
the Pacific side of Nicaragua, indigo, coffee, sugar, cacao,
and tobacco growing with the greatest luxuriance.

Nicaragua is thus divided into three longitudinal zones. The most easterly is covered by a great unbroken forest; the principal products being india-rubber and mahogany. The central zone is composed of grassed savannahs, on which are bred cattle, mules, and horses. It is essentially a pasturage country, though much maize and a little sugar and indigo are grown in some parts. The western zone skirts the Pacific, and is a country of fertile soil, where all the cultivated plants and fruits of the tropics thrive abundantly; the rich, fat land might, indeed, with a little labour, be turned into a Garden of Eden.

In the autumn of 1871, it became necessary for me to proceed to Granada to empower a lawyer there to act for us in a lawsuit in which we were engaged. Taking Velasquez and a servant with me, I rode over to Juigalpa on the 1st of November. We had intended to go by land to Granada, but we learnt that, through continued wet weather, much of the low land of the delta of the Malacatoya was impassable, so we determined to make for the lake, and try to get a boat to take us to Los Cocos, from which place there was a good road to Granada. We found at Juigalpa a Libertad storekeeper, named Señor Trinidad Ocon. He had already engaged a boat, and courteously offered, if we could not find one when we got to the lake, to give us a passage in his.

We started from Juigalpa the next morning; and for the first few miles our road lay down by the river, a deep branch of which we crossed. The alluvial plains bordering the river were covered with fine, though short, grass, amongst which were some beautiful flowers. The orange and black "sisitoté" (*Icterus pectoralis*, Wagl.) flew in

small flocks amongst the bushes; and the " sanaté "
(*Quiscalus*) was busy amongst the cattle. Their usual
plan of operations is for a pair of them to accompany one
of the cattle, one on each side, watching for grasshoppers
and other insects that are frightened up by the browsing
animal. They keep near the head, and fly after the
insects that break cover, but neither encroaches on the
hunting ground of the other.

We stopped at a little hacienda perched at the top of
a small hill. It was called " El Candelera," and was a
small cattle station, surrounded by plains. We then
crossed the valley, and made for a range of hills between
us and the lake. The ascent was steep and rocky; and
it took us two hours to get to the top. We then saw
the great lake, like a sea lying spread out before us, but
still at a considerable distance. The descent was very
steep, and we had to make long detours to avoid precipitous ravines. At last we reached level ground; but
it was even worse than the mountain roads to travel,
being in many parts wet and swampy. After missing
our way, and having to retrace our steps for more than
a mile, we reached Santa Claro, a cattle hacienda, at
dusk. Here we found Señor Ocon's boat, but there
was no other. The boatmen said we must embark at
once. We made an arrangement with a man who had
accompanied Ocon to take our mules to San Ubaldo, as
we proposed to return that way. The boat was small,
and there were seven of us; so that with our saddles and
luggage we were much cramped for room.

They poled the boat for two miles down a small river
that emptied into the lake, but just before we reached it,
the boatmen stopped and said it was too rough to proceed

that night, and notwithstanding our remonstrances they
tied the boat to some bushes.   Our cramped position
was very irksome ; the river was bordered by swamps,
so that we could not land, and thousands of mosquitoes
came about and rendered sleep impossible.   About midnight, the moon rose, and two hours later we prevailed
on the boatmen to set sail, but, notwithstanding their
excuse about it being too rough, there was so little wind
that we made slow progress.   At eight we went on shore,
where there was a hut built close by the lake below
Masaya.   The lake was flooded, and the water had been
over the floor of the hut during the night.   All around
were swamps, and the mosquitoes were intolerable.   We
could buy no food at the miserable shanty, and soon set
sail again.   A little more wind afterwards springing
up, we reached Los Cocos at eleven o'clock.   There is
a small village at this place, where we got breakfast
cooked, and did justice to it.   We hired horses to take
us to Granada ; but as the road for a league further on
was overflown by the lake, we went on in the boat, and
a boy took the horses round to meet us, swimming them
across the worst places.

   Glad we were to get on horseback again, and to canter
along a hard sandy road, instead of sitting cramped up
in a little boat, with the sun's rays pouring down on us.
The path led amongst the bushes, and was sometimes
overflowed, but the soil was sandy, and there was no
mud.   All the beach was submerged, or we should have
ridden along it.   The last time I had passed by this part
of the lake was in July 1868.   Then the waters of the
lake were low, and we rode along the sandy beach, black
in some parts with titanic iron sand.   The beach re-

sembled that of a sea-coast, with the waves rolling in
upon it, and to the south-east the water extended to the
horizon. Along the shore were strewn shells thrown
up by the surf; and on examining them, I found them
all to belong to well-known old-world genera—*Unio*,
Planorbis, *Ancylus*, and *Ampullari*.

On this journey, all the beach was, as I have said,
covered with water, and I saw no shells; but in the
pools on the road were water-beetles swimming about,
and these showed a surprising resemblance to the water-
beetles of Europe. *Gyrinidæ* swam round and round in
mazy circles; *Dytiscidæ* came up to the surface for a
moment, and dived down again to the depths below with
a globule of air glistening like a diamond. Amongst the
vegetation at the bottom and sides of the pools *Hydro-
philidæ* crawled about, just as in ponds in England.
Not only were those familiars there, but they were represented by species belonging to the typical genera
—*Gyrinus*, *Colymbetes*, and *Hydrophilus*. Over these
pools flew dragon-flies, whose larval stages are passed
in the water, closely resembling others all over the
world. All the land fauna was strikingly different
from that of other regions; but the water fauna was as
strikingly similar.

The sameness of fresh-water productions all over the
globe is not confined to animal life, but extends to plants
also. Alph. de Candolle has remarked that in large
groups of plants which have many terrestrial and only a
few aquatic species the latter have a far wider distribution than the former. It is well known to botanists
that many fresh-water and marsh plants have an immense range over continents, extending even to the most

remote islands.*   The close affinities of fresh-water
animals and plants have been noticed by many naturalists.   Darwin saw with surprise, in Brazil, the similarity of the fresh-water insects, shells, &c., and the
dissimilarity of the surrounding terrestrial beings compared with those of Britain.†   Dr. D. Sharp informs
me that water-beetles undoubtedly present the same
types all over the world.   He believes there is no
family of *Coleoptera* in which tropical or extra-tropical
species so closely resemble one another as in the
Dytiscidæ.   *Cybister* is found in Europe, Asia, Africa,
Australia, New Zealand, Brazil, and North America;
and the species have a very wide range.   Dr. Sharp
remarks that this wide distribution and great similarity of the *Dytiscidæ* is of special interest when we
recollect that they are nothing but *Carabidæ* fitted for
swimming, and yet that the *Carabidæ* are one of the
groups in which the tropical members differ widely from
the temperate ones.

For following up this branch of inquiry the study of
the distribution of the mollusca offers special advantages.
There are numerous marine, fresh-water, and terrestrial
species and genera.   They are slow moving; they have
not the means of transporting themselves great distances,
like insects, for example, that may easily and often pass
over arms of the sea, or fly from one country to another.
Their shells are the commonest of fossils ; and in islands
such as Madeira and St. Helena, where we have abundant
remains of extinct land shells, there are few, if any, of
extinct animals of other classes or of plants.

Taking the shells of Europe, we find a remarkable

* Darwin, " Origin of Species," p. 417.   † *Ibid.*, p. 414.

difference in the distribution of the land and fresh-water species. According to Mr. Lovell Reeve, who has specially studied this question, out of many hundreds of land mollusks inhabiting the Caucasian province at its centre in Hungary and Austria, only ninety extend to the British Isles, and of these thirty-five do not reach Scotland. Upwards of two hundred species of Clausilia are to be found in the centre of the province, and of these only four reach England, and only one Scotland. Out of five hundred and sixty species of Helix inhabiting the Caucasian province, there are but twenty-four in Britain.

Whilst the distribution of the terrestrial mollusks of Europe is thus restricted in range, though the species are numerous, the fresh-water shells are few in species, but of wide distribution. Quoting again from Mr. Reeve :— Of the *Lymnæacea* " there are not six species, it may be safely stated, in all Europe, more than there are in Britain. They have no particular centre of creation. There is no evidence to show whether the alleged progenitors of our British species were created in Siberia, Hungary, or Thibet. There is scarcely any variation either in the form or number of the species in those remote localities. Of *Planorbis* scarcely more than fifteen species inhabit the whole Caucasian province, and we have eleven of them in Britain."—" Of *Physa* and *Lymnæa*, it is extremely doubtful whether there are any species throughout the province more than we have in Britain. Neither of Ancylus, which lives attached, limpet-like, to sticks and stones, and has very limited facilities of migration, are there any species throughout the province more than we have in Britain." *

* Lovell Reeve, " British Land and Fresh-Water Mollusks," p. 225.

The wide distribution of species inhabiting fresh water compared with those living on land has not, as we have seen, escaped the comprehensive mind of Darwin, and in explanation of the fact, he has shown how fresh-water shells may be carried from pool to pool, or from one river or lake to others many miles distant, sticking to the feet of water-fowl, or to the elytra of water-beetles. Whilst the distribution of water-mollusks may be thus accounted for, the greater variety and more restricted range of the land species is not explained. They have at least equal means of dispersion, compared with the sluggish, mud-loving water-shells of our ponds and ditches. Why should the one have varied so much and the other so little? We might at first sight have expected the very reverse, on the theory of natural selection. In large lakes and in river systems isolated from others, we might look for the conditions most favourable for the variation of species, and for the preservation of the improved varieties.

It is evident that there must have been less variation, or that the varieties that arose have not been preserved. I think it probable that the variation of fresh-water species of animals and plants has been constantly checked by the want of continuity of lakes and rivers in time and space. In the great oscillations of the surface of the earth, of which geologists find so many proofs, every fresh-water area has again and again been destroyed. It is not so with the ocean—it is continuous—and as one part was elevated and laid dry, the species could retreat to another. On the great continents the land has probably never been totally submerged at any one time; it also is continuous over great areas, and as one part became uninhabitable, the land species could in most cases retreat to another. But for the inhabitants of lakes and rivers there was no retreat, and whenever the sea overflowed the land, vast numbers of fresh-water species must have been destroyed. A fresh-water fauna gave place to a marine one, and the former was annihilated so far as that area was concerned. When the land again rose from below the sea, the marine fauna was not destroyed—it simply retired farther back.

There is every reason to believe that the production of species is a slow process, and if fresh-water areas have not continued as a rule through long geological periods, we can see how variation has been constantly checked by the destruction, first in one part, then in another, of all the fresh-water species ; and on these places being again occupied by fresh water they would be colonised by forms from other parts of the world. Thus species of restricted range were always exposed to destruction because their habitat was temporary and their retreat impossible, and only families of wide distribution could be preserved. Hence I believe it is that the types of fresh-water productions are few and world-wide, whilst the sea has mollusks innumerable, and the land great variety and wealth of species. This variety is in the ratio of the continuity of their habitats in time and space.

It follows also, from the same reasoning, that old and wide-spread types are more likely to be preserved in fresh-water areas than on land or in the sea, for the destruction of wide-ranging species is effected more by the competition of improved varieties than by physical causes; so that when variation is most checked old forms will longest survive. Therefore I think it is that amongst fishes we find some old geological types still preserved in a few of the large rivers of the world.

To illustrate more clearly the theory I have advanced, I will take a supposititious case. In the southern states of America there is reason to suppose that since the glacial period there has been a great variation in the species of the fresh-water mollusk genus *Melania*, and in different rivers there are distinct groups of species. Now let us suppose that the glacial period were to return, and that the icy covering, gradually thickening in the north, should push down southward as it did once before. The great lakes of North America would be again filled with ice, and their inhabitants destroyed. As the ice advanced southward, the inhabitants of one river-system after another would be annihilated, and many groups of Melania entirely destroyed. On the retreat of the ice again the rivers and lakes would reappear, but the varieties of animals that had been developed in them would not, and their places would be taken by aquatic forms from other areas, so that the number of species would be thereby greatly reduced, and wide-spreading forms would be freed from the competition of many improved varieties.

Viewed in this light, the similarity of fresh-water productions all over the world, instead of being a difficulty in the way of the acceptance of the theory of natural selection, becomes a strong argument in favour of its truth; for we perceive that the number of marine, terrestrial, and fresh-water animals is in proportion to the more or less continuous development that was possible under the different conditions under which they lived.

The same line of argument might be used to explain
the much greater variety in some classes of terrestrial
animals than in others.   The land has often been submerged in geological history, and the classes that were
best fitted to escape the impending catastrophes would
be most likely to preserve the varieties that had been
developed.   The atmosphere has always been continuous, and the animals that could use it as a highway had great advantages over those that could not,
and so we find the slow-moving terrestrial mollusks few
in number compared with the multitudinous hosts of
strong-flying insects ; similarly, the mammals are far
outnumbered by the birds of the air, that can pass
from island to island, and from country to country,
unstopped by mighty rivers or wide arms of the sea.

CHAPTER XIX.

Iguanas and lizards—Granada—Politics—Revolution—Cacao cultivation—Masaya—The Lake of Masaya—The volcano of Masaya—
Origin of the lake basin.

THE road passed along a sandy ridge only a little
elevated above the waters of the lake, and the ground on
both sides was submerged. As we travelled on we were
often startled by hearing sudden plunges into the water
not far from us, but our view was so obstructed by
bushes that it was some time before we discovered the
cause. At last we found that the noise was made by
large iguana lizards, some of them three feet long, and
very bulky, dropping from the branches of trees, on
which they lay stretched, into the water. These iguanas
are extremely ugly, but are said to be delicious eating,
the Indians being very fond of them. The Carca
Indians, who live in the forest seven miles from Santo
Domingo, travel every year to the great lake to catch
iguanas, which abound on the dry hills near it. They
seize them as they lie on the branches of the trees, with
a loop at the end of a long stick. They then break the
middle toe of each foot, and tie the feet together, in
pairs, by the broken toes, afterwards sewing up the
mouth of the poor reptiles, and carrying them in this
state back to their houses in the forest, where they are

kept alive until required for food. The raccoon-like
" pisoti " is also fond of them, but cannot so easily
catch them. He has to climb every tree, and then,
unless he can surprise them asleep, they drop from the
branch to the ground and scuttle off to another tree.
I once saw a solitary " pisoti " hunting for iguanas
amongst some bushes near the lake where they were
very numerous, but during the quarter of an hour that
I watched him, he never caught one. It was like the
game of " puss in the corner." He would ascend a
small tree on which there were several ; but down they
would drop when he had nearly reached them, and rush
off to another tree. Master " pisoti," however, seemed
to take all his disappointments with the greatest coolness, and continued the pursuit unflaggingly. Doubtless experience had taught him that his perseverance
would ultimately be rewarded : that sooner or later he
would surprise a corpulent iguana fast asleep on some
branch, and too late to drop from his resting-place. In
the forest I always saw the " pisoti " hunting in large
bands, from which an iguana would have small chance
of escape, for some were searching along the ground
whilst others ranged over the branches of the trees.

Other tree-lizards also try to escape their enemies by
dropping from great heights to the ground. I was
once standing near a large tree, the trunk of which
rose fully fifty feet before it threw off a branch, when
a green *Anolis* dropped past my face to the ground,
followed by a long green snake that had been pursuing
it amongst the foliage above, and had not hesitated to
precipitate itself after its prey. The lizard alighted on
its feet and hurried away, the snake fell like a coiled-up

watch-spring, and opened out directly to continue the pursuit; but, on the spur of the moment, I struck at it with a switch and prevented it. I regretted afterwards not having allowed the chase to continue and watched the issue, but I doubt not that the lizard, active as it was, would have been caught by the swift-gliding snake, as several specimens of the latter that I opened contained lizards.

Lizards are also preyed upon by many birds, and I have taken a large one from the stomach of a great white hawk with its wings and tail barred with black (*Leucopternis ghiesbreghti*) that sits up on the trees in the forest quietly watching for them. Their means of defence are small, nor are they rapid enough in their movements to escape from their enemies by flight, and so they depend principally for their protection on their means of concealment. The different species of *Anolis* can change their colour from a bright green to a dark brown, and so assimilate themselves in appearance to the foliage or bark of trees on which they lie. Another tree-lizard, not uncommon on the banks of the rivers, is not only of a beautiful green colour, but has foliaceous expansions on its limbs and body, so that even when amongst the long grass it looks like a leafy shoot that has fallen from the trees above. I do not know of any lizard that enjoys impunity from attack by the secretion of any acrid or poisonous fluid from its skin, like the little red and blue frog that I have already described, but I was told of one that was said to be extremely venomous. As, however, besides the repute of giving off from the pores of its skin poisonous secretion, it was described to be of an inconspicuous brown colour, and to hide under logs, I should require some confirmation of the story by an experienced naturalist before believing it, for all my experience has led me to the opinion that any animal endowed with special means of protection from its enemies is always either conspicuously coloured, or in other ways attracts attention, and does not seek concealment.

About four o'clock we reached the city of Granada, and, passing along some wide streets and across a large square, found the hotel of Mons. Mestayer, where we engaged rooms for the night. The hotel, like most of the houses in the city, was built, in the Spanish style, around a large courtyard, in the centre of which was a flower-garden. Madame Mestayer was very fond of pets, and had macaws and parrots, a tame squirrel, a young white-faced monkey (*Cebus albifrons*), and several small long-haired Mexican dogs. I was interested in watching the monkey examining all the loose bark and curled-up leaves on a large fig-tree in search of insects. In this and other individuals of this species, a great variety of countenances could be distinguished, and I could easily have picked my own monkey out of all the others I have seen by the expression of its face. I was told that the one in the garden at Mons. Mestayer's did not touch the figs on the tree, and I believe it; the *Cebus* is much more of an animal than a vegetable feeder, whilst the spider-monkeys (*Ateles*) live principally on fruits.

Granada was entirely burnt down by Walker and his filibusters in 1856, and the present city is built on the ruins of that founded by Hernandez de Cordova in 1522. The streets are well laid out at right angles to each other, and there are many large churches, some of them in ruins. In one of the latter a company of mounte-banks performed every evening, and the circumstance did not seem to excite surprise or comment.

The streets are built in terraces, quite level for about fifty yards, then with a steep-paved declivity leading to another level portion. One has to be careful in riding down from one level to another, as horses and mules are very liable to slip on the smooth pavement. The houses are built of "adobe" or sun-dried brick. The walls are plastered and whitewashed, and the roofs and floors tiled. They are mostly of one storey, and the rooms surrounding the courtyards have doors opening both to the inside and to the street.

There are no factories in Granada, but many whole-sale stores, kept by merchants, who import goods from England and the United States, and export the produce of the country—indigo, hides, coffee, cacao, sugar, india-rubber, &c. Many of these merchants are very wealthy; but all deal retail as well as whole-sale; and the reputed wealthiest man of the town asked me if I did not want to buy a few boxes of candles. The highest ambition of every one seems to be to keep a shop, excepting when the revolutionary fever breaks out about every seven or eight years, when, for a few months, business is at a stand-still, and the popula-tion is divided into two parties, alternately pursuing and being pursued, but seldom engaging in a real battle.

There was one of these outbreaks whilst I was in Nicaragua, and the whole country was in a state of civil war for more than four months, nearly all the able-bodied men being drafted into the armies that were raised, but I believe there were not a score of men killed on the field of battle during the whole time; the town of Juigalpa was taken and retaken without any one receiving a scratch. The usual course pursued was for the two armies to manœuvre about until one thought it was weaker than the other, when it immediately took to flight. Battles were decided without a shot being fired, excepting after one side had run away.

Of patriotism I never saw a symptom in Central America, nothing but selfish partisanship, willing at any moment to set the country in a state of war if there was only a prospect of a little spoil. The states of Central America are republics in name only; in reality, they are tyrannical oligarchies. They have excellent constitutions and laws on paper, but both their statesmen and their judges are corrupt; with some honourable exceptions, I must admit, but not enough to stem the current of abuse. Of real liberty there is none. The party in power is able to control the elections, and to put their partisans into all the municipal and other offices. Some of the Presidents have not hesitated to throw their political opponents into prison at the time of an election, and I heard of one well-authenticated instance where an elector was placed, uncovered, in the middle of one of the plazas, with his arms stretched out to their full extent and each thumb thrust down into the barrel of an upright musket, and kept a few hours in the blazing sun until he agreed to vote according to the wish of the party in power. A change of rulers can only be effected by a so-called revolution; with all the machinery of a republic, the will of the people can only be known by the issue of a civil war.

With high-sounding phrases of the equality of man, the lower orders are kept in a state almost approaching to serfdom. The poor Indians toil and spin, and cultivate the ground, being almost the only producers. Yet, in the revolutionary outbreaks, they are driven about like cattle, and forced into the armies that are raised. Central America declared its independence of Spain in 1823, and constituted itself a republic, under the name of the United States of Central America. The confederacy, which consisted of Guatemala, San Salvador, Honduras, Nicaragua, and Costa Rica, was broken up in 1840, when each of the States became an independent republic. Ever since, revolutionary outbreaks have been periodical, and the States, with the exception of Costa Rica, have steadily decreased in wealth and produce.

It would be ungenerous of me, in this condemnation of the political parties of Central America, not to state that there are many individuals who view with alarm and shame the decadence of their country. Such, however, is the state of public opinion, that their voices are unheard, or listened to with indifference. There seems to be some radical incapacity in the Latin races to comprehend what we consider true political economy. The will of the majority is not the law of the land, but the will of the strongest in arms. They cannot understand that a republic has no more divine right than a monarchy ; that a country having an hereditary sovereign at its head, if it is governed in consonance with the wishes of the greatest number of its inhabitants, is freer than a republic where a minority rules by force of arms. They make a principle out of what is a mere detail of government—whether the chief of the state be elective or hereditary—but the fundamental principle of good government, namely, that the will of the majority shall be the law of the land, is trampled under foot and treated as the dream of an enthusiast.

The environs of Granada are very pretty; it is situated only a mile from the lake, and a few miles lower down the sleeping volcano of Mombacho juts boldly out, rising to a height of nearly 5000 feet, and clothed to the very summit with dark perennial verdure. The cacao of Granada and Rivas is said to be amongst the finest grown, and there are many large plantations of it. The wild cacao grows in the forests of the Atlantic slope, and when cultivated it still requires shade to thrive luxuriantly. This is provided at first by plantain trees, afterwards by the coral tree, a species of *Erythrina*, called by the natives Cacao madre, or the Cacao's mother, on account of the fostering shade it affords the cacao tree. The coral tree rises to a height of about forty feet, and when in flower, at the beginning of April, is one mass of bright crimson flowers, fairly dazzling the eyes of the beholder when the sun is shining on it.

One of the principal courts of law is held at Granada, and whilst we were there a priest was being tried for having seduced his own niece. He was afterwards convicted, and, to show the moral torpidity of the people, I may mention that his only punishment was banishment to Greytown, where he appeared to mix in Nicaraguan society as if he had not a spot on his character.

Having finished our business in Granada, we started for Masaya, where I wished to consult a lawyer, Senhor Rafael Blandino, who most deservedly bears a very high

character in Nicaragua for probity and ability. We had
a difficulty in obtaining horses, and did not get away
until noon. The road was a good one, having been
made by the late President, Señor Fernando Guzman,
who seems to have done what little lay in his power
to develop the resources of the country. The soil was
entirely composed of volcanic tufas, and was covered
with fine grass; but there were no springs or brooks,
all the moisture sinking into the porous ground. Lizards
were numerous, and on damp spots on the road there
were many fine butterflies, most of them of different
species from those of Chontales.

At four o'clock we entered Masaya, and passed down
a long road bordered with Indian huts and gardens.
The town is said to contain about 15,000 inhabitants,
nine-tenths of whom are Indians. It covers a great
space of ground, as the Indian houses are each surrounded by a garden or orchard; they stand back from
the road, and are almost hidden amongst the trees.
There was no water when I visited Masaya, excepting
what was brought up from the lake, which lies more
than 300 feet below the town, surrounded, excepting on
the western side, by precipitous cliffs, down which three
or four rocky paths have been cut. Up these, all day
long, and most of the night, women and girls are carrying water in Indian earthenware gourd-shaped jars,
which they balance on cushions on their heads, or sling
in nets on their backs. No men, or boys above ten
years of age, carry water, and the women seemed to
have all the labour to do. I believe it would have been
impossible to find ten men at work in Masaya at any
one time.

I spent the next day exploring around Masaya, as I was greatly interested with the geological structure of the country. One of the paths down to the lake has been made passable for animals taken down to drink. I rode my horse down, but in the steepest part he slipped on to his side, and I was content to lead him the rest of the way. The scene was one which is only possible in a half-civilised tropical land. Women, with the scantiest of clothing, or less, were washing linen, standing up to their waists in the water amongst the rocks, on which they thumped the clothes to be cleansed ; laughing and chatting to each other incessantly. Men with mules and horses were bathing themselves and their animals at a small sandy beach, and girls were carrying off great jars of water, which they obtained further down, where the water was less tainted with the ablutions. Great rocks, that had fallen from the cliffs above, lined the shore; and amongst these grew many shrubs and plants new to me. The cliffs themselves were, in some parts, green with lovely maiden-hair ferns, belonging to three different species.

On the opposite shore rises the cone of the volcano of Masaya, and the streams of lava that have flowed down to the lake and covered the old precipitous cliffs on that side are plainly visible. The cliff encircles the whole lake, excepting where concealed by the recent lava overflow. At the time of the conquest of Nicaragua, in 1522, the volcano of Masaya was in a state of activity. The credulous Spaniards believed the fiery, molten mass at the bottom of the crater to be liquid gold, and through great danger, amongst the smoke and fumes, were lowered down it until, with an iron chain and

bucket, they could reach the fiery mass, when the
bucket was melted from the chain, and the intrepid
explorers were drawn up half dead from amongst the
fumes.   Since then there have been several eruptions;
and so late as 1857 it threw out volumes of smoke, and
probably ashes.   The whole country is volcanic.   For
scores of miles every rock is trachytic, and the earth
decomposing tufas.

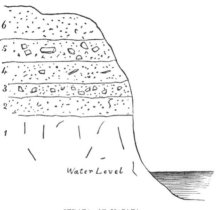

STRATA AT MASAYA.

The lake itself is like an immense crater with its
perpendicular cliffs.   I spent some time in making an
accurate section of the strata as exposed in the rocky
paths leading down to the water.   The whole section
exposed is 348 feet in height from the surface of the
lake to the top of the undulating plain on which
Masaya is built.   This measurement was kindly given
to me by Mr. Simpson, an enterprising American
engineer engaged in erecting a steam-pump to raise

the water for the supply of the town. At the bottom
are seen great cliffs of massive trachyte (No. 1 in
section). Above this is an ash bed, then a bed of
breccia containing fragments of trachyte, then another
bed of cinders, which looks like a rough sandstone, but
is pisolitic, and contains pebbles of the size of a bean.
This bed is surmounted by one that possesses great
interest (No. 5 in section). It is composed of fine tufa,
in which is imbedded a great number of large angular
fragments of trachyte, some of which are more than
three feet in diameter. It is the last bed but one, the
surface being composed of lightly coherent strata of
tufaceous ash, worn into an undulating surface by the
action of the elements.

I believe there is but one explanation possible of the
origin of these strata, namely, that the great bed of
trachyte at the base is an ancient lava bed; that this,
perhaps long after it was consolidated, was covered by
beds of ashes and *scoriæ* thrown out by a not far distant
volcano, and that at last a great convulsion broke
through the trachyte bed and hurled the fragments
over the country along with dense volumes of dust and
ashes. The angular blocks of trachyte imbedded in the
stratum No. 5 in section are exactly the same in composition as the great bed below, and in them I think
we see the fragments of the rocks that once filled the
perpendicular-sided hollow now occupied by the lake.
Looking at the vast force required to hollow out the
basin of the lake, by blasting out the whole contents
into the air—distributing them over the country so
that they have not been piled up in a volcanic cone
round the vent, but lie in comparatively level beds—I

cannot expect that this explanation will be readily received, nor should I myself have advanced it if I could in any other way account for the phenomena. Still, within historical times, there have been volcanic outbursts, not of such magnitude, certainly, as was required to excavate the basin of the lake of Masaya, but still of sufficient extent to show that such an origin is not beyond the limits of possibility.

Thus, in the same line of volcanic energy, not far from the boundary line of the States of Nicaragua and San Salvador, there was an eruption of the volcano of Cosaguina, on the 20th of January 1835, when dense volumes of dust and ashes, and fragments of rocks, were hurled up in the air and deposited over the country around. The vast quantity of material thrown out by this explosion may be gathered from the fact that, one hundred and twenty miles away, near the volcano of San Miguel, the dust was so thick that it was quite dark from four o'clock in the evening until nearly noon of the next day; and even at that distance there was deposited a layer of fine ashes four inches deep. The noise of the explosion was heard at the city of Guatemala, four hundred miles to the westward, and at Jamaica, eight hundred miles to the north-east.

In St. Vincent, in the West Indies, there was a great eruption on April 27th, 1812, which continued for three days, and was heard six hundred and thirty miles away on the llanos of Caracas. It has been so graphically narrated by Canon Kingsley that I shall once more quote from his eloquent pages. " That single explosion relieved an interior pressure upon the crust of the earth which had agitated sea and land from the Azores to the

West Indian islands, the coasts of Venezuela, the Cordillera of New Granada, and the valleys of the Mississippi and Ohio. For nearly two years the earthquakes had continued, when they culminated in one great tragedy, which should be read at length in the pages of Humboldt. On March 26th, 1812, when the people of Caracas were assembled in the churches, beneath a still and blazing sky, one minute of earthquake sufficed to bury, amid the ruins of churches and houses, nearly ten thousand souls. The same earthquake wrought terrible destruction along the whole line of the northern Cordilleras, and was felt even at Santa Fé de Bogota and Honda, one hundred and eighty leagues from Caracas. But the end was not yet. While the wretched survivors of Caracas were dying of fever and starvation, and wandering inland to escape from ever-renewed earthquake shocks, among villages and farms which, ruined like their own city, could give them no shelter, the almost forgotten volcano of St. Vincent was muttering in suppressed wrath. It had thrown out no lava since 1718, if, at least, the eruption spoken of by Moreau de Jonnés took place in the Souffrière. According to him, with a terrific earthquake, clouds of ashes were driven into the air, with violent detonations from a mountain situated at the eastern end of the island. When the eruption had ceased, it was found that the whole mountain had disappeared. Now there is no eastern end to St. Vincent nor any mountain on the east coast, and the Souffrière is at the northern end. It is impossible, meanwhile, that the wreck of such a mountain should not have left traces visible and notorious to this day. May not the truth

be, that the Souffrière had once a lofty cone, which was
blasted away in 1718, leaving the present crater-ring
of cliffs and peaks ; and that thus may be explained
the discrepancies in the accounts of its height, which
Mr. Scrope gives as 4940 feet, and Humboldt and Dr.
Davy at 3000, a measurement which seems to me to
be more probably correct? The mountain is said to
have been slightly active in 1785. In 1812, its old
crater had been for some years (and is now) a deep
blue lake, with walls of rock around, 800 feet in height,
reminding one traveller (Dr. Davy) of the lake of Albano.
But for twelve months it had given warning, by frequent
earthquake shocks, that it had its part to play in the
great subterranean battle between rock and steam; and
on the 27th April 1812 the battle began.

"A negro boy—he is said to be still alive in St.
Vincent—was herding cattle on the mountain-side. A
stone fell near him, and then another. He fancied that
other boys were pelting him from the cliffs above, and
began throwing stones in return. But the stones fell
thicker, and among them one and then another too large
to have been thrown by human hand. And the poor
fellow woke up to the fact that not a boy but the mountain was throwing stones at him ; and that the column of
black cloud which was rising from the crater above was
not harmless vapours, but dust, and ash, and stone. He
turned and ran for his life, leaving the cattle to their
fate, while the steam mitrailleuse of the Titans—to
which all man's engines of destruction are but pop-
guns—roared on for three days and nights, covering
the greater part of the island with ashes, burying crops,
breaking branches off the trees, and spreading ruin

from which several estates never recovered; and so the 30th of April dawned in darkness which might be felt.

" Meanwhile, on the same day, to change the scene of the campaign two hundred and ten leagues, ' a distance,' as Humboldt says, ' equal to that between Vesuvius and Paris,' the inhabitants, not only of Caracas, but of Calabozo, situate in the midst of the Llanos, over a space of four thousand square leagues, were terrified by a sub-terranean noise, which resembled frequent discharges of the loudest cannon. It was accompanied by no shock, and, what is very remarkable, was as loud on the coast as at eighty leagues inland; and at Caracas, as well as at Calabozo, preparations were made to put the place in defence against an enemy who seemed to be advancing with heavy artillery. They might as well have copied the St. Vincent herd-boy, and thrown their stones, too, at the Titans; for the noise was, there can be no doubt, nothing else than the final explosion in St. Vincent far away. The same explosion was heard in Venezuela, the same at Martinique and Guadaloupe; but there, too, there were no earthquake shocks. The volcanoes of the two French islands lay quiet, and left their English brother to do the work. On the same day, a stream of lava rushed down from the mountain, reached the sea in four hours, and then all was over. The earthquakes which had shaken for two years a sheet of the earth's surface larger than half Europe were stilled by the eruption of this single vent.

" The strangest fact about this eruption was, that the mountain did not make use of its old crater. The ori-ginal vent must have become so jammed and consolidated, in the few years between 1785 and 1812, that it could

z

not be reopened, even by a steam-force the vastness of
which may be guessed at from the vastness of the area
which it had shaken for two years. So when the eruption was over it was found that the old crater-lake,
incredible as it may seem, remained undisturbed, as far
as has been ascertained. But close to it, and separated
only by a knife-edge of rock some 700 feet in height, and
so narrow that, as I was assured by one who had seen it,
it is dangerous to crawl along it, a second crater, nearly
as large as the first, had been blasted out, the bottom of
which, in like manner, is now filled with water.

"The day after the explosion, 'Black Sunday,' gave
a proof, but no measure, of the enormous force which
had been exerted. Eighty miles to windward lies Barbadoes. All Saturday a heavy cannonading had been
heard to the eastward. The English and French fleets
were surely engaged. The soldiers were called out, the
batteries manned, but the cannonade died away, and all
went to bed in wonder. On the 1st of May the clocks
struck six; but the sun did not, as usual in the tropics,
answer to the call. The darkness was still intense, and
grew more intense as the morning wore on. A slow and
silent rain of impalpable dust was falling over the whole
island.

"The trade-wind had fallen dead; the everlasting
roar of the surf was gone; and the only noise was the
crashing of the branches snapped by the weight of the
clammy dust. About one o'clock the veil began to lift,
a lurid sunlight stared in from the horizon, but all
was black overhead. Gradually the dust-cloud drifted
away; the island saw the sun once more, and saw itself
inches deep in black, and in this case fertilising, dust.

"Those who will recollect that Barbadoes is eighty miles to windward of St. Vincent, and that a strong breeze from east-north-east is usually blowing from the former island to the latter, will be able to imagine, not to measure, the force of an explosion which must have blown the dust several miles into the air above the region of the trade-wind. Whether into a totally calm stratum or into that still higher one in which the heated south-west wind is hurrying continually from the tropics toward the pole." *

I have quoted this graphic account of the great volcanic eruption of St. Vincent in 1812 from Canon Kingsley's delightful work to impress on my readers, in more eloquent language than I can command, the fact of great explosions having taken place in recent times similar in character, though much inferior in extent and force, to that by which I believe the great basin of the Lake of Masaya and similar basins in the same and adjoining Pacific provinces have been blasted out. I do not shut my eyes to the fact that great as was the force in operation in 1812 at St. Vincent, that necessary to excavate the great chasm at Masaya was incomparably greater. No one is more disinclined than I am to invoke the aid of greater natural forces in former times than are now in existence. But I believe there is good reason to infer that at the close of the glacial period volcanic energy was much more intense than now. So strained is the earth's crust at some parts that it is surmised that even a great difference in the pressure of the atmosphere such as occurs during a cyclone, may be sufficient to bring on an earthquake or a volcanic eruption already immi-

* "At Last," by Charles Kingsley, vol. i. p. 90.

nent. Whether this be so or not, there can be no doubt
that at the melting away of the ice of the glacial period
there was an enormous change in the strains on the
earth's crust. Ice that had been piled up mountains
high at the poles and along the chain of the Andes all
through tropical America melted away and ran down to
the ocean beds. This great transference of weight could
not have been accomplished without many rendings of
the earth's crust and many outpourings of lava and volcanic outbursts. Let us reflect, too, that not only was an
enormous mass of matter, before lying over the poles, removed nearer to the equator, and many mountain-chains
relieved of the ice of thousands and tens of thousands of
years, but that there must have been an actual change
in the earth's centre of gravity. All our experience
shows that the ice was more developed on some meridians
than others; probably nowhere in the whole world did it
lie so thick as along the American continents; and everywhere it must have been greater over the land than over
the sea. When it assumed its liquid form, and arranged
itself freely according to its specific gravity, the centre of
gravity of the earth must have been effectively changed.
All who have studied the present statical condition of
the earth's crust will readily admit that such a change
might produce greater volcanic outbursts than any
known to history.

Then when we turn to the most ancient traditions of
the human race in both the old and the new worlds, and
find everywhere fire and water linked together in the
accounts of the great catastrophes that are said nearly to
have annihilated the human race, I for one am inclined
to accept them, and to believe; that when, in the " Leo

Amontli," as translated by Brasseur de Bourbourg, we read of "the volcanic convulsions that lasted four days and four nights," of "the thunder and lightning that came out of the sea," of "the mountains that were rising and sinking when the great deluge happened," and that when Plato on the other side of the Atlantic speaks of the earthquakes that accompanied the engulphment of Atlantis, we hear the dim echoes that have been sounding down through all time from that remote past, of the fearful volcanoes and earthquakes that terrified mankind at the time of the great cataclysm.

In these remarks on the origin of some of the lakes of Nicaragua I except the largest ones, namely, the lake of Managua and the great lake of Nicaragua, which probably occupy areas of depression produced by the large amount of material abstracted from below and thrown out by ancient volcanoes.

CHAPTER XX.

Indian population of the country lying between the great lakes of
Nicaragua and the Pacific—Discovery and conquest of Nicaragua
by the Spaniards—Cruelties of the Spaniards—The Indians of
Western Central America all belonged to one stock—Decadence
of Mexican civilisation before the arrival of the Spaniards—The
designation "Nahuatls" proposed to include all the Mexican,
Western Central American, and Peruvian races that had descended
from the same ancient stock—The Nahuatls distinct from the
Caribs on one side, and the Red Indians on the other—Discussion
of the question of the peopling of America.

I RODE for some distance around the Lake of Masaya,
and reached an Indian village named Nandasme, about
two leagues from the city. As usual the streets were
laid out at right angles, and the houses of the Indians
embowered in trees, many of which are grown entirely for
the beautiful odoriferous flowers they produce. There
are several other Indian villages around the lake, from
each of which paths have been cut through the forest
down to the water, along which the women are constantly ascending and descending to fill their vessels
for the supply of their houses.

All the fertile country lying between the great lakes
and the Pacific was densely populated at the time of the
conquest, and it was not far from Masaya that the great
chief, Diriangan, lived, who tried, but tried in vain, to
stem the onward course of the Spaniards. Gil Gonzales

de Avila was in command of the first expedition sent to explore the country of Nicaragua. He sailed from Panama with one hundred followers and four horses, the latter, auxiliaries whose aid was never dispensed with in these expeditions on account of the superstitious terror with which the unaccustomed sight of a man and a horse, apparently joined together, inspired the Indians. He landed somewhere on the Gulf of Nicoya, near which he entered the country of a powerful chief, after whom the gulf was named. Nicoya entertained the Spaniards courteously, supplied them with food, and embraced the Christian religion, being baptized himself along with all his people, six thousand in number.

Pushing on to the northward for fifty leagues, Gonzales entered the territories of a great chief named Nicaragua, whose country comprised the present province of Rivas. Nicaragua had been informed of " the sharpness of the Spanish swords " and received Gonzales with hospitality, presenting him with much gold, equal to " 25,000 pieces of eight," and garments and plumes of feathers. He asked the Spaniards many shrewd questions : about the flood, and about the sun, moon, and stars ; their motion, quality, and distance ; what was the cause of night and day and the blowing of the winds ? how the Spaniards got all their information about heaven ; who brought it to them, and if the messenger came down on a rainbow? We are told that " Gonzales answered to the best of his ability, commending the rest to God." Probably his interrogator knew more of the visible heavenly bodies than he did, for Nicaragua was of the Aztec race, a people who knew the true theory of eclipses, and possessed an astronomical calendar of great accuracy.

Pedrarias, who was then in command at Panama, stimulated by the accounts of the rich country that Gonzales had discovered, sent Hernando de Cordova in 1522 to subdue and settle the country of Nicaragua. Pascual de Andagoya tells the story of the rich land, "populous and fertile, yielding supplies of maize, and many fowls of the country, and certain small dogs which they also eat, and many deer and fish. This is a land of abundance of good fruits and of honey and wax, wherewith all the neighbouring countries are supplied. The bees are numerous, some of them yellow, and these do not sting." The poor Indians, too, could not sting, they were powerless with their coats of feathers and swords of stone against the arms of the Spaniards, who treated them like a hive of stingless bees, turning them out and eating up their riches. "They had a great quantity of cotton cloths, and they held their markets in the open squares, where they traded. They had a manufactory where they made cordage of a sort of *nequen*, which is like carded flax; the cord was beautiful and stronger than that of Spain, and their cotton canvas was excellent. The Indians were very civilised in their way of life, like those of Mexico, for they were a people who had come from that country, and they had nearly the same language."

They had even in one direction reached a pitch of civilisation that some of our philanthropists are only now hoping for. Women's rights were acknowledged, and, if anything, they appear to have had too much of them. Pascual says: "They had many beautiful women. The husbands were so much under subjection that if they made their wives angry they were turned out of doors, and the wives even raised their hands against

them." * Much have the Indians changed since then
under the dominion of the Spaniard, and now all the
toil and labour fall to the lot of the weaker sex. One
custom still remaining amongst the Masaya Indians
may be a relic of the old days of woman's superiority.
When they marry, the goods that the wife had before
her marriage still belong to her, and if she had a mule
or horse, and her husband had none, he cannot use hers
without her permission.

The poor Indians were ground down to the dust by
the Spaniards with pitiless barbarities. All their pos-
sessions were seized, and they themselves exported to
Panama and Peru, and sold as slaves to work at the
mines. Even in Pascual's time the country had been
greatly depopulated by these means. The people were
harmless and patient, but there was a noble independence about them that could not be eradicated, and the
Spaniards found it was cheaper to bring the negro from
Africa, with his light and careless nature, than to try to
enslave a people who did not resist, but who sought
a refuge from their persecutors in the grave rather than
continue in slavery. I shall not harrow the feelings of
my readers with the mass of treachery, avarice, blas-
phemy, and horrible cruelties with which the conquerors
rewarded the noble people who entertained them so
courteously. To me the conquest of Mexico, Central
America, and Peru appears one of the darkest pages in
modern history. One virtue indeed shone out—un-
daunted courage ; and the human mind is so constituted
that this single redeeming point irresistibly enlists our

* This and the other quotation are from the "Narrative of Pascual
de Andagoya," translated by C. R. Markham, Esq. Hakluyt Soc.

sympathies. But for this, Pizarro would be execrated as a monster of cruelty, and even the fame of Cortez, immeasurably superior as he was to the rest of the conquerors, would be tarnished with innumerable deeds of violence, cruelty, and treachery.

As has been already mentioned, the Pacific provinces of Nicaragua were inhabited by a people closely related to the Mexicans, and their language was nearly the same. According to Squier, who has more than any other traveller studied the different races, the Indians living at the island of Omotépec at the present time are of pure Mexican or Aztec stock. So many of the names of towns in the central provinces are also of Aztec origin, that they must have had a considerable footing there also. They called the older inhabitants, whom they had probably dispossessed and driven back to the interior, " Chontalli," " barbarians," and hence the name of the province of Chontales, where these tribes still existed in considerable numbers at the time of the conquest.

All these races, differing as they did in language and in the degree of civilisation at which they had arrived, were closely affiliated.* The American archæologist, Mr. John D. Baldwin, is of opinion that they were the descendants of indigenes. That at some very remote period, before they had attained a high degree of civilisation, they separated into two branches, one of which occupied Peru, the other Central America and Mexico. Both branches advanced greatly in civilisation, and both

* According to Prescott the Aztecs and cognate races believed their ancestors came from the north-west—and were preceded by the real civilisers—the Toltecs.

afterwards deteriorated by being conquered by ruder but more warlike people belonging to the same stock. From Mexico the ancient people spread northward and southward. The northern emigrants peopled the banks of the Mississippi, and were the mound-builders. The southern emigrants peopled Central America. Then came an immigration from the far north-west, of nomadic tribes from north-eastern Asia, who drove out the mound-builders. The latter retreated back to Mexico, that their fathers had left ages before, and were the ancient Toltecs. Later on, the Aztecs, who were the southern branch of the ancient Mexicans, invaded Mexico from the south, and supplanted the Toltecs. Another branch of the same ancient stock were the Mayas of Yucatan.*

Looking then far back we have, according to the old traditions, a few people who had escaped a great cataclysm, when fire and water both fought against mankind; remnants perhaps of many tribes, who, when the lowlands were overwhelmed, escaped to the mountains, speaking a variety of languages, and bringing with them some remembrances of the civilisation of their ancient homes. They increased and multiplied in their new abodes. Some in Mexico, some in Yucatan, and others in Peru arrived at a great pitch of civilisation. Ages passed away, they had developed into several distinct peoples, all showing traces of their common descent, but having branched off in different directions in their lines of progress; all underlaid by a few great principles : in their religion, by the worship of the heavenly bodies ; in their government, by complete and absolute obedience to their

* "Ancient America," by J. D. Baldwin, A.M.

kings and leaders ; in their mode of life all agriculturists
and dwellers in regular towns and villages. They spread
northward and occupied the valley of the Mississippi, and
in summer time sent off large bodies of workmen to
extract the copper of Lake Superior. Then came the
nomadic tribes from the north-west, the Red Indians
of the present day, and drove out the mound-builders,
who were turned back on their ancient home, of which
they had lost all recollection, and where they appeared
as immigrants and invaders. In the subjugation of the
ancient Choluans by the Toltecs, and afterwards the
Toltecs by the Aztecs, we see what has often occurred
in the world's history—a highly civilised race conquered
by a ruder people, who had advanced farther in the arts
of war, and so overcame the people who had advanced
farther in the arts of peace. Therefore the Choluans
were replaced by the more warlike Toltecs, the Toltecs
by the ruder Aztecs, and those who look at the miserable towns and villages of the present inhabitants alongside of the ruins of the grand edifices, the roads and
aqueducts of ancient Mexico and Peru, may say, the
Aztecs by the less civilised Spaniards.

The term Brown Indians has been proposed to distinguish the races of Mexico, Central and South America,
from the Red Indians of the north ; but it is a too general
term, as it includes not only the highly-civilised Aztecs,
Mayas, and Peruvians, but the much ruder Caribs of the
éastern coasts of South America and the Antilles, who
were widely removed from them in race and language.
Squier has proposed the term Nahuatls for the people
of Mexico and Central America, and if it might be
strained to include the Peruvians also, and all the

peoples descended from that ancient civilised race that
had spread northward and southward, it would supply a
want that I have greatly felt in studying these peoples.
The Nahuatls—I use the term in this extended sense—
are one of three great Indian races that occupy the
greater part of North and South America. They had
the Red Indians to the north of them, the savage Caribs
to the south-east. From both these races they were
profoundly different, though not in equal degrees. To
the Red Indian they have scarcely any affinity, excepting such as had been brought about by the nomads,
who came down from the north-west, taking the women
of the Nahuatls, whom they conquered, for their wives,
and thus bringing about some points of structural resemblance, such as are to be seen in a lesser degree in
the citizens of the United States, through whose veins
the blood of the half-breeds of the earlier settlements
still courses. In Florida, and around the northern side
of the Gulf of Mexico, there had probably been a greater
fusion of the two races. But in origin the two peoples
are distinct; the one came from north-eastern Asia, the
other, I believe, from a tropical country joined on to
the present continent, that was submerged at the breaking up of the glacial period.

Was that country to the east or the west of the
present continent ? Was it Atlantis, or was it a submerged country in the Pacific ? I am inclined to the
latter opinion, and to believe that the inhabitants of
ancient Atlantis were the ancestors of the warlike and
adventurous Caribs. The Nahuatls, in their peaceful
dispositions and agricultural pursuits, are much more
nearly allied to the Polynesians, and their present pre-

ponderance on the western coast favours the idea that they had a western origin.*

'The Caribs, who were found in possession of most of the West Indian Islands, and of the eastern coast of South America, were a warlike, fierce, and enterprising race. Even in Columbus's time they were found making long voyages to ravage the villages of the peace-loving Nahuatls. If there be any truth in the story told to Solon by the priests of Sais, they are a much more likely people to have invaded the countries around the Mediterranean than the Nahuatls. What seems foreign in the customs and beliefs of the latter appears to have come from the west—from China and Japan—whilst there are some few points of affinity between the Caribs and the peoples of Europe and Africa. Thus, Mr. Hyde Clarke states that the greater part of Brazil is covered by the Guarani or Tupi languages, which are allied to the Agaw of the Nile region, the Abkass of Caucasia, &c.

There is one singular custom amongst the Carib races of America, and amongst some ancient peoples in Asia, Europe, and Africa, the existence of which on both sides of the Atlantic cannot, I think, be explained excepting on the theory that there was a remote inter-course or affinity amongst the peoples who practised it. I allude to the singular custom of the " couvade," in which the father is put to bed on the birth of a child. I take the following account of this curious practice from Mr. Tylor's philosophical " Early History of Mankind." This couvade is developed to the highest degree in

* I have already at page 55 alluded to the fundamental difference in the food of the Nahuatls and the Caribs.

South America and the West Indies. The following
account is given by Du Tertre of the Carib couvade in
the West Indies. When a child is born, the mother
goes presently to work, but the father begins to com-
plain, and takes to his hammock, and there he is visited
as though he were sick, and undergoes a course of diet-
ing " which would cure of the gout the most replete of
Frenchmen." The imaginary invalid must repose and
take careful nursing and nourishing food. In Brazil,
on the birth of a child, the father was put to bed and
fed with light food, whilst the mother was unattended
to, and went about her work. The practice of the
couvade was universal, in some form or other, amongst
the Carib races, but was unknown amongst the peoples
whom I have called the Nahuatls.

On the other side of the Atlantic the couvade has
been noticed in West Africa, and "amongst the mountain
tribes known as the Miau-tsze, who are supposed to be
like the Sontals and Gonds of India, remnants of a race
driven into the mountains by the present dwellers of
the plains." "Another Asiatic people, recorded to have
practised the couvade, are the Tibareni of Pontus, at
the south of the Black Sea, among whom, when the
child was born, the father lay groaning in bed with his
head tied up, while the mother tended him with food
and prepared his baths." In Europe the couvade may
be traced up from ancient into modern times in the
neighbourhood of the Pyrenees. Above 1800 years ago
Strabo mentions the story that, among the Iberians of
the north of Spain, the women, after the birth of a
child, tend their husbands, putting them to bed instead
of going themselves ; and this account is confirmed by

the evidence of the practice amongst the modern Basques. In Biscay, says Michel, "in valleys whose population recalls in its usages the infancy of society, the women rise immediately after childbirth and attend to the duties of the household, while the husband goes to bed, taking the baby with him, and thus receives the neighbours' compliments." "It has been found also in Navarre, and on the French side of the Pyrenees. Legrand d'Aussy mentions that in an old French fable the king of Torelose is 'au lit et en couche' when Aucassin arrives and takes a stick to him and makes him promise to abolish the custom in his realm. The same author goes on to state that the practice is said still to exist in some cantons of Béarn, where it is called 'faire la couvade.' Lastly, Diodorus Siculus notices the same habit of the wife being neglected, and the husband put to bed and treated as the patient among the natives of Corsica about the beginning of the Christian era."

For a fuller account of the couvade I must refer my readers to Tylor's "Early History of Mankind," from which I have so largely quoted; his summing up of this curious custom is profound and philosophical. He says : "The isolated occurrences of a custom among particular races, surrounded by other races that ignore it, may be sometimes to the ethnologist like those outlying patches of strata from which the geologist infers that the formation they belong to once spread over intervening districts, from which it has been removed by denudation; or like the geographical distribution of plants, from which the botanist argues that they have travelled from a distant home. The way in which the couvade appears in the new and old worlds is especially interesting from this

point of view. Among the savage tribes of South America it is, as it were, at home, in a mental atmosphere,
at least, not so different from that in which it came into
being as to make it a mere meaningless, absurd super-
stition. If the culture of the Caribs and Brazilians, even
before they came under our knowledge, had advanced too
far to allow the couvade to grow up fresh among them,
they at least practised it with some consciousness of its
meaning; it had not fallen out of unison with their
mental state. Here we find, covering a vast compact
area of country, the mental stratum, so to speak, to
which the couvade most nearly belongs. But if we look
at its appearances across from China to Corsica the state
of things is widely different; no theory of its origin can
be drawn from the Asiatic and European accounts to
compete for a moment with that which flows naturally
from the observations of the missionaries, who found it
not a mere dead custom, but a live growth of savage
psychology. The peoples, too, who have kept it up in
Asia and Europe seem to have been, not the great progressive, spreading, conquering, civilising nations of the
Aryan, Semitic, and Chinese stocks. It cannot be
ascribed even to the Tartars, for the Lapps, Finns, and
Hungarians appear to know nothing of it. It would
seem rather to have belonged to that ruder population,
or series of populations, whose fate it has been to be
driven by the great races out of the fruitful lands to
take refuge in mountains and deserts. The retainers of
the couvade in Asia are the Miau-tsze of China and the
savage Tibareni of Pontus. In Europe they are the
Basque race of the Pyrenees, whose peculiar manners,
appearance, and language, coupled with their geo-

graphical position, favour the view that they are the remains of a people driven westward and westward, by the pressure of more powerful tribes, till they came to these last mountains, with nothing but the Atlantic beyond. Of what stock were the original barbarian inhabitants of Corsica we do not know; but their position, and the fact that they, too, had the couvade, would suggest their having been a branch of the same family who escaped their persecutors by putting out to sea and settling in their mountainous island." *

Let us now return to the Nahuatls, and see if they present any affinities to the nations of the old world. Humboldt's well-known argument, in which he sought to prove the Asiatic origin of the Mexicans, was based upon the remarkable resemblance of their system of reckoning cycles of years to that found in use in different parts of Asia. Both the Asiatic and Mexican systems of cycles are most artificial in their construction, and troublesome in practice, and they are very unlikely to have arisen independently on two continents. Humboldt says : " I inferred the probability of the western nations of the new continent having had communication with the east of Asia long before the arrival of the Spaniards from a comparison of the Mexican and Thibeto-Japanese calendars, —from the correct orientation of the steps of the pyramidal elevations towards the different quarters of the heavens, and from the ancient myths and traditions of the four ages or four epochs of destruction of the world, and the dispersion of mankind after a great flood of waters." †

* E. B. Tylor, " Early History of Mankind," pp. 288–297.
† Humboldt, " Aspects of Nature," vol. ii. 174.

Whilst there are undoubtedly many curious coincidences in the customs of the ancient Mexicans and the
peoples of eastern Asia, there are, on the other hand, so
many differences that I believe it is safer to infer that
they were essentially distinct in origin, and that there
had been communication between the two peoples in very
early times, but that the foreign influence in Mexico
was extremely feeble, and too weak to check the growth
of an essentially indigenous civilisation. Possibly sun
and serpent worship, baptism, and the use of the cross
as a sacred emblem, were the survival of religious
beliefs that had obtained in the very cradle of the
human race. We cannot, however, believe that mankind had, before the separation and dispersion of the
eastern and western nations, attained to any great
astronomical knowledge, and it is quite possible that
the extraordinary coincidences between the chronological and astronomical systems of the Nahuatls and
the eastern Asiatics might have been brought about
by some of the latter having been stranded on the
American shore.

Humboldt argued that, " as the western coasts of the
American continent trend from N.-W. to S.-E., and the
eastern coasts of Asia in the opposite direction, the distance between the two continents in 45° of latitude, or
in the temperate zone, which is most favourable to mental
development, is too considerable to admit of the probability of such an accidental settlement taking place in that
latitude. We must then assume the first landing to have
been made in the inhospitable climate of from 55° to 65°,
and that the civilisation thus introduced, like the general
movement of population in America, has proceeded by

successive stations from north to south." * If we are
obliged to assume that the people themselves came
from the old world, such an origin might be sought for
them as well as any other; but all research since Humboldt's time has favoured the idea that there are no signs
of the Nahuatls being a newer people than the nations
of Asia.   And if it is not the derivation of the people,
but of some coincidences in their observances and knowledge, we may seek for it some simpler solution than the
migration of a whole people down through North to
Central America.   That solution is, I believe, to be
found in the fact, not taken into consideration by Humboldt, that the great Japanese current, after traversing
the eastern coast of Japan, sends one large branch nearly
directly east across the Pacific to the coast of California,
and an offshoot from it passes southward along the
Mexican coast and as far as the western coast of Central
America.   In Kotzebue's narrative of his voyage round
the world, he says : " Looking over Adams' diary, I found
the following notice—' Brig Forester, March ·24, 1815,
at sea, upon the coast of California, latitude 32° 45′ N.
longitude 133° 3′ W.   We saw this morning, at a short
distance, a ship, the confused state of whose sails showed
that they wanted assistance.   We bent our course towards her, and made out the distressed vessel to be
Japanese, which had lost both mast and helm.   Only
three dying Japanese, the captain and two sailors, were
found in the vessel.   We took these unfortunate people
on board our brig, and, after four months' nursing, they
entirely recovered.   We learned from these people that
they had sailed from the harbour of Osaka, in Japan,

* Humboldt, "Aspects of Nature," vol. ii. 176.

bound for another seaport, but were overtaken by a storm, in which they lost the helm and mast. Till that day their ship had been drifting about, a mere butt for the winds and waves, during seventeen months; and of thirty-five men only three remained, all the others having died of hunger.'" Is it not likely that in ancient times such accidents may have occurred again and again, and that information of the astronomical and chronological systems of eastern Asia may thus have been brought to the Nahuatls, who, from the ease with which they embraced the religion of the Spaniards, are shown to have been open to receive foreign ideas?

The three arguments on which Humboldt principally relied to prove that a communication had existed between the east of Asia and the Mexicans may be explained without adopting his theory that the Nahuatls had travelled round from the old world. The remarkable resemblance of the Mexican and Thibeto - Japanese calendars might result from the accidental stranding of a Japanese or Chinese vessel on their shores, bringing to them some man learned in the astronomy of the old world. The correct orientation of the sides of their pyramidal temples was but the result of their great astronomical knowledge and of the worship of the sun. And the resemblance of their traditions of four epochs of destruction and of the dispersion of mankind after a great flood of waters, arose from the fact that the great catastrophes that befell the human race at the melting of the ice of the glacial period were universal over the world.

CHAPTER XXI.

HAVING finished our business at Masaya, we rode back to Granada on the evening of the second day, and the next morning took a passage in a fine steamboat that Mr. Hollenbeck, of Greytown, had placed on the lake to convey passengers and goods between Granada and San Carlos, at the head of the river San Juan. We arrived at San Ubaldo at two o'clock, and found our mules safe but foot-sore, through travelling over the rocky hills from Santo Claro. The San José plains were in a dreadfully muddy state, and for five miles we went plunging through the swamps. Most of the mules fell several times, and we had great difficulty in getting them up again. We passed two travellers with their mules up to their girths in mud, and incapable of extricating themselves, but could not help them, as we dared not allow ours to stand, or they would stick fast also. We had met, at San Ubaldo, the son of Dr. Seemann, on his way home to England. His pack-mule had stuck fast in the plains the night before, and he had passed the night sitting on his boxes, half sunk in the mud, and attacked by myriads of mosquitoes that had covered his hands, face, and neck with blisters.

It was two hours after dark before we got across the
weary plains. We found shelter for the night at a
small hut on their border, where, for a consideration,
the occupants gave up to us their mosquito curtains and
stretchers, and sat up themselves. I suppose in such
situations people get used to the mosquitoes, but to
us they were intolerable. They buzzed around us and
settled on our hands and face, if the former were not
incessantly employed driving them off. Those of our
party who had no curtains had a lively time of it. A
gentleman of colour, from Jamaica, who was returning
to the mines after escorting young Mr. Seemann to the
port, and who could find no place to rest in, excepting
an old hammock, kept his long arms going round like a
windmill, every now and then wakening every one up
with a loud crack, as he tried to bring his flat hand down
on one of his tormentors. A mosquito, however, is not
to be caught, even in the dark, in such a way. It holds
up its two hinder legs as feelers ; the current of air
driven before a descending blow warns it of the impending danger, and it darts off to one side, to renew
its attack somewhere else. The most certain way to
catch them in the dark is to move the outstretched
finger cautiously towards where one is felt, until a safe
striking distance is reached. But what is the use of
killing one when they are in myriads ? None whatever,
excepting that it is some occupation for the sleepless
victim. The black gentleman was a thinker and a
scholar, and used to amuse himself at the mines by
writing letters addressed to Mr. Jacob Elam, Esqre.
(himself), in which he informed himself that he had
been left legacies of ten, twenty, or thirty thousand

pounds, a few thousand more or less costing nothing. Pondering during that weary night over the purpose of creation, he startled me about one in the morning with the question, " Mr. Belt, sir, can you tell me what is the use of mosquitoes ? "

" To enjoy themselves and be happy, Jacob."

" Ah, sir! if I was only a mosquito! " said Jacob, as he came down with another fruitless whack.

At the first cock-crow we were up, and as the cheerful dawn lighted up the east, we were in our saddles, and the miseries of the night were but the jests of the morning. The mules even seemed to be eager to leave that dismal swamp, where malaria hung in the air, and mosquitoes did their best to drive mankind away. The dry savannahs were before us, our hearts were young as the morning, the tormenting spirits of the night had flown away with the darkness, and jest and banter enlivened the road. We reached Acoyapo at nine o'clock; my good friend Don Dolores Bermudez lent me a fresh mule, and riding all day, I reached Santo Domingo in the evening.

I have little more of interest to relate. Years had sped on at Santo Domingo; and the time approached when I should be set free from the worries and responsibilities attending the supervision of gold-mines, the products of which were just at that tantalising point, on the verge between profit and loss, that made their superintendence a most irksome and anxious duty. The difficulty of the task was vastly increased by the capital of the company having been originally wasted in the erection of machinery that proved to be useless ; so

that financial questions constantly retarded the completion of the works. This book has not been written,
however, to tell the story of the struggles of a mining
engineer; and I turn aside with pleasure from this
slight digression to say what little more I have to tell
of my natural-history experiences.

I did not, until near the conclusion of my stay, commence collecting the skins of birds, contenting myself
with watching and noting their habits. I obtained the
skins of ninety-two species only; but small as this collection was, it proved an important addition to the
knowledge of the bird-fauna of Nicaragua. The eminent ornithologist, Mr. Osbert Salvin, published in the
Ibis for July 1872 a list of seventy-three species that
I had up to that time sent to England. Altogether,
only one hundred and fifty species, including those that
I had collected, were known from Nicaragua. Frag-
mentary as our knowledge is, it is sufficient, in Mr.
Salvin's opinion, to indicate, with tolerable accuracy, to
which of the two sub-provinces of the Central American
fauna the forest region of Chontales belongs. The birds
I sent to England proved nearly conclusively that the
Costa-Rican sub-province included Chontales in Nicaragua, and that the boundary between it and the sub-
province of Southern Mexico and Guatemala must be
sought for more to the north-west.

Of the southern species, which in Chontales find their
northern limit, so far as is known, there are in my
small collection thirty-two species, whilst belonging to
the northern sub-province, and not known to range
further south, there are only seven species; showing
that the connection with Costa Rica and the south is

much closer than that with Guatemala and the north, and that the boundary between the two sub-provinces is not found, as was supposed, in the depression of the isthmus occupied by the great lakes and their outlet the San Juan river, but must exist further towards, if not in, Honduras. Mr. Salvin says, " What I suspect to be the case, though I cannot as yet bring evidence to prove it, is, that the forests of Chontales spread uninterruptedly into Costa Rica, but that towards the north and north-west a decided break occurs, and that this break determines the range of the prevalent Costa Rican and Guatemalan forest forms." * I can confirm Mr. Salvin's supposition. The San Juan river forms no greater break in the forest than a dozen other rivers that run through it and fall into the Atlantic. But a decided interruption does occur to the north-west. It is found in the valleys of Humuya and Goascoran in Honduras, which, along with the central plain of Comayagua, constitute a great transverse valley running north and south from sea to sea, and cutting completely through the chain of the Cordilleras.† The highest point of this pass is 2850 feet above the sea, and the country around is composed of undulating savannahs and plains covered with grass. The Gulf of Honduras, cutting deeply into the continent, also plays an important part in preventing the intermingling of the faunas of the two sub-provinces, but the principal barrier is the termination of the great Atlantic forest north-westward, which even at Cape Gracias begins to give place to plains and savannahs next the coast.

* *The Ibis*, July 1872, p. 312.
† Squier, " States of Central America," p. 681.

My entomological collections were much more complete than my collections of birds, especially those of the butterflies and beetles. Mr. W. C. Hewitson has described 25 new species, but no list of the whole of the butterflies known from Nicaragua has yet been published. In Coleoptera I made large collections, but the extensive families of the Elateridæ, Lamellicorns, and others are still uncatalogued, and very many species remain to be described. The only beetles that have been catalogued as yet with sufficient completeness to warrant any general conclusions are the Longicorns. I collected about 300 different species, and Mr. H. W. Bates has enumerated 242 of these in a paper " On the Longicorn Coleoptera of Chontales, Nicaragua," published in the " Transactions of the Entomological Society for 1872." In an interesting summary of the results he gives the following analysis of the range of the species :—

Peculiar to Chontales	133	species.
Common to Chontales and Mexico . . .	38	,,
,, Do. and the West India Islands .	5	,,
,, Do. and the United States . .	5	,,
,, Do. and New Grenada or Venezuela	24	,,
,, Do. and the Amazon Region . .	22	,,
,, Do. and South Brazil . . .	10	,,
Generally distributed in Tropical America . .	5	,,
	242	,,

Omitting the peculiar species and those generally distributed in Tropical America, we have thus forty-three that are found in Chontales and in Mexico or the United States, and sixty-one that are found in Chontales and countries lying to the southward. The preponderance of southern forms is not so great as in the birds, but when we reflect on the large number of peculiar species, and that the Longicorns of the Atlantic slope of Costa Rica are yet scarcely known, it appears likely that many of the Chontales species will be found ranging southward across the San Juan river, and that the Insect fauna will be shown to have the same relations as the Bird fauna; for, as the Atlantic forest continues unbroken much further southward than northward, so will the insects peculiar to the forest region have a greater range in that direction.

Mr. Hollick has beautifully drawn on wood a few of the characteristic Longicorns of Chontales, all of them, with one exception (*Polyraphis Fabricii*), being as yet only known from that province, but probably extending into Costa Rica.

One of these, the lovely little *Cosmisoma Titania*, No. 7 in Plate, has been appropriately named after the Queen of the Fairies by Mr. Bates. It was first found by Mr. Janson, junior, who came out to Chontales purposely to collect insects; and I afterwards obtained it in great numbers. The use of the curious brushes on the antennæ is not known. Another longicorn, about the same size (*Coremia hirtipes*), has its two hindmost legs greatly lengthened, and furnished with brushes: one I saw on a branch was flourishing these in the air, and I thought at first they were two black flies hovering over the branch, my attention being taken from the body of the beetle by the movement of the brushes.

Another fine longicorn, figured in Plate, *Deliathis nivea*, looks as if made of pure white porcelain spotted with black. It is a rare beetle, one or two specimens

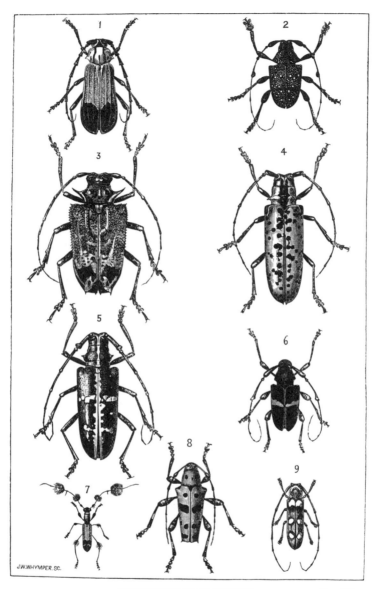

LONGICORN BEETLES OF CHONTALES. Page 380.

1. *Evander nobilis*, Bates.   2. *Gymnocerus Beltii*, Bates.   3. *Polyrhaphis Fabricii*, Thom.
4. *Deliathis nivea*, Bates.   5. *Tœniotes præclarus*, Bates.   6. *Chalastinus rubrocinctus*, Bates.
7. *Cosmisoma Titania*, Bates.   8. *Carneades superba*, Bates.   9. *Amphionyca princeps*, Bates.

each season being generally all that are taken. It is usually found on the leaves of young trees, from twelve to twenty feet from the ground. I have taken the rather heavy-bodied female by throwing a stone at it and causing it to fall within reach, but the male is more active on the wing, and it was long before I obtained a specimen.

LEAF INSECT.

Amongst the insects of Chontales none are more worthy of notice than the many curious species of Orthoptera that look like green and faded leaves of trees. I have already described one species that resembles a green leaf, and so much so that it even deceived the acute senses of the foraging ants; other species, belonging to a closely-

related genus (*Pterochroza*), imitate leaves in every
stage of decay, some being faded-green, blotched with
yellow; others, as in the species figured, resemble a
brown withered leaf, the resemblance being increased by
a transparent hole through both wings that looks like a
piece taken out of the leaf. In many butterflies that
resemble leaves on the under side of their wings, the
wings being raised and closed together when at rest so
as to hide the bright colours of the upper surface, there
are similar transparent spots that imitate holes; and

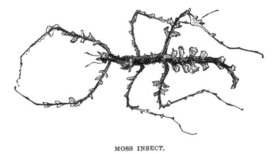

MOSS INSECT.

others again are jagged at the edge, as if pieces had
been taken out of them. Many chrysalides also have
mirror-like spots that resemble holes; and one that I
found hanging from the under side of a leaf had a real
hole through it, formed by a horn that projected from
the thorax and doubled back to the body, leaving a space
between. Another insect, of which I only found two
specimens, had a wonderful resemblance to a piece of
moss, amongst which it concealed itself in the daytime,
and was not to be distinguished except when accidentally
shaken out. It is the larval stage of a species of *Phasma*.

The extraordinary perfection of these mimetic resemblances is most wonderful.   I have heard this urged as a reason for believing that they could not have been produced by natural selection, because a much less degree of resemblance would have protected the mimetic species. To this it may be answered, that natural selection not only tends to pick out and preserve the forms that have protective resemblances, but to increase the perceptions of the predatory species of insects and birds, so that there is a continual progression towards a perfectly mimetic form.   This progressive improvement in means of defence and of attack may be illustrated in this way. Suppose a number of not very swift hares and a number of slow-running dogs were placed on an island where there was plenty of food for the hares but none for the dogs, except the hares they could catch ; the slowest of the hares would be first killed, and the swifter preserved. Then the slowest-running dogs would suffer, and having less food than the fleeter ones, would have least chance of living, and the swiftest dogs would be preserved; thus the fleetness of both dogs and hares would be gradually but surely perfected by natural selection, until the greatest speed was reached that it was possible for them to attain.   I have in this supposed example confined myself to the question of speed alone, but in reality other means of pursuit and of escape would come into play and be improved.   The dogs might increase in cunning, or combine together to work in couples or in packs by the same selective process ; and the hares on their part might acquire means of concealment or stratagem to elude their enemies ; but, on both sides, the improvement would be progressive until the highest form of excellence was reached. Viewed in this light, the wonderful perfection of mimetic forms is a natural consequence of the selection of the individuals that, on the one side, were more and more mimetic, and on the other (that of their enemies) more and more able to penetrate through the assumed disguises. It has doubtless happened in some cases that species, having many foes, have entirely thrown off some of them through the disguises they have been brought to assume, but others they still cannot elude.

Since Mr. Bates first brought forward the theory of mimetic resemblances its importance has been more and more demonstrated, as it has been found how very largely animal life has been influenced in form and colour by the natural selection of the varieties that were preserved from their enemies, or enabled to approach their prey, through the resemblance they bore to something else. So general are these deceptive resemblances throughout nature, that it is often difficult to determine whether sexual preferences or the preservation of mimetic forms has been most potent in moulding the form and coloration of species, and in some the two forces are seen to be opposed in their operation. Thus in some butterflies that mimic the Heliconidæ, the females only are mimetic, the males retaining the normal form and coloration of the group to which they belong. In such cases it appears as if the females have not been checked in gradually assuming the disguise they wear, and it is important that they should be protected, as they are more exposed to destruction while seeking for places to deposit their eggs ; but that both sexes should not have inherited the change in form and colour when it would have been beneficial to

both can only be explained, I think, on the supposition
that the females had a choice of mates and preferred
those that retained the primordial appearance of the
group. This view is supported by the fact that many of the
males of the mimetic *Leptalides* have the upper half of the
lower wing of a pure white, whilst all the rest of the wings
is barred and spotted with black, red, and yellow, like
the species they mimic. The females have not this white
patch, and the males usually conceal it by covering it
with the upper wing, so that I cannot imagine its being
of any other use to them excepting as an attraction in
courtship, to exhibit to the females, and thus gratify a
deep-seated preference for the normal colour of the order
to which the Leptalides belong.

I finally left the mines September 6th, 1872, on my
way to England. I was accompanied through the forest
by several of the mining officials. Though glad to return
to Europe, it was not without some feeling of regret that
I rode for the last time through the forest where I had
so often wandered during the years I had been at Santo
Domingo. The woods had become as familiar to me as
home scenes. No more should I see the white-headed
ruby humming-bird come darting down the brook, chasing away the green-throat from its bathing-place; no
more watch the flocks of many-coloured birds hunting
the insects in the forests, or admire the wonderful
instincts of the tropical ants. I listened with pleasure
to the last hoarse cries of the mot-mots, and tried to
impress on my memory the curious forms of vegetation
—the palms, the gigantic arums, the tangled lianas,
and perching epiphytes.

After reaching Pital I rode rapidly over the savannahs, where the swallows were skimming over the top of the long grass to frighten up the insects which rested there. After another flounder across the San José plains, I reached San Ubaldo without incident, excepting a tumble with my mule in the mud. Much of the land between Pital and the lake is well fitted for the cultivation of maize, sugar, and plantains, and near the river at Acoyapo the soil is very fertile. Little of it is occupied, and it is open to any one to squat down on it and fence it in. All that is required is that the form shall be gone through of obtaining permission from the alcalde of the township, which is never refused. Nicaragua offers a tempting field for the emigrant, but there are some other considerations which should not be lost sight of. When a man finds he can live easily without much work, that all his neighbours are contented with the scantiest clothing, the coarsest food, and the poorest dwellings, he is very apt to fall into the same slothful habits. Even if he himself has innate energy enough to ward off the insidious foe, he will see his children growing up exposed to all the temptations to lead an easy life that a tropical climate offers, and without any example of industry or enterprise around them to arouse or cultivate a spirit of emulation. The consequence is that nearly all the foreign settlers in Nicaragua from amongst the European and North American labouring classes have fallen into the same lazy habits as the Nicaraguans, and whenever I have been inclined to blame the natives for their indolence, some recollection of a fellow-countryman who has succumbed to the same influences has arrested my harsher judgment. I cannot recommend Nicaragua, with

all its natural wealth, its perpetual summer, its magnificent lakes, and its teeming soil, as a place of emigration
for isolated families, and even for larger schemes of
colonisation I do not think it so suitable as our own
colonies and the United States. A large body of emigrants would carry with them the healthful influence of
the good and industrious, and the spirit of emulation and
progress might be preserved if the community could be
kept together, but I fear this could not be. After a
while the tastes of one individual would lead in one,
those of another in an opposite direction. Where all
were free to choose, the idle would go away from the influences that urged them to industry, the sensual from the
restraints of morality. Many will, however, smile at the
objection I have to emigration to Nicaragua, when they
perceive that it is founded only on the ease with which
people can live in plenty there. There is one form of
colonisation that will be successful, and that is the
gradual moving down southward of the people of the
United States. When the destiny of Mexico is fulfilled,
with one stride the Anglo-American will bound to the
Isthmus of Panama, and Central America will be filled
with cattle estates, and with coffee, sugar, indigo, cotton,
and cacao plantations. Railways will then keep up a
healthful and continuous intercourse with the enterprising North, and the sluggard and the sensual will not be
able to stand before the competition of the vigorous and
virtuous. Nor will the Anglo-American long be stayed
by the Isthmus, in his progress southward. Unless some
such catastrophe happens as a few years ago threatened
to cover North America with standing armies as in
Europe, which God forbid, not many centuries will roll

over before the English language will be spoken from
the frozen soil of the far north to Tierra del Fuego in
the south.

The fine steamer that the enterprise of Mr. Hollenbeck
had placed on the lake, and which he had named the
Elizabeth after his amiable wife, had been wrecked a
short time before I left the country, and Mr. Hollenbeck's own health had greatly suffered by the labours he
undertook in endeavouring to get the vessel off the
sunken rock on which it had struck.   Notwithstanding
this and other misfortunes, enough to try a man's mettle
to its foundation, his native pluck carried him through
all his difficulties, and he was away to the States to get
new vessels and blow another blast at fortune's iron gates.
Whilst I write these last few pages I learn that a new
steamer ploughs the lake, and that his transit service is
again in complete working order.   Success attend him.

The result of the wreck of the *Elizabeth,* so far as
I was concerned, was that I had to take a passage down
the lake to San Carlos in a bungo packet, so full as to
necessitate closer acquaintanceship with many amiable
Nicaraguans than was agreeable to my insular prejudices.
When in the middle of the night an old woman tried
to roll me off the soft plank I had found for myself
into a litter of crying babies, I indulged in some bitter
reflections on the race, that, I am happy to say, were as
transitory as the inconvenience to which I was put.   At
San Carlos we changed to the river steamer under my
old friend Captain Birdsall.   As I have already described the scenery of the San Juan in the account of my
journey up, I shall not repeat the story, but simply state

that we reached Greytown on the 11th September, and
on the 16th embarked on the West Indian Mail Packet.
I arrived in England within a month, to find my
native town (Newcastle) wealthier and dirtier than
ever, with thousands of furnaces belching out smoke
and poisonous gases ; to find the people of England
fretting about the probable exhaustion of her coal-fields
in a few hundred years, actually dreading the time when
she will no longer be the smithy of the world, but the
centre of the science, philosophy, literature, and art of
the Anglo-Saxon race—that race whose sons all over the
globe will then look up to her with loving reverence as
the mother of nations, the coloniser of the world, the
pioneer of freedom, progress, and morality.

SKETCH MAP
of
NICARAGUA

English Miles

0 3 10 20 30 40 50 60 70 80

INDEX.

—◂◂—

2 C

THE END.